Anonymous

Reformed Church Hymnal

With Tunes

Anonymous

Reformed Church Hymnal
With Tunes

ISBN/EAN: 9783337296605

Printed in Europe, USA, Canada, Australia, Japan

Cover: Foto ©Lupo / pixelio.de

More available books at **www.hansebooks.com**

THE REFORMED CHURCH HYMNAL.

WITH TUNES.

For "The Service of Song in the House of the Lord."
1 Chron. 6: 31.

"*In Psalms and Hymns and Spiritual Songs, singing with grace in your hearts to the Lord.*"—Col. 3: 16.

CLEVELAND, O.
H. J. RUETENIK, 991 Scranton Avenue.

PREFACE.

In preparing this book for the use of congregations and families, we have returned to the old usage of the Continental Churches, now so widely followed by other Denominations, in printing the Tunes on the same pages with the Hymns. It is hoped, in this way, to improve "the service of Song in the House of the Lord." But to reach this end, so greatly desired by all, it is of still greater importance to understand the true meaning and intent of Singing, as a part of Cultus, or Public Worship. This, expressed in the fewest words, *is, and ought always to be an act of Prayer or Praise, by the congregation as a whole and by every individual worshipper.* Prayer is the elevation of the soul to God, in the various forms of Praise, Adoration, Confession, Thanks-giving, Petition and Supplication. All these come forward in our Hymns and Psalms. Those are perverted and defective views, therefore, which regard Singing in Public Worship as directed, not to God, but to Men, and as intended either to call forth sacred emotions, or to produce pleasure by the beauty of the melody or harmony. Not to men, but to God, should our hearts be lifted up in our sacred songs. All who possibly can do so, should unite in these prayers. And where the power of uniting audibly is wanting, each worshipper should regard it as a privilege and a duty to unite with the Congregation in making melody to God in his heart (Eph. 5. 19). In this way this delightful part of worship can be restored to its true place, and will bring its true blessing to the worshippers.

In the preparation of this work, both in the selection of the Hymns and the Tunes, we have been guided mainly by the above *fundamental principle*. We have, also, regarded it as of far more importance to have respect to *the quality*, than *the quantity* of either the Hymns or the Tunes. *The Hymns should be true prayers, and the Tunes should be fit vehicles and bearers of these prayers to the throne of Almighty God.* The Tunes should serve, mainly, to enable the worshippers to make the exercise of singing *a common prayer*, and so in unison, and in a pleasing way, to give utterance to the emotions and longings of the soul. The attention of all worshippers, and especially of all choirs, cannot be drawn

PREFACE.

too strongly to this point, because the general decay of congregational singing must be ascribed, mainly, to the fact that this fundamental principle has been lost sight of. If choirs, singers, congregations and ministers will reflect upon this subject, they will come to see that the true way to restore congregational singing, is to select devotional hymns, devotional tunes, and to train all to sing, not as rendering music unto men, but as praying unto God.

In the arrangement of the Hymns and Tunes we have endeavored to adapt the book, as well as possible, to the needs of practical use. Wherever the book is opened, the Hymns on the two pages are usually of the same metre, for which two Tunes are given, either one of which may be selected, at the discretion of the minister or the leader. The proper Doxology is generally found at the foot of the second page.

Our special thanks are due to Prof. George Kingsley, the composer of so many beautiful tunes, for the use of a large number of his compositions. The Tunes "*Hallet,*" "*Lambic,*" "*Reiter,*" "*Mease,*" "*Good,*" and "*Go to Thy Rest in Peace,*" are by Mr. Kingsley, and have never before been published. They cannot be used, therefore, by others, without special permission.

The book is published in the humble hope and prayer that it may be accepted of God, and prove of service to his Church.

J. H. GOOD,
I. H. REITER, } COMMITTEE.
SAMUEL MEASE,

INDEX OF SUBJECTS.

I. HYMNS OF ADORATION AND PRAISE.

To God.—Hymns 3, 5, 6, 7, 8, 9, 10, 11, 12, 14, 15, 16, 17, 18, 19, 20, 21, 22, 23, 24, 25, 26, 27, 28, 29, 30, 32, 33, 34, 35, 36, 37, 38, 39, 41, 44, 93, 94, 577, 613, 616, 625, 640.

To the Redeemer (or, Jesus Hymns)—42, 43, 45, 46, 48, 49, 50, 51, 52, 53, 54, 55, 56, 57, 58, 59, 60, 61, 62, 63, 64, 65, 66, 67, 68, 69, 70, 71, 72, 73, 74, 75, 76, 77, 78, 79, 80, 81, 82, 83, 84, 85, 86, 87, 88, 89, 90, 91, 92, 96, 97, 99, 100, 101, 102, 103, 104, 473, 567, 570, 573, 574, 578, 580, 581, 582, 583, 596, 597, 598, 602, 605, 614.

To the Holy Spirit.—Hymns 13, 31, 40, 98, 126, 196, 197, 208, 209, 210, 211, 212, 213, 214, 215, 216, 217.

The Trinity.—Hymns 4, 35, 223, 224, 226, 227, 234, 625.

The Holy Scriptures.—Hymns 106, 107, 113, 124, 125.

The Lord's Day.—Hymns 47, 108, 109, 110, 111, 112, 114, 115, 116, 117, 118, 119, 120, 121, 122, 123, 156, 380.

II. HYMNS FOR THE CHURCH YEAR.

The Advent Season.—Hymns 127, 128, 129, 130, 132, 133, 137, 143, 144, 145, 582.

The Second Advent.—Hymns 95, 134, 135, 136, 147, 235, 236.

The Christmas Season.—Hymns 131, 138, 139, 142, 148, 149, 150, 153, 154, 620.

New Year.—Hymns 140, 141, 151, 152, 186.

The Epiphany Season.—Hymns 79, 97, 130, 146, 154, 158, 159, 165, 230, 231, 232, 248, 255, 556, 560, 582.

The Lenten and Passion Season.—Hymns 105, 160, 161, 162, 163, 164, 166, 167, 168, 169, 170, 171, 172, 173, 174, 175, 176, 177, 178, 179, 181, 182, 183, 184, 187, 188, 189,

The Lenten and Passion Season.—190, 191, 225, 287, 376, 377, 378, 379, 555, 573, 574, 604, 607, 622, 626, 627.

The Easter Season.—Hymns 185, 192, 198, 199, 204, 205, 206, 207.

Ascension.—Hymns 193, 194, 195, 200, 201, 202, 203, 222, 559, 601.

The Pentecost Season.—Hymns 13, 31, 40, 98, 196, 197, 209, 210, 211, 212, 213, 214, 215, 216, 217, 559, 630.

Trinity.—Hymns 4, 35, 223, 224, 226, 234, 625.

The Church.—Hymns 218, 219, 220, 227, 228, 229, 239, 240, 241, 245, 408, 558.

The Communion of Saints.—Hymns 155, 221, 242, 243, 244, 246.

Missions.—Hymns 10, 69, 230, 231, 232, 233, 247, 248, 249, 250, 251, 252, 253, 254, 255, 258, 259, 277, 409, 594, 608, 615.

III. HYMNS FOR THE ORDINANCES OF THE CHURCH.

Baptism and Covenant Relation.—Hymns 89, 262, 263, 264, 265, 266, 268, 269, 270, 472, 473.

Confirmation.—Hymns 55, 271, 272, 275, 276, 376.

The Lord's Supper.—Hymns 163, 164, 166, 175, 260, 261, 267, 281, 282, 283, 284, 285, 286, 288, 289, 290, 291, 292, 293, 294, 338, 376, 377, 378, 566, 579, 585.

Ordination and Installation of Ministers.—Hymns 218, 222, 223, 224, 231, 233, 248, 277, 278.

Ordination and Installation of Church Officers.—Hymns 240, 244, 256, 260.

Laying of a Corner-stone.—Hymns 157, 273, 239, 245, 279.

Consecration of a Church.—Hymns 3, 12, 239, 240, 245, 274, 280.

INDEX OF SUBJECTS.

Burial of the Dead.—Hymns 287, 295, 296, 297, 298, 299, 300, 301, 302, 303, 304, 305, 306, 307, 308, 309, 310, 311, 312, 313, 314, 315, 316, 317, 318, 319, 503, 576, 611, 617, 618, 619.

Harvest and Thanksgiving Festivals.—Hymns 3, 323, 324, 325, 326, 327, 328, 329, 330, 333, 334, 335, 557, 572, 629.

National Humiliation and Fasts.—Hymns 331, 332, 179, 188.

IV. HYMNS OF CHRISTIAN EXPERIENCE.
(The New Life in Christ).

Invitations.—Hymns 339, 340, 341, 342, 343, 346, 347, 348, 352, 353, 354, 355, 359, 555, 575,

Conviction of Sin.—Hymns 344, 345, 351, 357, 358, 360, 632.

Penitence and Conversion.—Hymns 349, 350, 356, 361, 362, 363, 364, 365, 366, 367, 368, 369, 370, 371, 372, 373, 374, 375.—171, 172, 178, 179, 183, 189.

Faith.—Hymns 225, 376, 381, 382, 383, 387, 388, 390, 607, 621.

Adoption.—Hymns 384, 385, 386, 393, 394, 395, 405, 472, 473.

Union with Christ.—Hymns 396, 397, 398, 579, 522, 626.

Justification.—Hymns 389, 391, 392, 575, 607.

Joy, Hope and Trust in God.—Hymns 399, 400, 402, 410, 411, 412, 413, 414, 415, 416, 418, 419, 420, 421, 422, 423, 424, 425, 426, 427, 428, 429, 459, 561, 565, 566, 567, 568, 570, 578, 585, 589, 599, 600, 603.

The Christian Warfare.—Hymns 104, 401, 402, 430, 431, 432, 433, 434, 435, 436, 437, 438, 439, 440, 441, 442, 443, 444, 445, 446, 447, 448, 449, 571, 588, 592, 597, 598, 599, 600, 603, 612.

Love to God and Man.—Hymns 450, 451, 452, 453, 454, 455.

Longing.—Hymns 320, 321, 322, 406, 407, 417, 456, 457, 458, 460, 461, 462, 463, 464, 465, 466, 467, 468, 469, 470, 471, 558, 564, 573, 593, 595, 606.

Prayer.—Hymns 257, 403, 404, 472, 474, 475, 476, 477, 478, 479, 480, 596, 628,

Shortness of Life.—Hymns 297, 311, 317, 610.

Comfort in Afflictions.—Hymns 8, 19, 20, 45, 77, 102, 287, 295, 306, 310, 336, 337, 482, 483, 484, 487, 488, 489, 490, 491, 492, 494, 495, 496, 497, 565, 568, 585, 590.

V. HYMNS RELATING TO THE LAST THINGS.

Death.—Hymns 301, 302, 303, 308, 314, 315, 316, 493, 498, 499, 500, 501, 502, 503.

Resurrection.—Hymns 507, 508, 509, 512, 513, 516.

Judgment.—Hymns 235, 236, 504, 505, 506, 510, 514, 515, 572.

Eternal Life and Heaven.—Hymns 309, 322, 469, 485, 486, 511, 517, 518, 519, 520, 521, 522, 523, 524, 525, 526, 527, 528, 529, 564, 584, 586, 587, 591, 606, 609, 623, 624.

VI. MORNING AND EVENING HYMNS.
(For Family Devotions and Church Use.)

Morning Hymns.—Hymns 530, 531, 532, 536, 537, 538, 542, 543, 544, 545, 549, 550, 551.

Evening Hymns.—Hymns 533, 534, 535, 539, 540, 541, 546, 547, 548, 552, 553, 554.

VII. MISCELLANEOUS.

Temperance.—Hymns 344, 366, 412, 629.

Marriage.—Hymn 569.

On the Sea.—Hymns 562, 563.

Pilgrimage.—Hymns 237, 406, 465, 597, 610, 621, 624, 626, 627, 633, 634.

Closing Hymns.—Hymns 180, 237, 238, 625, 635, 636, 637, 638, 639, 640.

Chants.—Hymns 1, 619, 620, 621, 622, 623, 624, 625, 633, 640.

The Seasons.—Hymns 140, 141, 151, 152, 186, 325, 326, 327, 330.

Prayer Meetings.—Hymns 1—126, 158—188, 257, 320—326, 339—529, 558, 560, 561, 565, 566, 567, 570, 571, 573, 574, 577, 578, 580, 581, 584, 585, 586, 587, 591, 593, 594, 595, 597, 598, 600, 602, 604, 607, 609, 610, 612, 613—616, 620—625, 626, 627, 628, 629, 630, 631, 632, 633, 634.

Doxologies.—640.

Index of First Lines and Authors.—Page 230.

Metrical Index of Tunes and Authors.—Page 237.

THE LORD'S PRAYER.

1. Our Father who art in heaven, Hallowed .... be thy name.
   Give us this day our .... dai - - ly bread.
   And lead us not into temptation, but deliver .... us from evil.
   Thy kingdom come. Thy will be done in .... earth as it is in heaven.
   And forgive us our debts as .... we for - - give our debtors.
   For thine is the kingdom, and the power, and the glo - ry, for - - - ever. A - men.

THE APOSTLES' CREED.

2

1. I believe in God the Father Almighty, Maker of | heaven and | earth,
   And in Jesus Christ his | only | Son our | Lord;

2. Who was conceived by the Holy Ghost, born of the Virgin Mary,
   suffered under Pontius Pilate, was crucified, | dead and | buried;
   He descended into hell; the third day he | rose | from the | dead.

3. He ascended into heaven, and sitteth at the right hand of God the | Father
   Al | mighty;
   From thence he shall come to | judge the | quick and the | dead.

4. I believe in the | Holy | Ghost;
   The holy catholic Church; the communion of saints; the forgiveness of
   sins: the resurrection of the body: and the | life— | ever | lasting. ‖
   A | men.

ADORATION AND PRAISE.

OLD HUNDRED. L. M.

3   *"Before Jehovah's awful throne."*
         Psalm 100.   **L. M.**

1 BEFORE Jehovah's awful throne,
  Ye nations, bow with sacred joy;
  Know that the Lord is God alone;
  He can create, and he destroy.

2 His sovereign power, without our aid,
  Made us of clay, and formed us men;
  And when, like wand'ring sheep, we strayed,
  He brought us to his fold again.

3 We are his people, we his care,
  Our souls, and all our mortal frame;
  What lasting honors shall we rear,
  Almighty Maker, to thy name?

4 We'll crowd thy gates with thankful songs,
  High as the heaven our voices raise;
  And earth, with her ten thousand tongues,
  Shall fill thy courts with sounding praise.

5 Wide as the world is thy command,
  Vast as eternity, thy love;
  Firm as a rock thy truth shall stand,
  When rolling years shall cease to move.

4   *"The blessed Trinity."*   **L. M.**

1 GREAT One in Three, great Three in One,
  Thy wondrous name we sound abroad;
  Prostrate we fall before Thy throne,
  O Holy, Holy, Holy Lord!

2 Thee, Holy Father, we confess;
  Thee, Holy Saviour, we adore;
  And Thee, O Holy Ghost, we bless
  And praise and worship evermore.

3 Thou art by heaven and earth adored;
  Thy universe is full of Thee,
  O Holy, Holy, Holy Lord!
  Great Three in One, great One in Three!

5   *"God only wise."*   **L. M.**

1 AWAKE, my tongue, thy tribute bring,
  To him who gave thee power to sing;
  Praise him, who has all praise above,
  The source of wisdom and of love.

2 How vast his knowledge! how profound!
  A depth where all our thoughts are drowned!
  The stars he numbers, and their names
  He gives to all those heavenly flames.

3 Through each bright world above, behold
  Ten thousand, thousand charms unfold;
  Earth, air, and mighty seas combine,
  To speak his wisdom all divine.

4 But in redemption, oh, what grace!
  Its wonders, oh, what thought can trace!
  Here wisdom shines forever bright;
  Praise him, my soul, with sweet delight.

6   *"Hallelujah."*
                Psalm 150.   **L. M.**

1 PRAISE ye the Lord; all nature join
  In work and worship so divine;
  Let heaven and earth unite, and raise
  High hallelujahs to his praise.

2 While realms of joy, and worlds around,
  Their hallelujahs high resound,
  Let saints below, and saints above,
  Exulting sing redeeming love.

3 As instruments well tuned and strung,
  We'll praise the Lord with heart and tongue;

ADORATION AND PRAISE.

SESSIONS. L. M.

While life remains we'll loud proclaim,
High hallelujahs to his name.

4 Beyond the grave, in nobler strains,
When freed from sorrow, sin and pains,
Eternally the church will raise
High hallelujahs to his praise.

7 *"Bless the Lord, O my soul"*
Psalm 103 **L. M.**

1 BLESS, O my soul! the living God;
Call home thy thoughts that rove abroad;
Let all the powers within me join
In work and worship so divine.

2 Bless, O my soul! the God of grace,
His favors claim thy highest praise;
Why should the wonders he hath wrought
Be lost in silence, and forgot?

3 'Tis he, my soul, that sent his Son
To die for crimes which thou hast done;
He owns the ransom, and forgives,
The hourly follies of our lives.

4 Let every land his power confess;
Let all the earth adore his grace:
My heart and tongue with rapture join
In work and worship so divine.

8 *"I will praise Thee with my whole heart."—Psalm 138.* **L. M.**

1 With all my powers of heart and tongue,
I'll praise my Maker in my song;
Angels shall hear the notes I raise.
Approve the song, and join the praise.

2 To God I cried when troubles rose;
He heard me, and subdued my foes:
He did my rising fears control,
And strength diffused thro' all my soul.

3 Amid a thousand snares, I stand
Upheld and guarded by thy hand;
Thy words my fainting soul revive,
And keep my dying faith alive.

4 I'll sing thy truth and mercy, Lord,
I'll sing the wonders of thy word;
Not all thy works and names below
So much thy power and glory show.

9 *"God's Majesty." Ps. 68.* **L. M.**

1 Kingdoms and thrones to God belong;
Crown him, ye nations! in your song;
His wondrous names and powers rehearse;
His honors shall enrich your verse.

2 He rides, and thunders through the sky;
His name, Jehovah, sounds on high;
Sing to his name, ye sons of grace!
Ye saints! rejoice before his face.

3 Proclaim him King, pronounce him blest;
He's your defence, your joy, your rest
When terrors rise and nations faint,
God is the strength of every saint.

Doxology. **L. M.**

Praise God, from whom all blessings flow,
Praise him, all creatures here below;
Praise him above, ye heavenly host,
Praise Father, Son, and Holy Ghost.

ADORATION AND PRAISE.

STIRLING. L. M.

10 *"Thy Kingdom Come."* Rev. 11: 15. **L. M.**

1 Ascend thy throne, Almighty King,
And spread thy glories all abroad;
Let thine own arm salvation bring,
And be thou known the gracious God.

2 Let millions bow before thy seat,
Let humble mourners seek thy face,
Bring daring rebels to thy feet,
Subdu'd by thy victorious grace.

3 O let the kingdoms of the world
Become the kingdoms of the Lord;
Let saints and angels praise thy name,
Be thou through heav'n and earth ador'd.

11 *The hand that made us is Divine.* **L. M.**
Ps. 19.

1 The spacious firmament on high,
With all the blue ethereal sky,
And spangled heavens, a shining frame,
Their great Original proclaim.

2 Th' unwearied sun, from day to day,
Does his Creator's power display,
And publishes to every land
The work of an Almighty hand.

3 Soon as the evening shades prevail,
The moon takes up the wondrous tale,
And nightly to the listening earth
Repeats the story of her birth;

4 While all the stars that round her burn,
And all the planets in their turn,
Confirm the tidings as they roll,
And spread the truth from pole to pole.

5 What though, in solemn silence all
Move round this dark, terrestrial ball?
What though no real voice nor sound
Amid their radiant orbs be found?

6 In reason's ear they all rejoice,
And utter forth a glorious voice;
For ever singing as they shine,
"The hand that made us is Divine."

12 *"Surely the Lord is in this place."* **L. M.**
Gen. 28: 16.

1 Lo, God is here!—let us adore,
And own how dreadful is this place!
Let all within us feel his power,
And silent bow before his face!

2 Lo, God is here!—him, day and night,
United choirs of angels sing;
To him, enthroned above all height,
Let saints their humble worship bring.

3 Lord God of hosts! Oh, may our praise
Thy courts with grateful incense fill!
Still may we stand before thy face,
Still hear and do thy sovereign will!

13 *"The Comforter."* John 16: 13. **L. M.**

1 Eternal Spirit! we confess
And sing the wonders of thy grace;
Thy power conveys our blessings down
From God, the Father, and the Son.

2 Enlightened by thy heavenly ray,
Our shades and darkness turn to day;
Thine inward teachings make us know
Our danger, and our refuge too.

ADORATION AND PRAISE.

HURSLEY. L. M.

3 Thy power and glory work within,
And break the chains of reigning sin,
Do our imperious lusts subdue,
And form our wretched hearts anew.

4 The troubled conscience knows thy voice,
Thy cheering words awake our joys;
Thy words allay the stormy wind,
And calm the surges of the mind.

14 *"The Scriptures" Thess. 1: 5.* **L. M.**

1 Now let my soul, Eternal King,
To Thee its grateful tribute bring;
My knee, with humble homage, bow;
My tongue perform its solemn vow.

2 All nature sings Thy boundless love,
In worlds below and worlds above
But in Thy blessed word I trace
Diviner wonders of Thy grace.

3 There Jesus bids my sorrows cease,
And gives my laboring conscience peace;
Raises my grateful passions high,
And points to mansions in the sky.

4 For love like this, oh let my song,
Through endless years, Thy praise prolong;
Let distant climes Thy name adore,
Till time and nature are no more.

15 *The Lord God omnipotent reigneth.* **L. M.**
Rev. 19: 6.

1 The Lord is King! lift up thy voice,
O earth, and all ye heavens, rejoice!
From world to world the joy shall ring:
"The Lord omnipotent is King!"

2 The Lord is King! who then shall dare
Resist his will, distrust his care?
Holy and true are all his ways,
Let every creature speak his praise.

3 The Lord is King! exalt your strains;
Ye saints, your God, your Father reigns;
One Lord one empire all secures:
He reigns, and life and death are yours.

4 Oh, when his wisdom can mistake,
His might decay, his love forsake,
Then may his children cease to sing,
"The Lord omnipotent is King!"

16 *"Return, O God of Hosts."* **L. M.**

1 Lord, in the temples of thy grace
Thy saints behold thy smiling face;
And oft have seen thy glory shine,
With power and majesty divine.

2 Come, dearest Lord, thy children cry,
Our graces droop our comforts die:
Return, and let thy glory rise
Again to our admiring eyes:

3 Till filled with light, and joy, and love,
Thy courts below, like those above,
Triumphant hallelujahs raise,
And heaven and earth resound thy praise.

Doxology. **L. M.**

To God, the Father, God the Son,
And God the Spirit, Three in One,
Be honor, praise, and glory given,
By all on earth, and all in heaven.

ADORATION AND PRAISE.

UXBRIDGE. L. M.

17 *"Being of God."* Heb 11:6. **L. M.**

1 There is a God, all nature speaks,
Thro' earth and air, and seas, and skies;
See, from the clouds, his glory breaks,
When the first beams of morning rise.

2 The rising sun, serenely bright,
O'er the wide world's extended frame,
Inscribes in characters of light,
His mighty Maker's glorious name.

3 The flow'ry tribes all blooming rise
Above the weak attempts of art;
The smallest worms, the meanest flies,
Speak sweet conviction to the heart.

4 Ye curious minds who roam abroad,
And trace creation's wonders o'er,
Confess the footsteps of your God,
Bow down before him, and adore.

18 *"Omnipresence of God."* **L. M.**

1 Lord of all being! throned afar,
Thy glory flames from sun and star;
Centre and soul of every sphere,
Yet to each loving heart how near!

2 Sun of our life! thy quickening ray
Sheds on our path the glow of day;
Star of our hope! thy softened light
Cheers the long watches of the night.

3 Our midnight is thy smile withdrawn;
Our noontide is thy gracious dawn;
Our rainbow arch thy mercy's sign;
All save the clouds of sin are thine.

4 Lord of all life! below, above,
Whose light is truth, whose warmth is love,
Before thy ever-blazing throne
We ask no luster of our own.

5 Grant us thy truth to make us free,
And kindling hearts that burn for thee,
Till all thy living altars claim
One holy light, one heavenly flame.

19 *"Wisdom of Providence."* **L. M.**
Ps. 46: 10.

1 Wait, O my soul, thy Maker's will,
Tumultuous passions, all be still!
Nor let a murm'ring thought arise,
His providence and ways are wise.

2 He in the thickest darkness dwells,
Performs the work, the cause conceals;
But though his methods are unknown,
Judgment and truth support his throne.

3 In heav'n and earth, and air and seas,
He executes his firm decrees;
And by his saints it stands confessed,
That what he does is ever best.

4 Wait then, my soul, submissive wait,
Prostrate before his awful seat;
And midst the terrors of his rod,
Trust in a wise and gracious God.

20 *"We rely on God our Father."* **L. M.**

1 Beneath a num'rous train of ills,
Our feeble flesh and heart may fail;
Yet shall our hope in thee, our God,
O'er ev'ry gloomy fear prevail.

ADORATION AND PRAISE.

HARMONY GROVE. L. M.

2 Parent and Husband, Guard and Guide,
Thou art each tender name in one;
On thee we cast our heavy cares;
And comfort seek from thee alone.

3 Our Father, God, to thee we look,
Our Rock, our Portion, and our Friend;
And on thy cov'nant, love and truth,
Our trusting souls shall still depend.

21 *"Thou art from everlasting."* **L. M.**
Psalm 93.

1 Jehovah reigns! He dwells in light,
Girded with majesty and might;
The world, created by his hands,
Still on its firm foundation stands.

2 But ere this spacious world was made,
Or had its first foundation laid,
Thy throne eternal ages stood,
Thyself the ever-living God.

3 Like floods the angry nations rise,
And aim their rage against the skies;
Vain floods, that aim their rage so high!
At thy rebuke the billows die.

4 For ever shall thy throne endure:
Thy promise stand for ever sure;
And everlasting holiness
Becomes the dwelling of thy grace.

22 *"The Glory of Jehovah."* **L. M.**
Psalm 97.

1 Jehovah reigns; his throne is high,
His robes are light and majesty:
His glory shines with beams so bright,
No mortal can sustain the sight.

2 His terrors keep the world in awe;
His justice guards his holy law;
His love reveals a smiling face;
His truth and promise seal the grace.

3 Thro' all his works what wisdom shines!
He baffles Satan's deep designs;
His power is sovereign to fulfill
The noblest counsels of his will.

4 And will this glorious Lord descend
To be my Father and my Friend?
Then let my songs with angels join,
Heaven is secure, if God is mine.

23 *"Oh, that men would praise the Lord!"* **L. M.**
Psalm 107.

1 Give thanks to God; he reigns above;
Kind are his thoughts, his name is love:
His mercy ages past have known,
And ages long to come shall own.

2 He feeds and clothes us all the way,
He guides our footsteps lest we stray;
He guards us with a powerful hand,
And brings us to the heavenly land.

3 Oh, let the saints with joy record
The truth and goodness of the Lord!
How great his works! how kind his ways!
Let every tongue pronounce his praise.

Doxology. **L. M.**

Praise God, from whom all blessings flow,
Praise him all creatures here below;
Praise him above, ye heav'nly host,
Praise Father, Son, and holy Ghost.

ADORATION AND PRAISE.

AVON. C. M.

24 *"Thrice Holy Lord."* Ps. 111: 9. C. M.

1 Holy and reverend is the name
Of our eternal King:
"Thrice holy Lord!" the angels cry;
"Thrice holy!" let us sing.

2 The deepest reverence of the mind,
Pay, O my soul! to God;
Lift, with thy hands, a holy heart,
To his sublime abode.

3 With sacred awe pronounce his name,
Whom words nor thoughts can reach;
A broken heart shall please him more
Than noblest forms of speech.

4 Thou holy God! preserve our souls
From all pollution free;
The pure in heart are thy delight,
And they thy face shall see.

25 *"The Love of God."* C. M.
1 John 4: 8.

1 Come ye that know and fear the Lord,
And lift your souls above;
Let ev'ry heart and voice accord,
To sing, that "God is love."

2 This precious truth his word declares,
And all his mercies prove;
Jesus, the gift of gifts, appears
To show, that "God is love."

3 In all his doctrines and commands,
His counsels and designs,
In ev'ry work his hands have fram'd,
His love supremely shines.

4 Angels and men the news proclaim,
Thro' earth and heav'n above,
The joyful and transporting news,
That God, the Lord, is love.

26 *"The Goodness of God."* C. M.

1 Ye humble souls, approach your God,
With songs of sacred praise;
For he is good, immensely good,
And kind are all his ways.

2 All nature owns his guardian care,
In him we live and move;
But nobler benefits declare
The wonders of his love.

3 He gave his Son, his only Son,
To ransom rebel worms;
'Tis here he makes his goodness known
In its diviner forms.

4 To this dear refuge, Lord, we come;
'Tis here our hope relies;
A safe defence, a peaceful home,
When storms of trouble rise.

27 *"The voice of praise.* Ps. 66. C. M.

1 Lift up to God the voice of praise,
Whose breath our souls inspired;
Loud and more loud the anthems raise,
With grateful ardor fired.

2 Lift up to God the voice of praise,
Whose goodness, passing thought,
Loads every moment, as it flies,
With benefits unsought.

ADORATION AND PRAISE.

DENFIELD. C. M.

3 Lift up to God the voice of praise,
From whom salvation flows:
Who sent his Son our souls to save
From everlasting woes.

4 Lift up to God the voice of praise,
For hope's transporting ray,
Which lights through darkest shades of death
To realms of endless day.

28   *An ancient Hymn to the Trinity.*   **C. M.**

1 To God be glory, peace on earth,
To all mankind good will;
We bless, we praise, we worship thee,
And glorify thee still;

2 And thanks for thy great glory give,
That fills our souls with light:
O Lord, our heavenly King, the God
And Father of all might!

3 And thou, begotten Son of God,
Before all time begun;
O Jesus Christ, thou Lamb of God,
The Father's only Son;

4 Thou who the sins of all the world
Dost fully take away,
Have mercy, Saviour of mankind,
And hear us when we pray!

5 O thou, who sitt'st at God's right hand,
Upon the Father's throne,
Have mercy on us, thou, O Christ,
Who art the Holy One!

6 Thou, only with the Holy Ghost,
Whom earth and heaven adore,
In glory of the Father art
Most high for evermore!

29   *Te Deum laudamus.*   **C. M.**

1 O God, we praise Thee and confess
That Thou the only Lord
And everlasting Father art,
By all the earth adored.

2 To Thee all Angels cry aloud;
To Thee the Powers on high,
Both Cherubim and Seraphim,
Continually do cry:

3 O Holy, Holy, Holy Lord,
Whom heavenly hosts obey,
The world is with the glory filled
Of Thy majestic sway.

4 The Apostles' glorious company,
And Prophets crowned with light,
With all the Martyrs' noble host,
Thy constant praise recite.

5 The Holy Church throughout the world,
O Lord, confesses Thee,
That Thou the Eternal Father art
Of boundless majesty.

Doxology.   **C. M.**

To Father, Son, and Holy Ghost,
The God whom we adore;
Be glory, as it was, is now,
And shall be evermore.

ADORATION AND PRAISE.

PLEYEL'S HYMN. 7s.

30   *Gloria in excelsis.*   7s.

1 Glory be to God on high,
God, whose glory fills the sky;
Peace on earth to man forgiven,
Man, the well-beloved of Heaven.

2 Sovereign Father, heavenly King,
Thee we now presume to sing;
Glad, thine attributes confess,
Glorious all, and numberless.

3 Hail, by all thy works adored!
Hail, the everlasting Lord!
Thee, with thankful hearts we prove
Lord of power, and God of love.

4 Christ our Lord and God we own,
Christ, the Father's only Son;
Lamb of God, for sinners slain,
Saviour of offending man.

5 Bow thine ear, in mercy bow;
Hear, the world's Atonement thou!
Jesus, in thy name we pray,
Take, O take our sins away.

6 Hear, for thou, O Christ, alone
Art with thy great Father One;
One, the Holy Ghost with thee;
One supreme, eternal three.

31   *Prayer for the Indwelling of the Spirit.*   7s.

1 Holy Spirit! Love Divine!
Let thy light within me shine;
Breathe thyself into my breast:
Earnest of immortal rest.

2 Let me never from thee stray,
Keep me in the narrow way:
Keep me thine, forever thine;
Let thy love and joy be mine.

32   *"All the sons of God shouted for joy."*   7s.

1 Songs of praise the angels sang,
Heaven with hallelujahs rang,
When Jehovah's work begun,
When he spake, and it was done.

2 Songs of praise awoke the morn,
When the Prince of Peace was born:
Songs of praise arose, when he
Captive led captivity.

3 Heaven and earth must pass away;
Songs of praise shall crown that day:
God will make new heavens and earth;
Songs of praise shall hail their birth.

4 Saints below, with heart and voice,
Still in songs of praise rejoice;
Learning here, by faith and love,
Songs of praise to sing above.

5 Borne upon their latest breath
Songs of praise shall conquer death;
Then, amid eternal joy,
Songs of praise their powers employ.

33   *"Holy, holy, holy is the Lord of Hosts."*   7s.

1 Holy, holy, holy Lord,
Be thy glorious name adored!
Lord, thy mercies never fail;
Hail, celestial Goodness, hail!

ADORATION AND PRAISE.

TELEMANN'S CHANT. 7s.

2 Though unworthy, Lord, thine ear,
Deign our humble songs to hear;
Purer praise we hope to bring,
When around thy throne we sing.

3 While on earth ordained to stay,
Guide our footsteps in thy way,
Till we come to dwell with Thee,
Till we all thy glory see.

4 Then with angel-harps again
We will wake a nobler strain;
There, in joyful songs of praise,
Our triumphant voices raise.

34 *"Within the Vail." Ps. 29: 2.* **7s.**

1 To thy temple I repair;
Lord, I love to worship there,
When within the vail I meet
Thee before the mercy seat.

2 While thy glorious praise is sung,
Touch my lips, unloose my tongue;
That my joyful soul may bless
Thee, the Lord, my Righteousness.

3 While the prayers of saints ascend,
God of love! to mine attend:
Hear me, for thy Spirit pleads;
Hear, for Jesus intercedes.

4 While I hearken to thy law,
Fill my soul with humble awe,
Till thy Gospel bring to me
Life and immortality.

5 From thine house when I return,
May my heart within me burn;
And at evening let me say,
"I have walked with God to-day."

35 *Te Deum laudamus.* **7s.**

1 God eternal, mighty King,
Unto Thee our praise we bring;
All the earth doth worship Thee;
We amid the throng would be.

2 Holy, Holy, Holy! cry,
Angels round Thy throne on high:
Lord of all the heavenly Powers,
Be the same loud anthem ours.

3 Glorified Apostles raise,
Night and day, continual praise;
Hast not Thou a mission too
For Thy children here to do?

4 With the Prophet's goodly line
We in mystic bond combine;
For Thou hast to us revealed
Things that to the wise were sealed.

5 Martyrs, in a noble host,
Of the cross are heard to boast;
Oh that we our cross may bear,
And a crown of glory wear!

6 God eternal, mighty King,
Unto Thee our praise we bring;
To the Father, and the Son,
And the Spirit, Three in One.

Doxology. **7s.**

Sing we to our God above,
Praise eternal as his love;
Praise him, all ye heavenly host,
Father, Son, and Holy Ghost.

ADORATION AND PRAISE.

WILMOT. 8s & 7s.

36 *Psalm 148.* 8s & 7s.

1 Praise the Lord! ye heavens, adore him;
Praise him, angels in the height;
Sun and moon, rejoice before him;
Praise him, all ye stars of light!

2 Praise the Lord—for he hath spoken;
Worlds his mighty voice obeyed;
Laws which never shall be broken,
For their guidance he hath made.

3 Praise the Lord—for he is glorious;
Never shall his promise fail;
God hath made his saints victorious,
Sin and death shall not prevail.

4 Praise the God of our salvation;
Hosts on high, his power proclaim;
Heaven and earth, and all creation,
Laud and magnify his Name!

37 *Brief Ascription of Praise.* 8s & 7s.

1 Worship, honor, glory, blessing,
Lord, we offer to thy name;
Young and old their thanks expressing,
Join thy goodness to proclaim:

2 As the hosts of heaven adore thee,
We, too, bow before thy throne;
As the angels serve before thee,
So on earth thy will be done.

38 *Praise to the Creator.—Ps. 107: 31.* 8s & 7s.

1 Praise to thee, thou great Creator!
Praise to thee from every tongue:
Join, my soul, with every creature,
Join the universal song.

2 Father, Source of all compassion,
Pure, unbounded grace is thine:
Hail the God of our salvation!
Praise him for his love divine.

3 For ten thousand blessings given,
For the hope of future joy,
Sound his praise thro' earth and heaven,
Sound Jehovah's praise on high.

4 Joyfully on earth adore him,
Till in heaven our song we raise;
There, enraptured, fall before him,
Lost in wonder, love, and praise.

39 *"And David said, 'Blessed be Thou.'"—1 Chron. 29: 10-23.* 8s & 7s.

1 Blest be thou, O God of Israel!
Thou, our Father and our Lord!
Majesty is thine forever;
Ever be thy name adored.

2 Thine, O Lord, are power and greatness;
Glory, vict'ry, are thine own;
All is thine in earth and heaven,
Over all thy boundless throne.

3 Riches come of thee, and honor;
Power and might to thee belong;
Thine it is to make us prosper,
Only thine to make us strong.

4 Lord, our God, for these, thy bounties,
Hymns of gratitude we raise;
To thy name, forever glorious,
Ever we address our praise.

ADORATION AND PRAISE.

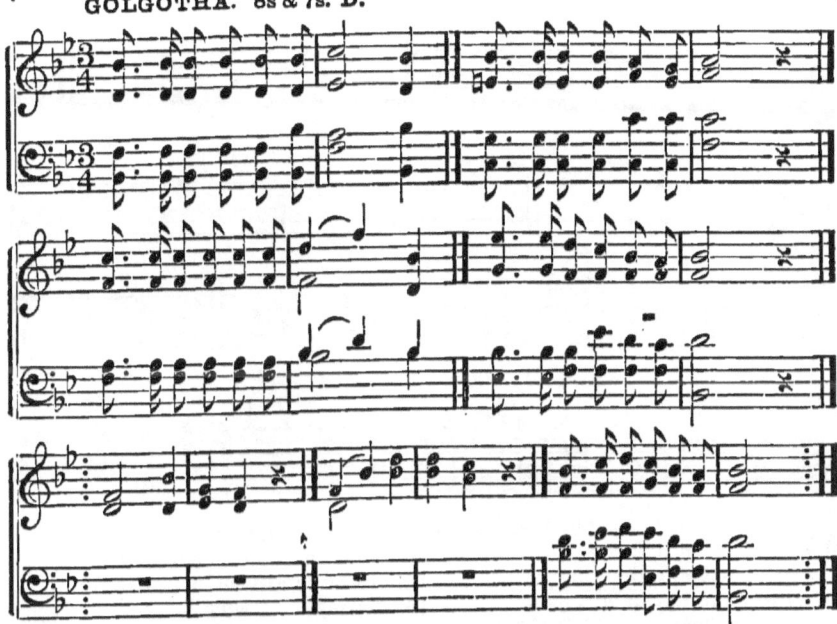

GOLGOTHA. 8s & 7s. D.

40 "*The Comforter.*" 8s & 7s.

1 Holy Ghost! dispel our sadness,
Pierce the clouds of sinful night;
Come, thou source of joy and gladness!
Breathe thy life and spread thy light.

2 Come, thou best of all donations
God doth give when men implore!
Having thy sweet consolations,
We need wish for nothing more.

3 Author of the new creation!
Let us now thine influence prove;
Make our hearts thy habitation,
Shed abroad a Saviour's love.

4 From that height that knows no measure
As a gracious rain descend,
Bringing down the richest treasure
We can ask or God can send.

5 Manifest thy love for ever,
Fence us in on every side;
In distress be our Reliever,
Guard and teach, support and guide.

6 Hear, oh hear our supplication,
Blessed Spirit! God of peace!
Rest upon this congregation
With the fulness of thy grace.

41 "*Heaven and earth are full of the majesty of thy glory.*" 8s & 7s.

1 Round the Lord in glory seated,
Cherubim and seraphim
Filled His temple and repeated
Each to each the alternate hymn:

2 "Lord, Thy glory fills the heaven,
Earth is with its fulness stored;
Unto Thee be glory given,
Holy, Holy, Holy, Lord!"

3 Heaven is still with glory ringing;
Earth takes up the angels' cry,
"Holy, Holy, Holy," singing,
"Lord of Hosts, the Lord most High."

4 With his seraph train before Him,
With His holy Church below,
Thus conspire we to adore Him,
Bid we thus our anthem flow:

5 "Lord, Thy glory fills the heaven,
Earth is with its fulness stored;
Unto Thee be glory given,
Holy, Holy, Holy, Lord!"

Doxology. 8s & 7s.

Praise the Father, earth and heaven,
Praise the Son, the Spirit praise,
As it was, and is, be given
Glory through eternal days.

THE REDEEMER.

SILVER STREET. S. M.

42 *"The song of Moses and the Lamb."* **S. M.**
  Rev. 15: 3, 4.

1 Awake and sing the song
Of Moses and the Lamb:
Wake ev'ry heart and ev'ry tongue,
To praise the Saviour's name.

2 Sing of his dying love,
Sing of his rising pow'r;
Sing how he intercedes above,
For those whose sins he bore.

3 Sing on your heav'nly way,
Ye ransom'd sinners sing;
Sing on rejoicing, ev'ry day,
In Christ, th' exalted King.

4 Soon shall our raptur'd tongue
His endless praise proclaim;
And sweeter voices tune the song
Of Moses and the Lamb.

43 *"To the only wise God, our Saviour."* **S. M.**
  Jude 24, 25.

1 To God, the only wise,
Our Saviour and our King,
Let all the saints below the skies
Their humble praises bring.

2 'Tis his Almighty love,
His counsel and his care,
Preserves us safe from sin and death,
And every hurtful snare.

3 He will present our souls,
Unblemished and complete,
Before the glory of his face,
With joys divinely great.

4 To our Redeemer, God,
Wisdom and power belong,
Immortal crowns of majesty,
And everlasting song.

44 *"Make a joyful noise unto Him with psalms."* **S. M.**
  Ps. 95.

1 Come, sound his praise abroad,
And hymns of glory sing:
Jehovah is the sovereign God,
The universal King.

2 He formed the deeps unknown;
He gave the seas their bound;
The watery worlds are all his own,
And all the solid ground.

3 Come, worship at his throne,
Come, bow before the Lord:
We are his work and not our own;
He formed us by his word.

4 To-day attend his voice,
Nor dare provoke his rod;
Come, like the people of his choice,
And own your gracious God.

45 *"The Lord is my Shepherd."* **S. M.**
  Ps. 23.

1 The Lord my Shepherd is;
I shall be well supplied:
Since he is mine, and I am his,
What can I want beside?

2 He leads me to the place
Where heavenly pasture grows;
Where living waters gently pass,
And full salvation flows.

THE REDEEMER.

LABAN. S. M.

3 If e'er I go astray,
He doth my soul reclaim;
And guides me, in his own right way,
For his most holy name.

4 While he affords his aid,
I cannot yield to fear;
Though I should walk through death's dark shade,
My Shepherd's with me there.

5 In spite of all my foes,
Thou dost my table spread;
My cup with blessings overflows,
And joy exalts my head.

6 The bounties of thy love
Shall crown my future days;
Nor from thy house will I remove,
Nor cease to speak thy praise.

46 *"All that call upon the name of Jesus Christ, our Lord."*—1 Cor 1: 2. S. M.

1 O Jesus, God and Man,
On this Thy holy day,
To Thee for precious gifts of grace
Thy ransomed people pray.

2 We pray for childlike hearts,
For gentle, holy love,
For strength to do Thy will below,
As angels do above.

3 We pray for simple faith,
For hope that never faints,
For true communion evermore
With all Thy blessed saints.

4 On friends around us here
O let Thy blessing fall;
We pray for grace to love them well,
But Thee beyond them all.

5 O joy to live for Thee!
O joy in Thee to die!
O very joy of joys to see
Thy Face eternally.

47 *Lord's day morning.—Psalm 84.* S. M.

1 Welcome sweet day of rest
That saw the Lord arise;
Welcome to this reviving breast,
And these rejoicing eyes.

2 The King himself comes near,
And feasts his saints to-day;
Here we may sit, and see him here,
And love, and praise, and pray.

3 One day amidst the place,
Where my great God hath been,
Is sweeter than ten thousand days
Of pleasurable sin.

4 My willing soul would stay
In such a frame as this,
And sing, and bear herself away
To everlasting bliss.

Doxology. S. M.

Ye angels round the throne,
And saints that dwell below,
Worship the Father, praise the Son,
And bless the Spirit too.

THE REDEEMER.

CORONATION. C. M.

48 *The Coronation.—Phil.* 2: 10. 11. **C. M.**

1 All hail, the power of Jesus' name!
Let angels prostrate fall:
Bring forth the royal diadem,
And crown him Lord of all!

2 Crown him, ye martyrs of our God,
Who from his altar call;
Extol the stem of Jesse's rod,
And crown him Lord of all!

3 Ye chosen seed of Israel's race,
A remnant weak and small,
Hail him who saves you by his grace,
And crown him Lord of all!

4 Ye Gentle sinners, ne'er forget
The wormwood and the gall;
Go, spread your trophies at his feet,
And crown him Lord of all!

5 Let every kindred, every tribe,
On this terrestrial ball,
To him all majesty ascribe,
And crown him Lord of all!

6 Oh, that with yonder sacred throng,
We at his feet may fall!
We'll join the everlasting song,
And crown him Lord of all!

2 Thee we acknowledge God and Lord,
The Lamb for sinners slain;
Who art by heaven and earth adored,
Worthy o'er both to reign!

3 To thee all angels cry aloud,
Through heaven's extended coasts;
Hail, holy, holy, holy Lord
Of glory and of hosts!

4 The prophets' goodly fellowship,
In radiant garments dressed,
Praise thee, thou Son of God, and reap
The fullness of thy rest.

5 Th' apostles' glorious company
Thy righteous praise proclaim;
The martyred army glorify
Thine everlasting name.

6 Throughout the world thy churches join
To call on thee, their Head,—
Brightness of Majesty divine,
Who every power hast made!

7 Among their number, Lord, we love
To sing thy precious blood:
Reign here, and in the worlds above,
Thou holy Lamb of God!

49 *An ancient Hymn of Praise to Christ.* **C. M.**

1 We sing to thee, thou Son of God,
Thou source of life and grace!
We praise thee, Son of Man, whose blood
Redeemed our fallen race!

50 *"The Way, and the Truth, and the Life."—John* 14: 6. **C. M.**

1 Thou art the Way: to thee alone
From sin and death we flee;
And he who would the Father seek,
Must seek him, Lord, by thee.

THE REDEEMER.

ARMENIA. C. M.

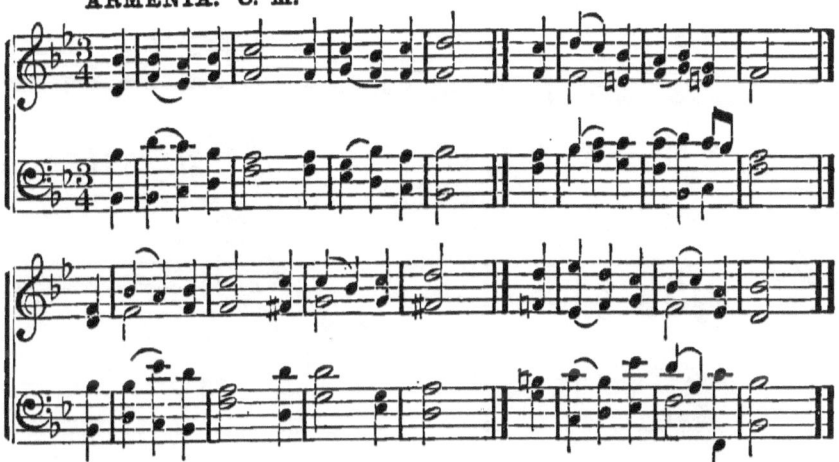

2 Thou art the Truth: thy word alone
True wisdom can impart;
Thou only canst instruct the mind,
And purify the heart.

3 Thou art the life: the rending tomb
Proclaims thy conqu'ring arm;
And those who put their trust in thee
Nor death nor hell shall harm.

4 Thou art the Way, the Truth, the Life;
Grant us to know that Way;
That Truth to keep, that Life to win,
Which leads to endless day.

51   *"This is my Friend."*   C. M.
       Cant 5: 10—16.

1 Majestic sweetness sits enthroned
Upon the Saviour's brow;
His head with radiant glories crowned,
His lips with grace o'erflow.

2 No mortal can with him compare,
Among the sons of men;
Fairer is he than all the fair
That fill the heavenly train.

3 He saw me plunged in deep distress,
He flew to my relief;
For me he bore the shameful cross,
And carried all my grief.

4 To him I owe my life and breath,
And all the joys I have;
He makes me triumph over death,
He saves me from the grave.

5 To heaven, the place of his abode,
He brings my weary feet;
Shows me the glories of my God,
And makes my joy complete.

6 Since from his bounty I receive
Such proofs of love divine,
Had I a thousand hearts to give,
Lord! they should all be thine.

52   *"Hosanna."—Matt 21: 9.*   C. M.

1 Hosanna! raise the pealing hymn
To David's Son and Lord;
With cherubim and seraphim
Exalt the Incarnate Word.

2 Hosanna! Master, lo, we bring
Our offerings to Thy throne;
Not gold, nor myrrh, nor mortal thing,
But hearts to be Thine own.

3 Hosanna! once Thy gracious ear
Approved a lisping throng;
Be gracious still, and deign to hear
Our poor but grateful song.

4 O Saviour, if redeemed by Thee,
Thy temple we behold,
Hosannas through eternity
We'll sing to harps of gold.

Doxology.   C. M.

To praise the Father and the Son,
And Spirit all divine,
The One in Three, and Three in One;
Let saints and angels join.

THE REDEEMER.

WARD. L. M.

53 *The example of Christ.—Rom 8: 29.* **L. M.**

1 My dear Redeemer, and my Lord!
I read my duty in thy word:
But, in thy life the law appears,
Drawn out in living characters.

2 Such was thy truth, and such thy zeal,
Such def'rence to thy Father's will,
Thy love and meekness so divine,
I would transcribe and make them mine.

3 Cold mountains and the midnight air
Witness'd the fervor of thy pray'r:
The desert thy temptations knew,
Thy conflict and thy vic'try too.

4 Be thou my pattern; let me bear
More of thy gracious image here:
Then God the judge shall own my name
Among the foll'wers of the Lamb.

54 *Delight in Christ.* **L. M.**

1 Jesus, thou Joy of loving hearts!
Thou Fount of Life! thou Light of men!
From the best bliss that earth imparts,
We turn unfilled to thee again.

2 Thy truth unchanged hath ever stood;
Thou savest those that on thee call;
To them that seek thee thou art good,
To them that find thee—All in All!

3 We taste thee, O thou Living Bread,
And long to feast upon thee still:
We drink of thee, the Fountain Head,
And thirst our souls from thee to fill.

4 Our restless spirits yearn for thee,
Where'er our changeful lot is cast;
Glad, when thy gracious smile we see,
Blest, when our faith can hold thee fast.

5 O Jesus, ever with us stay,
Make all our moments calm and bright;
Chase the dark night of sin away,—
Shed o'er the world thy holy light.

55 *Not ashamed of Christ.—Mark 8: 38.* **L. M.**

1 Jesus! and shall it ever be
A mortal man asham'd of thee?
Asham'd of thee, whom angels praise,
Whose glories shine through endless days?

2 Asham'd of Jesus: sooner far
Let ev'ning blush to own a star:
He sheds the beams of light divine
O'er this benighted soul of mine.

3 Asham'd of Jesus! just as soon
Let midnight be asham'd of noon;
'Tis midnight with my soul till he,
Bright Morning-Star! bid darkness flee.

4 Asham'd of Jesus! that dear friend
On whom my hopes of heav'n depend!
No; when I blush—be this my shame,
That I no more revere his name.

5 Asham'd of Jesus! yes I may,
When I've no guilt to wash away,
No tear to wipe, no good to crave,
No fears to quell, no soul to save.

THE REDEEMER.

LOVING-KINDNESS. L. M.

6 Till then,—nor is my boasting vain—
Till then I boast a Saviour slain!
And O may this my glory be,
That Christ is not asham'd of me!

56 *Ps. 36: 7.* **L. M.**

1 Awake, my soul, in joyful lays,
And sing thy great Redeemer's praise;
He justly claims a song from thee,
His loving-kindness, oh, how free!

2 He saw me ruined in the fall,
Yet loved me notwithstanding all;
He saved me from my lost estate,
His loving-kindness, oh, how great!

3 Though num'rous hosts of mighty foes,
Though earth and hell my way oppose,
He safely leads my soul along,
His loving-kindness, oh, how strong!

4 When trouble, like a gloomy cloud,
Has gathered thick, and thundered loud,
He near my soul has always stood,
His loving-kindness, oh, how good!

5 Often I feel my sinful heart
Prone from my Saviour to depart;
But, though I oft have him forgot,
His loving-kindness changes not.

6 Soon shall I pass the gloomy vale,
Soon all my mortal powers must fail;
Oh, may my last expiring breath
His loving-kindness sing in death.

57 *"Unto the Lamb for ever."* **L. M.**
Rev. 1: 5. 6.

1 What equal honors shall we bring
To thee, O Lord our God, the Lamb,
When all the notes that angels sing
Are far inferior to thy name?

2 Worthy is he who once was slain,
The Prince of Peace, who groaned and died;
Worthy to rise, and live and reign
At his almighty Father's side.

3 Blessings for ever on the Lamb,
Who bore the curse for wretched men;
Let angels sound his sacred name,
And every creature say, Amen!

58 *Rev. 5: 11. 12.* **L. M.**

1 Around the Saviour's lofty throne,
Ten thousand times ten thousand sing;
They worship him as God alone,
And crown him—everlasting King.

2 Approach, ye saints! this God is yours;
'Tis Jesus fills the throne above:
Ye cannot want while God endures;
Ye cannot fail while God is love.

3 Jesus, thou everlasting King!
To thee the praise of heaven belongs;
Yet, smile on us who fain would bring
The tribute of our humble songs.

4 Though sin defile our worship here,
We hope ere long thy face to view;
And when our souls in heaven appear,
We'll praise thy name as angels do.

THE REDEEMER.

ST. MARTINS. C. M.

59 *"The chiefest among ten thousand."* **C. M.**
1 Tim. 1: 15.

1 The Saviour! oh, what endless charms
Dwell in that blissful sound!
Its influence every fear disarms,
And spreads sweet comfort round.

2 Here pardon, life, and joys divine,
In rich effusion flow,
For guilty rebels lost in sin,
And doomed to endless woe.

3 The almighty Former of the skies
Stooped to our vile abode;
While angels viewed with wondering eyes,
And hailed th' incarnate God.

4 O, the rich depths of love divine!
Of bliss, a boundless store!
Dear Saviour, let me call thee mine:
I cannot wish for more.

5 On thee alone my hope relies;
Beneath thy cross I fall;
My Lord, my life, my sacrifice,
My Saviour, and my all!

60 *"Thou shalt call his name Jesus."* **C. M.**
Matt. 1: 21.

1 Oh, for a thousand tongues to sing
My dear Redeemer's praise,
The glories of my God and King,
The triumphs of his grace!

2 My gracious Master and my God,
Assist me to proclaim,
To spread through all the earth abroad
The honors of thy name.

3 Jesus! the name that calms our fears,
That bids our sorrows cease—
'Tis music to my ravished ears,
'Tis life, and health, and peace.

4 He breaks the power of reigning sin,
He sets the prisoner free;
His blood can make the foulest clean:
His blood availed for me.

5 He speaks, and, listening to his voice,
New life the dead receive;
The mourning, broken hearts rejoice,
The humble poor believe.

6 Hear him, ye deaf! his praise, ye dumb,
Your loosened tongues employ!
Ye blind, behold your Saviour come,
And leap, ye lame, for joy!

61 *"The love of Christ constraineth us."* **C. M.**
2 Cor. 5: 14.

1 Jesus, in thy transporting name
What blissful glories rise!
Jesus—the angels' sweetest theme!
The wonder of the skies!

2 Well might the skies with wonder view
A love so strange as thine!
No thought of angels ever knew
Compassion so divine!

3 Jesus, and didst thou leave the sky
To bear our sins and woes?
And didst thou bleed, and groan, and die
For vile, rebellious foes?

THE REDEEMER.

HEBER. C. M.

4 Is there a heart that will not bend
To thy divine control?
Descend, O sovereign Love, descend,
And melt the stubborn soul!

5 Oh, may our willing hearts confess
Thy sweet, thy gentle sway!
Glad captives of resistless grace,
Thy pleasing rule obey.

6 Come, dearest Lord, extend thy reign,
Till rebels rise no more:
Thy praise all nature then shall join,
And heaven and earth adore.

62   *"My Jesus and my God."*   **C. M.**
       1 Cor 1: 22-24.

1 Dearest of all the names above,
My Jesus and my God,
Who can resist thy heavenly love,
Or trifle with thy blood?

2 'T is by the merits of thy death
Thy Father smiles again;
'T is by thine interceding breath
The Spirit dwells with men.

3 Till God in human flesh I see,
My thoughts no comfort find:
The holy, just, and sacred Three
Are terror to my mind.

4 But if Immanuel's face appear,
My hope, my joy, begin:
His name forbids my slavish fear;
His grace removes my sin.

5 While Jews on their own law rely,
And Greeks of wisdom boast,
I love th' incarnate Mystery,
And there I fix my trust.

63   *An ancient hymn to Christ.*   **C. M.**

1 O Jesus, King most wonderful,
Thou Conqueror renowned,
Thou sweetness most ineffable,
In whom all joys are found!

2 When once thou visitest the heart,
Then truth begins to shine;
Then earthly vanities depart;
Then kindles love divine.

3 O Jesus, Light of all below!
Thou Fount of life and fire!
Surpassing all the joys we know,
All that we can desire,

4 May every heart confess thy name,
And ever thee adore;
And seeking thee, itself inflame
To seek thee more and more.

5 Thee may our tongues for ever bless;
Thee may we love alone;
And ever in our lives express
The image of thine own.

             Doxology.   **C. M.**

To Father, Son and Holy Ghost,
One God whom we adore,
Be glory as it was, is now,
And shall be evermore.

THE REDEEMER.

ARLINGTON. C. M.

64 *The name of Jesus.*—1 Pet. 2: 7. **C. M.**

1 How sweet the name of Jesus sounds
In a believer's ear!
It soothes his sorrows, heals his wounds,
And drives away his fear.

2 It makes the wounded spirit whole,
And calms the troubled breast;
'Tis manna to the hungry soul,
And to the weary rest.

3 Dear name! the rock on which I build,
My shield and hiding-place;
My never-failing treas'ry, fill'd
With boundless stores of grace.

4 Jesus! my Shepherd, Husband, Friend,
My Prophet, Priest, and King,
My Lord, my Life, my Way, my End,
Accept the praise I bring.

5 Weak is the effort of my heart,
And cold my warmest thought;
But when I see thee as thou art,
I'll praise thee as I ought.

6 Till then I would thy love proclaim
With ev'ry fleeting breath;
And may the music of thy name
Refresh my soul in death.

65 *Luke 23: 42.* **C. M.**

1 Jesus, Thou art the sinner's Friend;
As such I look to Thee:
Now in the fulness of Thy love,
O Lord, remember me.

2 Remember Thy pure word of grace,
Remember Calvary;
Remember all Thy dying groans,
And then remember me.

3 Thou wondrous Advocate with God,
I yield myself to thee;
While thou art sitting on thy throne,
Dear Lord, remember me.

4 Lord, I am guilty, I am vile,
But thy salvation's free;
Then in thine all-abounding grace,
Dear Lord, remember me.

5 And, when I close my eyes in death,
When creature-helps all flee,
Then, O my dear Redeemer-God,
I pray, remember me.

66 *Christ our only joy.* Math 17: 8. **C. M.**

1 Jesus! the very thought of thee
With gladness fills my breast;
But dearer far thy face to see,
And in thy presence rest.

2 Nor voice can sing, nor heart can frame,
Nor can the memory find
A sweeter sound than thy blest name,
O Saviour of mankind!

3 O Hope of every contrite heart,
O Joy of all the meek!
To those who fall, how kind thou art,
How good to those who seek!

THE REDEEMER.

CROSS AND CROWN. C. M.

4 And those who find thee, find a bliss
Nor tongue nor pen can show:
The love of Jesus—what it is,
None but his loved ones know.

5 Jesus, our only joy be thou!
As thou our prize wilt be;
Jesus, be thou our glory now,
And through eternity!

67 *"He reviled not again."* 1 Pet 2: 21-23. **C. M.**

1 What grace, O Lord, and beauty shone,
Around thy steps below;
What patient love was seen in all
Thy life and death of woe.

2 For, ever on thy burdened heart,
A weight of sorrow hung;
Yet no ungentle, murmuring word
Escaped thy silent tongue.

3 Thy foes might hate, despise, revile,
Thy friends unfaithful prove;
Unwearied in forgiveness still,
Thy heart could only love.

4 Oh, give us hearts to love like thee!
Like thee, O Lord, to grieve
Far more for others' sin than all
The wrongs that we receive.

5 One with thyself, may every eye,
In us, thy brethren, see
The gentleness and grace that spring
From union, Lord, with thee.

68 *Christ is our strength and righteousness. Psalm 71.* **C. M.**

1 My Saviour, my Almighty Friend,
When I begin thy praise,
Where will the growing numbers end,
The numbers of thy grace?

2 Thou art my everlasting trust,
Thy goodness I adore!
And since I knew thy graces first,
I speak thy glories more.

3 My feet shall travel all the length
Of the celestial road,
And march with courage in thy strength
To see my Father, God.

4 When I am filled with sore distress
For some surprising sin,
I'll plead thy perfect righteousness,
And mention none but thine.

5 How will my lips rejoice to tell
The vict'ries of my King!
My soul, redeem'd from sin and hell,
Shall thy salvation sing.

6 My tongue shall all the day proclaim
My Saviour and my God;
His death hath brought my foes to shame,
And sav'd me by his blood.

Doxology. **C. M.**

Let God the Father, and the Son,
And Spirit, be adored,
Where there are works to make him known,
Or saints to love the Lord!

THE REDEEMER.

TALLIS' EVENING HYMN. L. M.

69   *"I am the Light of the world."*   L. M.
           John 8: 12.

1 O Christ, our true and only light!
Illumine those who sit in night;
Let those afar now hear thy voice,
And in thy fold with us rejoice.

2 And all who else have strayed from thee,
Oh, gently seek! thy healing be
To every wounded conscience given,
And let them also share thy heaven.

3 Oh make the deaf to hear thy word,
And teach the dumb to speak, dear Lord,
Who dare not yet the faith avow,
Though secretly they hold it now.

4 Shine on the darkened and the cold,
Recall the wanderers from thy fold;
Unite those now who walk apart,
Confirm the weak and doubting heart.

5 So they, with us, may evermore
Such grace with wondering thanks adore,
And endless praise to thee be given,
By all thy Church in earth and heaven.

70   *"No other name."—Acts. 4: 12.*   L. M.

1 Jesus, the spring of joys divine
Whence all our hopes and comforts flow,
Jesus, no other name but thine
Can save us from eternal woe.

2 In vain would boasting reason find
The way to happiness and God:
Her weak directions leave the mind
Bewildered in a dubious road.

3 No other name will heaven approve;
Thou art the true, the living way,
Ordained by everlasting love,
To the bright realms of endless day.

4 Safe lead us through this world of night,
And bring us to the blissful plains,
The regions of unclouded light,
Where perfect joy for ever reigns.

71   *"Thine wholly—Thine alone."*   L. M.

1 Jesus! thy boundless love to me
No thought can reach, no tongue declare;
Unite my thankful heart to thee,
And reign without a rival there.

2 Thy love, how cheerful is its ray!
All pain before its presence flies;
Care, anguish, sorrow, melt away
Where'er its healing beams arise.

3 Oh, let thy love my soul inflame,
And to thy service sweetly bind;
Transfuse it through my inmost frame,
And mould me wholly to thy mind.

4 Thy love, in sufferings, be my peace;
Thy love, in weakness, make me strong:
And when the storms of life shall cease,
Thy love shall be in heaven my song.

72   *"The one thing needful."*   L. M.
           Luke 10: 42.

1 Jesus! engrave it on my heart
That thou the one thing needful art;
I could from all things parted be,
But never, never, Lord, from thee.

THE REDEEMER.

MIGDOL. L. M.

2 Needful is thy most precious blood
To reconcile my soul to God,
Needful is thy indulgent care,
Needful thy all-prevailing prayer.

3 Needful thy presence, dearest Lord,
True peace and comfort to afford,
Needful thy promise, to impart
Fresh life and vigor to my heart.

4 Needful art thou, my Guide, my Stay,
Through all life's dark and weary way;
Nor less in death thou'lt needful be
To bring my spirit home to thee.

5 Then needful still, my God, my King,
Thy name eternally I'll sing!
Glory and praise be ever his—
The one thing needful Jesus is!

73 *"He hath done all things well." Mark 7: 37.* **L. M.**

1 Now, in a song of grateful praise,
To my dear Lord my voice I'll raise;
With all his saints I'll join to tell
That Jesus hath done all things well.

2 Wisdom, and power, and love divine,
In all his works, unrivaled, shine,
And force the wondering world to tell
That he alone did all things well.

3 Howe'er mysterious are his ways,
Or dark and sorrowful my days;
And though my spirit oft rebel,
I know he still doth all things well.

4 And when I stand before his throne,
And all his ways are fully known,
This note in sweetest strains shall swell,
That Jesus hath done all things well.

74 *Hosanna.* **L. M.**

1 Hosanna to the living Lord!
Hosanna to th' incarnate Word!
To Christ, Creator, Saviour, King,
Let earth, let heaven, Hosanna sing;—

2 "Hosanna! Lord!" thine angels cry,
"Hosanna! Lord!" thy saints reply;
Above, beneath us, and around,
The dead and living swell the sound.

3 O Saviour! with protecting care,
Return to this thy house of prayer,
Assembled in thy sacred name,
Where we our parting promise claim.

4 But, chiefest, in our cleansed breast,
Eternal! bid thy Spirit rest,
And make our secret soul to be
A temple pure, and worthy thee.

5 So, in the last and dreadful day,
When earth and heaven shall melt away,
Thy flock redeemed from sinful stain,
Shall swell the sound of praise again.

Doxology. **L. M.**

To God the Father, God the Son,
And God the Spirit, Three in One,
Be honor, praise, and glory given,
By all on earth and all in heaven.

THE REDEEMER.

MARTYN. 7s. Double.

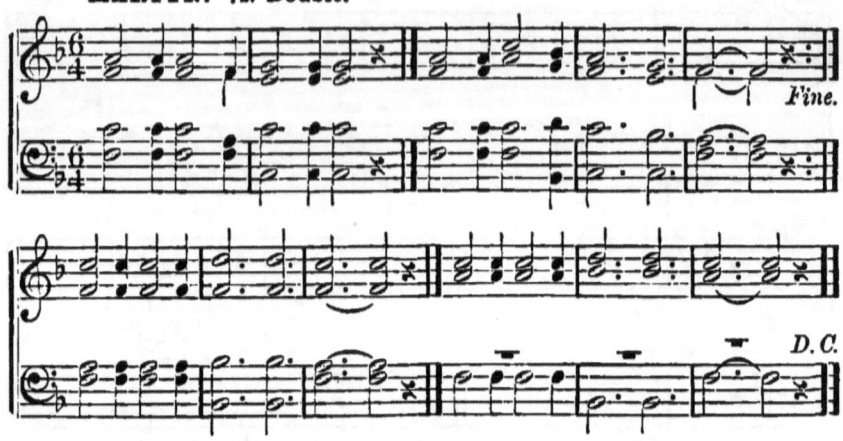

75   *"Jesus, Lover of my soul."*
           Psalm 57: 1.

1 Jesus, Lover of my soul,
Let me to thy bosom fly,
While the waters near me roll,
While the tempest still is high:
Hide me, O my Saviour, hide,
Till the storm of life is past;
Safe into the haven guide:
Oh, receive my soul at last!

2 Other refuge have I none;
Hangs my helpless soul on thee:
Leave, ah! leave me not alone;
Still support and comfort me;
All my trust on thee is stayed,
All my help from thee I bring,
Cover my defenseless head
With the shadow of thy wing.

76   *"I lay down my life for the sheep,"*   7s.
           John 10: 15.

1 Shepherd of the ransomed flock,
Lead us to the shadowing rock,
Where the cooling waters flow,
Where the freshening pastures grow.
Grant, O Lord, that we may be
Ever glad to follow thee;
And with thankful hearts rejoice,
When we hear thy gracious voice.

2 Saviour, when thy loved ones stray,
From the new and living way,
Gently call thine own by name;
All our wand'ring steps reclaim.

7s. Jesus, who thy life didst give,
Dying that thy sheep might live;
Let us in thy presence rest,
With eternal comfort blest.

77   *"Looking unto Jesus."*   7s.
           Heb. 12: 2.

1 When, along life's thorny road,
Faints the soul beneath the load,
By its cares and sins oppressed,
Finds on earth no peace or rest;
When the wily tempter's near,
Filling us with doubts and fear,
Jesus, to thy feet we flee;
Jesus, we will look to thee.

2 Thou, our Saviour, from the throne
List'nest to thy people's moan:
Thou, the living Head, dost share
Every pang thy members bear:
Full of tenderness thou art,
Thou wilt heal the broken heart;
Full of power, thine arm shall quell
All the rage and might of hell.

3 Mighty to redeem and save,
Thou hast overcome the grave:
Thou the bars of death hast riven,
Opened wide the gate of heaven:
Soon in glory thou shalt come,
Taking thy poor pilgrims home:
Jesus, then we all shall be
Ever, ever, Lord, with thee!

THE REDEEMER.

HOLLEY. 7s.

78 *Wonders of God's Condescension.*
   Psalm 113.   **7s.**

1 Hallelujah! raise, oh, raise
To our God the song of praise:
All his servants join to sing,
God, our Saviour and our King.

2 Blessed be for evermore
That dread name which we adore:
O'er all nations, God alone,
Higher than the heavens his throne.

3 Yet to view the heavens he bends;
Yea, to earth he condescends;
Passing by the rich and great
For the low and desolate.

4 He can raise the poor to stand
With the princes of the land;
Wealth upon the needy shower;
Set the lowliest high in power.

5 He the broken spirit cheers,
Turns to joy the mourner's tears,
Such the wonders of his ways:
Praise his name, for ever praise.

79 *"The Light and the Life of men."*
   John 1: 4.   **7s.**

1 Light of life!—seraphic Fire!
Love divine!—thyself impart;
Every fainting soul inspire;
Shine in every drooping heart.
Every mournful sinner cheer;
Scatter all our guilty gloom:
Saviour—Son of God! appear;
To thy human temples come.

7s. 2 Come, in this accepted hour,
Bring thy heavenly kingdom in;
Fill us with thy glorious power—
Rooting out the love of sin.
Nothing more can we require,
We will covet nothing less;
Be thou all our heart's desire,
All our joy and all our peace.

80   *Isa. 35: 8—10.*   **7s.**

1 Children of the Heavenly King,
As ye journey sweetly sing;
Sing your Saviour's worthy praise,
Glorious in His works and ways.

2 We are travelling home to God
In the way the fathers trod;
They are happy now, and we
Soon their happiness shall see.

3 Fear not, brethren; joyful stand
On the borders of your land;
Jesus Christ, your Father's Son,
Bids you undismayed go on.

7s. 4 Lord, obediently we go,
Gladly leaving all below;
Only thou our Leader be,
And we still will follow Thee!

Doxology.   **7s.**

Father, Son, and Holy Ghost,
Blessing, honor, glory be
Given by all the heavenly host,
And by all on earth, to Thee!

THE REDEEMER.

COVENTRY. C. M.

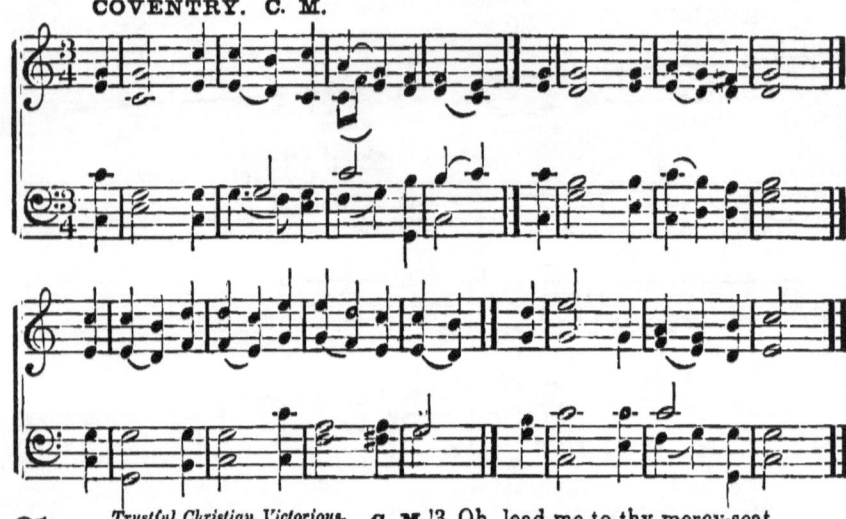

81 *Trustful Christian Victorious.*
Cant. 2: 16. C. M.

1 My God! the spring of all my joys,
The life of my delights,
The glory of my brightest days,
And comfort of my nights!

2 In darkest shades if he appear,
My dawning is begun:
He is my soul's sweet morning star,
And he my rising sun.

3 The opening heavens around me shine,
With beams of sacred bliss,
While Jesus shows his heart is mine,
And whispers, I am his!

4 My soul would leave this heavy clay
At that transporting word,
Run up with joy the shining way,
T" embrace my dearest Lord.

5 Fearless of hell, and ghastly death,
I'd break through every foe;
The wings of love and arms of faith
Should bear me conqu'ror through.

82 *Luke 10: 39.* C. M.

1 Jesus, My Saviour! bind me fast
In cords of heavenly love;
Then sweetly draw me to thy breast,
Nor let me thence remove.

2 Draw me from all created good,
From self, the world and sin,
To the dear fountain of thy blood,
And make me pure within.

3 Oh, lead me to thy mercy-seat,
Attract me nearer still:
Draw me, like Mary, to thy feet,
To sit and learn thy will.

4 Oh, draw me by thy providence,
Thy Spirit and thy word,
From all the things of time and sense,
To thee, my gracious Lord.

83 *Love to Christ desired.—Titus 2: 11.* C. M.

1 Thou lovely source of true delight,
Whom I unseen adore,
Unveil thy beauties to my sight,
That I may love thee more.

2 Thy glory o'er creation shines,
But in thy sacred word
I read, in fairer, brighter lines,
My bleeding, dying Lord.

3 'Tis here whene'er my comforts droop,
And sin and sorrow rise,
Thy love, with cheerful beams of hope,
My fainting breast supplies.

4 Jesus, my Lord, my Life, my Light!
Oh! come with blissful ray;
Break radiant through the shades of night,
And chase my fears away.

5 O may my soul with rapture trace
The wonders of thy love!
But the full glories of thy face
Are only known above.

THE REDEEMER.

MERTON. C. M.

84 *Living with Christ.—Cant. 1: 4.* **C. M.**

1 O could I find from day to day,
A nearness to my God!
Then should my hours glide sweet away,
While leaning on his word.

2 Lord, I desire with thee to live
Anew from day to day;
In joys the world can never give,
Nor ever take away.

3 Blest Jesus! come and rule my heart,
And make me wholly thine,
That I may never more depart,
Nor grieve thy love divine.

4 Thus, till my last, expiring breath,
Thy goodness I'll adore;
And when my frame dissolves in death,
My soul shall love thee more.

85 *"Thou shalt call his name Jesus." Matt. 1: 21.* **C. M.**

1 Jesus! I love thy charming name;
'Tis music to mine ear:
Fain would I sound it out so loud,
That earth and heaven should hear.

2 All that my loftiest powers can wish,
In thee doth richly meet:
Not to mine eyes is light so dear,
Nor friendship half so sweet.

3 Thy grace still dwells upon my heart,
And sheds its fragrance there—
The noblest balm of all my wounds,
The cordial of my care.

4 I'll speak the honors of thy name
With my last lab'ring breath;
Then, speechless, clasp thee in mine arms,
The conqueror of death.

5 When death these mortal eyes shall seal,
And still this throbbing heart,
The rending vail shall thee reveal,
All glorious as thou art!

86 *Christ loved Unseen. 1 Peter 1: 8.* **C. M.**

1 Jesus, these eyes have never seen
That radiant form of thine!
The vail of sense hangs dark between
Thy blessed face and mine!

2 I see thee not, I hear thee not,
Yet art thou oft with me;
And earth hath ne'er so dear a spot,
As where I meet with thee.

3 Like some bright dream that comes unsought,
When slumbers o'er me roll,
Thine image ever fills my thought,
And charms my ravished soul.

4 Yet though I have not seen, and still
Must rest in faith alone;
I love thee, dearest Lord!—and will,
Unseen, but not Unknown.

Doxology. **C. M.**

To Father, Son, and Holy Ghost,
One God, whom we adore,
Be glory as it was, is now,
And shall be evermore.

THE REDEEMER.

ITALIAN HYMN. 6s & 4s.

87 *"He first loved us.—1 John 4: 19.* **6s & 4s.**

1 Jesus! thy name I love
All other names above,
Jesus, my Lord!
Oh, thou art all to me!
Nothing to please I see,
Nothing apart from thee,
Jesus, my Lord!

2 Thou, blessed Son of God!
Hast bought me with thy blood,
Jesus, my Lord!
Oh, how great is thy love,
All other loves above—
Love that I daily prove,
Jesus, my Lord!

3 When unto thee I flee,
Thou wilt my refuge be,
Jesus, my Lord!
What need I now to fear?
What earthly grief or care,
Since thou art ever near?
Jesus, my Lord!

4 Soon thou wilt come again;
I shall be happy then,
Jesus, my Lord!
Then thine own face I'll see,
Then I shall like thee be,
Then evermore with thee,
Jesus, my Lord!

88 *"The Lamb that was slain.*
Rev. 5. **6s & 4s.**

1 Glory to God on high!
Let heaven and earth reply,
"Praise ye his name!"
His love and grace adore,
Who all our sorrows bore;
Sing loud forever more,
"Worthy the Lamb!"

2 While they around the throne
Cheerfully join in one,
Praising his name,—
Ye, who have felt his blood
Sealing your peace with God,
Sound his dear name abroad,
"Worthy the Lamb!"

3 Join, all ye ransomed race,
Our Lord and God to bless:
Praise ye his name!
In him we will rejoice,
And make a joyful noise,
Shouting with heart and voice,
"Worthy the Lamb!"

4 Soon must we change our place,
Yet will we never cease
Praising his name:
To him our songs we bring;
Hail him our gracious King;
And through all ages sing,
"Worthy the Lamb!"

THE REDEEMER.

NEW HAVEN. 6s & 4s.

89   6s & 4s.

1 Shepherd of tender youth,
Guiding in love and truth
Through devious ways —
Christ, our triumphant King,
We come thy name to sing,
And here our children bring,
To shout thy praise.

2 Thou art our holy Lord,
O all-subduing Word,
Healer of strife:
Thou didst thyself abase,
That from sin's deep disgrace
Thou mightest save our race,
And give us life.

3 Ever be near our side,
Our Shepherd and our Guide,
Our staff and song;
Jesus, thou Christ of God,
By thine enduring word
Lead us where thou hast trod;
Make our faith strong.

4 So now, and till we die,
Sound we thy praises high,
And joyful sing:
Let all the holy throng,
Who to thy Church belong,
Unite and swell the song
To Christ our King!

90   *"Worthy is the Lamb."—Rev. 5.*   6s & 4s.

1 Come, all ye saints of God,
Wide through the earth abroad
Spread Jesus' fame:
Tell what his love hath done;
Trust in his name alone;
Shout to his lofty throne,
"Worthy the Lamb!"

2 Hence, gloomy doubts and fears!
Dry up your mournful tears;
Swell the glad theme:
To Christ, our gracious King,
Strike each melodious string;
Join heart and voice to sing,
"Worthy the Lamb!"

3 Hark! how the choirs above,
Filled with the Saviour's love,
Dwell on his name!
There, too, may we be found,
With light and glory crowned,
While all the heavens resound,
"Worthy the Lamb!"

Doxology.   6s & 4s.

To the great One in Three,
The highest praises be,
Hence, evermore;
His sovereign majesty
May we in glory see,
And to eternity
Love and adore.

THE REDEEMER.

BREMEN. C. P. M.

91   *"The unsearchable riches of Christ.."*—1 Pet. 2: 7.   C. P. M.

1 O could I speak the matchless worth,
O could I sound the glories forth
Which in my Saviour shine!
I'd soar, and touch the heavenly strings,
And vie with Gabriel, while he sings,
In notes almost divine.

2 I'd sing the precious blood he spilt,
My ransom from the dreadful guilt
Of sin and wrath divine:
I'd sing his glorious righteousness,
In which all perfect, heavenly dress,
My soul shall ever shine.

3 I'd sing the characters he bears,
And all the forms of love he wears,
Exalted on his throne;
In loftiest songs of sweetest praise,
I would to everlasting days
Make all his glories known.

4 Well, the delightful day will come
When my dear Lord will bring me home,
And I shall see his face;
Then with my Saviour, Brother, Friend,
A blest eternity I'll spend,
Triumphant in his grace.

92   *"The love of Christ, which passeth knowledge."*—Eph. 3: 19.   C. P. M.

1 O Love divine, how sweet thou art!
When shall I find my willing heart
All taken up by thee?
I thirst, I faint, I die to prove
The greatness of redeeming love,
The love of Christ to me!

2 O that I could, with favor'd John,
Recline my weary head upon
The dear Redeemer's breast!
From care, and sin, and sorrow free,
Give me, O Lord, to find in Thee
My everlasting rest!

3 Only Thy love do I require,
Nothing on earth below desire,
But this in heav'n above;
Let earth, and heav'n, and all things go,
Give me Thy only love to know,
Impart to me Thy love.

93   Matt. 25: 46.   C. P. M.

1 O thou that hear'st the prayer of faith,
Wilt thou not save a soul from death
That casts itself on thee?
I have no refuge of my own,
But fly to what my Lord has done
And suffered once for me.

2 Slain in the guilty sinner's stead,
His spotless righteousness I plead,
And his availing blood;
Thy merit, Lord, my robe shall be,
Thy merit shall atone for me,
And bring me near to God.

THE REDEEMER.

WADE. C. P. M.

3 Then snatch me from eternal death,
The spirit of adoption breathe,
His consolation send:
By him some word of life impart,
And sweetly whisper to my heart,
"Thy Maker is thy Friend."

4 The king of terrors then would be
A welcome messenger to me,
That bids me come away;
Unclogg'd by earth or earthly things,
I'd mount upon his sable wings
To everlasting day.

94 *Praise from all creatures.* **C. P. M.**
Psalm 148.

1 Begin, my soul, th' exalted lay,
Let each enraptur'd thought obey,
And praise th' Almighty's name;
Let heav'n and earth, and seas and skies,
In one melodious concert rise,
To swell th' inspiring theme.

2 Ye angels catch the thrilling sound,
While all th' adoring thrones around
His boundless mercy sing;
Let ev'ry list'ning saint above,
Wake all the tuneful soul of love,
And touch the sweetest string.

3 Let man, by nobler passions sway'd,
The feeling heart, the judging head,
In heav'nly praise employ;
Spread His tremendous Name around,
While heaven's broad arch rings back the sound,
The gen'ral burst of joy.

95 *Second Advent.* **C. P. M.**
"Remember Thou me."
Matt. 25: 46.

1 When thou, my righteous Judge, shalt come,
To take thy ransomed people home,
Shall I among them stand?
Shall such a worthless worm as I,
Who sometimes am afraid to die,
Be found at thy right hand?

2 I love to meet among them now,
Before thy gracious feet to bow,
Though vilest of them all;
But—can I bear the piercing thought?—
What if my name should be left out,
When thou for them shalt call!

3 Prevent, prevent it by thy grace;
Be thou, dear Lord, my hiding-place,
In this th' accepted day:
Thy pard'ning voice, oh, let me hear,
To still my unbelieving fear;
Nor let me fall, I pray!

4 Let me among thy saints be found,
Whene'er th' archangel's trump shall sound,
To see thy smiling face;
Then loudest of the throng I'll sing,
While heaven's resounding mansions ring
With shouts of sovereign grace.

Doxology. **C. P. M.**

To Father, Son, and Holy Ghost,
The God, whom Heaven's triumphant host
And saints on earth adore,
Be glory as in ages past,
Is now, and shall forever last,
When time shall be no more!

THE REDEEMER.

FERGUSON. S. M.

96 *"Your life is hid with Christ in God."—Col. 3: 3*

1 I bless the Christ of God;
I rest on love divine;
And with unfaltering lip and heart
I call this Saviour mine.

2 His cross dispels each doubt;
I bury in his tomb
Each thought of unbelief and fear,
Each lingering shade of gloom.

3 I praise the God of grace;
I trust his truth and might;
He calls me his, I call him mine,
My God, my joy, my light.

4 'Tis he who saveth me,
And freely pardon gives!
I love because he loveth me,
I live because he lives.

5 My life with him is hid,
My death has passed away,
My clouds have melted into light,
My midnight into day.

97 *Christ is All.* S. M.

1 O everlasting Light!
Shine graciously within;
Brightest of all on earth that's bright,
Come, shine away my sin!

2 O everlasting Truth!
Truest of all that's true,
Sure guide of erring age or youth,
Lead me and teach me too.

3 O everlasting Strength!
Uphold me in the way;
Bring me, in spite of foes, at length,
To joy, and light, and day.

4 O everlasting Love!
Well-spring of grace and peace,
Pour down thy fullness from above;
Bid doubt and trouble cease.

5 O everlasting rest!
Lift off life's load of care;
Relieve, revive this burdened breast,
And every sorrow bear.

6 Thou art in heaven our all;
Our all on earth art thou;
Upon thy glorious name we call:
Lord Jesus, bless us now!

98 *Rom. 8: 16.* S. M.

1 O Holy Spirit! come
And Jesus' love declare;
Oh! tell us of our heavenly home,
And guide us safely there.

2 Our unbelief remove,
By Thine almighty breath;
Oh! work the wondrous work of love,
The mighty work of faith.

3 Thy sceptre, Lord! extend,
Pity our deep distress;
Thou art the contrite sinner's Friend,
Thy waiting servants bless.

4 We bless Thee for Thy grace,
And Thine almighty power;
We bless Thee for Thy holy place,
And this accepted hour.

THE REDEEMER.

MORNINGTON. S. M.

99   *"Give thanks unto the Lord."*   **S. M.**
Psalm 92.

1 Sweet is the work, O Lord,
Thy glorious acts to sing,
To praise thy name, and hear thy word,
And grateful offerings bring.

2 Sweet, at the dawning light,
Thy boundless love to tell;
And, when approach the shades of night,
Still on the theme to dwell.

3 Sweet, on this day of rest,
To join in heart and voice
With those who love and serve thee best,
And in thy name rejoice.

4 To songs of praise and joy
Be every Sabbath given,
That such may be our blest employ
Eternally in heaven.

100   *"Bless the Lord, O my soul."*   **S. M.**
Psalm 103.

1 O bless the Lord, my soul!
Let all within me join,
And aid my tongue to bless his name,
Whose favors are divine.

2 O bless the Lord, my soul!
Nor let his mercies lie
Forgotten in unthankfulness,
And without praises die.

3 'T is he forgives thy sins;
'T is he relieves thy pain;
'T is he that heals thy sicknesses,
And makes thee young again.

4 He crowns thy life with love,
When ransomed from the grave;
He, who redeemed my soul from hell,
Hath sovereign power to save.

101   *Praise for the Redeemer.*   **S. M.**

1 Ye saints, proclaim abroad
The honors of your King;
To Jesus, your Incarnate God,
Your songs of praises sing.

2 Not angels round the throne
Of majesty above,
Are half so much obliged as we,
To our Immanuel's love.

3 They never sank so low,
They are not raised so high;
They never knew such depths of wo,
Such heights of majesty.

4 The Saviour did not join
Their nature to His own;
For them He shed no blood divine,
Nor breathed a single groan.

5 May we with angels vie,
The Saviour to adore;
Our debts are greater far than theirs,
O be our praises more!

Doxology.   **S. M.**

Praise to the Father be;
Praise to His Only Son;
Praise to the blessed Paraclete,
While endless ages run.

THE REDEEMER.

PORTUGUESE HYMN. 11s.

102   *Psalm* 23.   **11s.**

1 The Lord is my Shepherd; no want shall I know;
I feed in green pastures; safe folded I rest;
He leadeth my soul where the still waters flow,
Restores me when wandering, redeems when oppressed.

2 Through the valley and shadow of death though I stray,
Since thou art my Guardian, no evil I fear;
Thy rod shall defend me, thy staff be my stay:
No harm can befall with my Comforter near.

3 In the midst of affliction my table is spread;
With blessings unmeasured my cup runneth o'er;
With perfume and oil thou anointest my head;
Oh, what shall I ask of thy providence more?

4 Let goodness and mercy, my bountiful God!
Still follow my steps till I meet thee above;
I seek, by the path which my forefathers trod
Through the land of their sojourn, thy kingdom of love.

103   *"Abide with us."—Luke* 24: 29.   **11s.**

1 Come, Jesus, Redeemer! abide thou with me,
Come gladden my spirit, that waiteth for thee;
Thy smile every shadow shall chase from my heart,
And soothe every sorrow, though keen be the smart.

2 Without thee but weakness, with thee I am strong;
By day thou shalt lead me, by night be my song;
Though dangers surround me, I still every fear,
Since thou, the Most Mighty, my Helper, art near.

THE REDEEMER.

EXPOSTULATION. 11s.

3 Thy love, oh how faithful! so tender, so pure;
Thy promise, faith's anchor, how steadfast and sure!
That love, like sweet sunshine, my cold heart can warm,
That promise make steady my soul in the storm.

4 Breathe, breathe on my spirit, oft ruffled, thy peace,
From restless vain wishes bid thou my heart cease;
In thee all its longings henceforward shall end,
Till glad to thy presence my soul shall ascend.

5 Oh then, blessed Jesus! who once for me died,
Made clean in the fountain that gushed from thy side,
I shall see thy full glory, thy face shall behold,
And praise thee for ever with raptures untold.

104 *"Faint, yet pursuing."—Judges 8: 4.* **11s.**

1 Though faint, yet pursuing, we go on our way;
The Lord is our Leader, his word is our stay;
Though suffering, and sorrow, and trial be near,
The Lord is our refuge, and whom can we fear?

2 He raiseth the fallen, he cheereth the faint;
The weak, and oppressed—he will bear their complaint;
The way may be weary, and thorny the road,
But how can we falter? our help is in God!

3 And to his green pastures our footsteps he leads;
His flock in the desert how kindly he feeds!
The lambs in his bosom he tenderly bears,
And brings back the wanderers all safe from the snares.

4 Though clouds may surround us, our God is our light;
Though storms rage around us, our God is our might;
So faint, yet pursuing, still onward we come;
The Lord is our Leader, and heaven is our home!

105 *Passion week.*
Matt. 26: 42. **11s.**

1 O garden of Olives, thou dear honored spot,
The fame of thy wonders shall ne'er be forgot;
The theme most transporting to seraphs above;
The triumph of sorrow,—the triumph of love!

2 Come, saints, and adore him; come, bow at his feet;
Oh, give him the glory, the praise that is meet:
Let joyful hosannas unceasing arise,
And join the full chorus that gladdens the skies!

THE HOLY SCRIPTURES, AND

WINCHESTER. L. M.

106 *The Works and the Word of God.* **L. M.**
Psalm 19.

1 The heavens declare thy glory, Lord;
In every star thy wisdom shines;
But when our eyes behold thy word,
We read thy name in fairer lines.

2 The rolling sun, the changing light,
And night, and day, thy power confess:
But the blest volume thou hast writ,
Reveals thy justice and thy grace.

3 Sun, moon, and stars convey thy praise
Round the whole earth, and never stand;
So when thy truth began its race,
It touched and glanced on every land.

4 Nor shall thy spreading gospel rest,
Till through the world thy truth hath run;
Till Christ hath all the nations blest
That see the light, or feel the sun.

5 Great Sun of Righteousness, arise!
Bless the dark world with heavenly light;
Thy gospel makes the simple wise,
Thy laws are pure, thy judgments right.

6 Thy noblest wonders here we view
In souls renewed, and sins forgiven;
Lord, cleanse my sins, my soul renew,
And make thy word my guide to heaven.

107 *2 Cor. 4: 3.* **L. M.**

1 God, in the gospel of his Son,
Makes his eternal counsels known;
'T is here his richest mercy shines,
And truth is drawn in fairest lines.

2 Here sinners of a humble frame
May taste his grace and learn his name,
May read in characters of blood
The wisdom, power and grace of God.

3 The prisoner here may break his chains;
The weary rest from all his pains;
The captive feel his bondage cease;
The mourner find the way of peace.

4 Here faith reveals to mortal eyes
A brighter world beyond the skies:
Here shines the light which guides our way
From earth to realms of endless day.

5 O grant us grace, almighty Lord!
To read and mark thy holy word;
Its truth with meekness to receive,
And by its holy precepts live.

108 *Psalm 92.* **L. M.**

1 Sweet is the work, my God, my King,
To praise Thy name, give thanks and sing,
To show thy love by morning light,
And talk of all thy truth at night.

2 Sweet is the day of sacred rest;
No mortal care shall seize my breast;
Oh, may my heart in tune be found,
Like David's harp of solemn sound!

3 My heart shall triumph in my Lord,
And bless his works, and bless His word:
Thy works of grace, how bright they shine!
How deep Thy counsels, how divine!

THE LORD'S DAY.

109 *The Lord's day.* L. M.

1 Come, dearest Lord, and bless this day,
Come bear our thoughts from earth away,
Now, let our noblest passions rise
With ardor to their native skies.

2 Come, Holy Spirit, all divine,
With rays of light upon us shine;
And let our waiting souls be blest,
On this sweet day of sacred rest.

3 Then when our Sabbaths here are o'er,
And we arrive on Canaan's shore,
With all the ransom'd, we shall spend
A Sabbath which shall never end.

110 *"Let us worship and bow down."* L. M.
Psalm 95.

1 O come, loud anthems let us sing,
Loud thanks to our almighty King!
For we our voices high should raise,
When our salvation's Rock we praise.

2 Into his presence let us haste,
To thank him for his favors past;
To him address in joyful songs
The praise that to his name belongs.

3 O let us to his courts repair,
And bow with adoration there!
Down on our knees, devoutly, all
Before the Lord, our Maker, fall.

111 *The Lord's day.* L. M.

1 Return, my soul, enjoy thy rest,
Improve the day thy God has bless'd;
Another six days' work is done,
Another Sabbath is begun.

2 Come bless the Lord, whose love assigns
So sweet a rest to wearied minds;
Provides a blest foretaste of heav'n,
On this day more than all the sev'n.

3 O that our thoughts and thanks may rise,
As grateful incense to the skies;
And draw from Christ that sweet repose,
Which none but he that feels it, knows.

4 This heavenly calm, within the breast,
Is the dear pledge of glorious rest,
Which for the Church of God remains,
The end of cares, the end of pains.

112 *"I will that men pray everywhere."* L. M.
John 4: 21.

1 Jesus, where'er thy people meet,
There they behold thy mercy-seat;
Where'er they seek thee, thou art found,
And every place is hallowed ground.

2 For thou, within no walls confined,
Inhabitest the humble mind;
Such ever bring thee where they come,
And going, take thee to their home.

3 Great Shepherd of thy chosen few!
Thy former mercies here renew;
Here to our waiting hearts proclaim
The sweetness of thy saving name.

Doxology. L. M.

Praise God, from whom all blessings flow,
Praise him, all creatures here below;
Praise him above, ye heavenly host;
Praise Father, Son and Holy Ghost.

MARLOW. C. M.

113 *The inspired word, a system of knowledge and joy.*—Ps. 119. **C. M.**

1 How precious is the book divine,
By inspiration giv'n!
Bright as a lamp its doctrines shine,
To guide our souls to heav'n.

2 It sweetly cheers our drooping hearts
In this dark vale of tears;
Life, light and joy, it still imparts,
And quells our rising fears.

3 This lamp, through all the tedious night
Of life, shall guide our way,
Till we behold the clearer light
Of an eternal day.

114 *"The day the Lord hath made."* Psalm 118. **C. M.**

1 This is the day the Lord hath made;
He calls the hours his own:
Let heaven rejoice, let earth be glad,
And praise surround the throne.

2 To-day he rose, and left the dead,
And Satan's empire fell;
To-day the saints his triumph spread,
And all his wonders tell.

3 Hosanna to th' anointed King,
To David's holy Son:
Help us, O Lord! Descend, and bring
Salvation from thy throne.

4 Blest be the Lord who comes to men
With messages of grace;
Who comes, in God his Father's name,
To save our sinful race.

5 Hosanna in the highest strains
The church on earth can raise;
The highest heavens, in which he reigns,
Shall give him nobler praise.

115 *"Peace be within thy walls."* Psalm 122. **C. M.**

1 With joy we hail the sacred day
Which God hath called his own;
With joy the summons we obey
To worship at his throne.

2 Thy chosen temple, Lord, how fair!
Where willing votaries throng
To breathe the humble, fervent prayer,
And pour the choral song.

3 Spirit of grace! Oh, deign to dwell
Within thy church below;
Make her in holiness excel,
With pure devotion glow.

4 Let peace within her walls be found
Let all her sons unite
To spread, with grateful zeal, around
Her clear and shining light.

5 Great God, we hail the sacred day
Which thou hast called thine own:
With joy the summons we obey
To worship at thy throne.

116 **C. M.**

1 Come, dearest Lord, and feed thy sheep,
On this sweet day of rest;
Oh bless this flock, and make this fold
Enjoy a heavenly rest!

THE LORD'S DAY.

VALENTIA. C. M.

2 Welcome and precious to my soul
Are these sweet days of love;
But what a Sabbath shall I keep
When I shall rest above!

3 I come, I wait, I hear, I pray;
Thy footsteps, Lord, I trace;
Here, in Thine own appointed way,
I wait to see Thy face.

117 *Lev. 19: 30.* **C. M.**

1 Frequent the day of God returns
To shed its quick'ning beams;
And yet how slow devotion burns,
How languid are its flames!

2 Accept our faint attempts to love,
Our frailties, Lord, forgive;
We would be like thy saints above,
And praise thee while we live.

3 Increase, O Lord, our faith and hope,
And fit us to ascend,
Where the assembly ne'er breaks up,
The Sabbath ne'er shall end.

4 There we shall breathe in heav'nly air,
With heav'nly lustre shine;
Before the throne of God appear,
And feast on love divine.

118 *Isa. 56: 7.* **C. M.**

1 Again our earthly cares we leave,
And in thy courts appear;
Again with joyful feet we come
To meet our Saviour here.

2 Show us some token of thy love
Our fainting hope to raise,
And pour thy blessing from above
That we may render praise.

119 *Psalm 5.* **C. M.**

1 Lord, in the morning Thou shalt hear
My voice ascending high;
To Thee will I direct my prayer,
To Thee lift up mine eye:

2 Up to the hills where Christ is gone
To plead for all His saints,
Presenting at His Father's throne
Our songs and our complaints.

3 Thou art a God before whose sight
The wicked shall not stand;
Sinners shall ne'er be Thy delight
Nor dwell at Thy right hand.

4 But to Thy house will I resort
To taste Thy mercies there;
I will frequent Thy holy court,
And worship in Thy fear.

5 Oh may Thy Spirit guide my feet
In ways of righteousness!
Make every path of duty straight
And plain before my face.

Doxology. **C. M.**

Glory to God the Father be,
Glory to God the Son,
Glory to God the Holy Ghost,
Glory to God alone.

THE LORD'S DAY, AND

MIGDOL. L. M.

120 *Heb. 4: 9.* L. M.

1 Thine earthly Sabbaths, Lord, we love,
But there's a nobler rest above:
To that our longing souls aspire,
With cheerful hope and strong desire.

2 No more fatigue, no more distress,
Nor sin nor hell shall reach the place;
No groans to mingle with the songs
Which warble from immortal tongues.

3 No rude alarms of raging foes;
No cares to break the long repose;
No midnight shade, no clouded sun,—
But sacred, high, eternal noon!

4 O long-expected day, begin!
Dawn on these realms of woe and sin;
Fain would we leave this weary road,
And sleep in death, to rest with God.

121 *"Remember the Sabbath day, to keep it holy."* L. M.

1 Another six days' work is done;
Another Sabbath is begun:
Return, my soul, unto thy rest;
Enjoy the day thy God hath blest.

3 Oh that our thoughts and thanks may rise,
As grateful incense to the skies!
And draw from heaven that calm repose,
Which none but he who feels it knows;

3 That heavenly calm within the breast!
It is the pledge of that dear rest
Which for the church of God remains,—
The end of cares, the end of pains.

4 In holy duties let the day,
In holy pleasures, pass away,
How sweet a Sabbath thus to spend,
In hope of one that ne'er shall end!

122 *Psalm 5: 3.* L. M.

1 My opening eyes with rapture see
The dawn of thy returning day;
My thoughts, O God, ascend to thee,
While thus my early vows I pay.

2 Oh, bid this trifling world retire,
And drive each carnal thought away;
Nor let me feel one vain desire—
One sinful thought through all the day.

3 Then, to thy courts when I repair,
My soul shall rise on joyful wing,
The wonders of thy love declare,
And join the strains which angels sing.

123 *Joy in the House of God. Psalm 84.* L. M.

1 Great God, attend, while Zion sings
The joy that from thy presence springs:
To spend one day with thee on earth,
Exceeds a thousand days of mirth.

2 Might I enjoy the meanest place
Within thy house, O God of grace,
Not tents of ease, nor thrones of power
Should tempt my feet to leave thy door.

3 God is our sun—he makes our day;
God is our shield—he guards our way
From all th' assaults of hell and sin,
From foes without and foes within.

THE HOLY SCRIPTURES.

VANHALL'S HYMN. L. M.

4 All needful grace will God bestow,
And crown that grace with glory too;
He gives us all things, and withholds
No real good from upright souls.

5 O God, our King, whose sovereign sway
The glorious host of heaven obey,
Display thy grace, exert thy power,
Till all on earth thy name adore!

4 While I am here, these leaves supply
His place, and tell me of his love;
I read with faith's discerning eye,
And gain a glimpse of joys above.

5 I know in them the Spirit breathes
To animate his people here;
Oh, may these truths prove life to all,
Till in his presence we appear!

124 *Psalm 19.* **L. M.**

1 Great Sun of Righteousness, arise!
Oh, bless the world with heavenly light!
Thy gospel makes the simple wise:
Thy laws are pure, thy judgments right.

2 Thy noblest wonders here we view,
In souls renewed and sins forgiven:—
Lord, cleanse my sins, my soul renew,
And make thy word my guide to heaven.

125 *Rev. 10: 2.* **L. M.**

1 I love the sacred book of God!
No other can its place supply;
It points me to his own abode;
It gives me wings, and bids me fly.

2 Sweet Book! in thee my eyes discern
The very image of my Lord;
From thine instructive page I learn
The joys his presence will afford.

3 In thee I read my title clear
To mansions that will ne'er decay;—
Dear Lord, oh, when wilt thou appear,
And bear thy prisoner away?

126 *Gal. 4: 6.* **L. M.**

1 Come, O Creator Spirit blest!
And in our souls take up thy rest;
Come, with thy grace and heavenly aid,
To fill the hearts which thou hast made.

2 Great Comforter! to thee we cry;
O highest gift of God most high!
O fount of life! O fire of love!
Send sweet anointing from above!

3 Kindle our senses from above,
And make our hearts o'erflow with love;
With patience firm, and virtue high,
The weakness of our flesh supply.

4 Far from us drive the foe we dread,
And grant us thy true peace instead;
So shall we not, with thee for guide,
Turn from the path of life aside.

Doxology. **L. M.**

Praise God, from whom all blessings flow;
Praise him, all creatures here below;
Praise him above, ye heavenly host;
Praise Father, Son and Holy Ghost.

ADVENT, AND

ANTIOCH. C. M.

127 *Christ's Mission.*
Isa. 61: 1—3. C. M.

1 Hark, the glad sound! the Saviour comes,
The Saviour promised long;
Let every heart prepare a throne,
And every voice a song.

2 He comes, the prisoner to release,
In Satan's bondage held;
The gates of brass before him burst,
The iron fetters yield.

3 He comes, from thickest films of vice
To clear the mental ray,
And on the eyes long closed in night
To pour celestial day.

4 He comes, the broken heart to bind,
The bleeding soul to cure,
And, with the treasures of his grace,
Enrich the humble poor.

5 Our glad hosannas, Prince of Peace,
Thy welcome shall proclaim,
And heaven's eternal arches ring
With thy beloved name.

128 *"O let the nations be glad and sing for joy."—Ps. 98.* C. M.

1 Joy to the world, the Lord is come!
Let earth receive her King;
Let every heart prepare Him room,
And heav'n and nature sing.

2 Joy to the earth, the Saviour reigns;
Let men their songs employ;
While fields and floods, rocks, hills, and plains,
Repeat the sounding joy.

3 No more let sins and sorrows grow,
Nor thorns infest the ground:
He comes to make His blessings flow
Far as the curse is found.

4 He rules the world with truth and grace,
And makes the nations prove
The glories of His righteousness,
And wonders of His love.

129 *The Incarnation of Christ.*
Luke 2: 13. C. M.

1 Mortals, awake, with angels join
And chant the solemn lay;
Joy, love, and gratitude, combine
To hail th' auspicious day.

2 In heav'n the rapt'rous song began,
And sweet seraphic fire
Through all the shining legions ran,
And strung and tun'd the lyre.

3 Swift through the vast expanse it flew,
And loud the echo roll'd;
The theme, the song, the joy was new,
'Twas more than heav'n could hold.

4 Down through the portals of the sky
Th' impetuous torrent ran;
And angels flew with eager joy
To bear the news to man.

5 Hark! the cherubic armies shout,
And glory leads the song;
Good-will and peace are heard throughout
Th' harmonious heav'nly throng.

CHRISTMAS.

CHRISTMAS. C. M.

6 With joy the chorus we'll repeat,
"Glory to God on high!
"Good-will and peace are now complete;
"Jesus was born to die."

130 *The first and second coming of Christ.—Ps. 96.* **C. M.**

1 Sing to the Lord, ye distant lands,
Ye tribes of ev'ry tongue;
His rich display of grace demands
A new and nobler song.

2 Say to the nations, Jesus reigns,
God's own almighty Son;
His pow'r the sinking world sustains,
And grace surrounds his throne.

3 Let heav'n proclaim the joyful day;
Joy through the earth be seen;
Let cities shine in bright array,
And fields in cheerful green.

4 Let an unusual joy surprise
The islands of the sea:
Ye mountains sink, ye valleys rise;
Prepare the Lord his way.

5 Behold, he comes! he comes to bless
The nations as their God;
To show the world his righteousness,
And send his truth abroad.

6 But when his voice shall raise the dead,
And bid the world draw near,
How will the guilty nations dread,
To see their Judge appear!

131 *"On earth peace." Luke 2: 14.* **C. M.**

1 Calm, on the listening ear of night,
Come heaven's melodious strains,
Where wild Judea stretches far
Her silver-mantled plains.

2 Celestial choirs, from courts above,
'Mid sacred glories there;
And angels, with their sparkling lyres,
Make music on the air.

3 The answering hills of Palestine
Send back the glad reply;
And greet, from all their holy heights,
The day-spring from on high.

4 O'er the blue depths of Galilee
There comes a holier calm;
And Sharon waves, in solemn praise,
Her silent groves of palm.

5 "Glory to God!" the sounding skies
Loud with their anthems ring;
"Peace to the earth — good will to men,
From heaven's eternal King."

Doxology. **C. M.**

To Father, Son, and Holy Ghost,
The God whom we adore,
Be glory as it was, is now,
And shall be evermore.

ADVENT, CHRISTMAS, AND

BOYLSTON. S. M.

132   *John 1: 4.*   S. M.

1 O Saviour of our race,
Welcome indeed Thou art,
Blessed Redeemer, Fount of grace,
To this my longing heart!

2 Light of the world, abide
Through faith within my heart;
Leave me to seek no other guide,
Nor e'er from Thee depart.

3 Thou art the Life, O Lord!
Sole Light of life Thou art!
Let not Thy glorious rays be poured
In vain on my dark heart.

4 Star of the East, arise!
Drive all my clouds away;
Guide me till earth's dim twilight dies
Into the perfect day.

133   *The First and Second Coming of Christ.*   S. M.

1 The Advent of our God
Our prayers must now employ,
And we must meet Him on His road
With hymns of holy joy.

2 The Everlasting Son
Incarnate deigns to be:
Himself a servant's form puts on,
To set His people free.

3 Daughter of Zion, rise,
And greet thy lowly King,
And do not wickedly despise
The mercies He will bring.

4 As Judge, in clouds of light,
He will come down again,
And all His scattered saints unite
With Him in Heaven to reign.

5 Before that dreadful day
May all our sins be gone;
May the old man be put away,
And the new man put on!

6 Praise to the Saviour-Son,
From all the angel host;
Like praise be to the Father done,
And to the Holy Ghost.

134   *"When the Son of Man shall come in His glory."*   S. M.

1 The Son of Man shall come
With angel hosts around,
'Mid darkening sun and falling stars,
And trumpet's solemn sound.

2 Awake, ye slumbering souls,
It is no time for rest;
He comes, as comes the lightning flash
Shining from east to west.

3 Thy servants, Lord, prepare
For that tremendous day;
Fill every heart with watchful care,
And stir us up to pray.

4 Help us to wait the hour
In toil and holy fear,
When, manifested with Thy saints,
Thou shalt again appear.

THE SECOND ADVENT.

5 Then, when the wailing earth
Thy sign in heaven shall see,
Thou shalt send forth Thine angel band
To gather us to Thee.

135 *"Even so, come, Lord Jesus."*
Rev. 22: 20. **S. M.**

1 Come, Lord! and tarry not;
Bring the long-looked-for day;
Oh! why these years of waiting here,
These ages of delay?

2 Come, for Thy saints still wait:
Daily ascends their sigh;
The Spirit and the Bride say, Come!
Dost thou not hear the cry?

3 Come! for love waxes cold,
Its steps are faint and slow;
Faith now is lost in unbelief;
Hope's lamp burns dim and low.

4 Come! for creation groans,
Impatient of thy stay,
Worn out with these long years of ill,
These ages of delay.

5 Come, and make all things new;
Build up this ruined earth;
Restore our faded Paradise—
Creation's second birth!

6 Come, and begin thy reign
Of everlasting peace;
Come, take the kingdom to thyself,
Great King of righteousness!

136 *"How long, O Lord, holy and true."* **S. M.**

1 The Church has waited long
Her absent Lord to see;
And still in loneliness she waits,
A friendless stranger she.

2 How long, O Lord our God,
Holy and true and good,
Wilt thou not judge thy suffering church,
Her sighs and tears and blood?

3 Saint after saint on earth
Has lived, and loved, and died;
And as they left us one by one,
We laid them side by side.

4 We laid them down to sleep,
But not in hope forlorn;
We laid them but to ripen there,
Till the last glorious morn.

5 We long to hear thy voice,
To see thee face to face,
To share thy crown and glory then,
As now we share thy grace.

6 Come, Lord! and wipe away
The curse, the sin, the stain,
And make this blighted world of ours
Thine own fair world again.

Doxology. **S. M.**

The Father and the Son
And Spirit we adore;
We praise, we bless, we worship thee,
Both now and evermore!

WATCHMAN. 7s. Double.

137 *"Watchman, what of the night."* Isaiah 21: 11. **7s.**

1 Watchman, tell us of the night,
What its signs of promise are.
Traveler, o'er yon mountain's height,
See that glory-beaming star!

2 Watchman, does its beauteous ray
Aught of joy or hope foretell?
Traveler, yes: it brings the day,
Promised day of Israel.

3 Watchman, tell us of the night:
Higher yet that star ascends.
Traveler, blessedness and light,
Peace and truth, its course portends.

4 Watchman, will its beams alone
Gild the spot that gave them birth?
Traveler, ages are its own:
See! it bursts o'er all the earth!

5 Watchman, tell us of the night,
For the morning seems to dawn.
Traveler, darkness takes its flight,
Doubt and terror are withdrawn.

6 Watchman, let thy wand'rings cease;
Hie thee to thy quiet home.
Traveler, lo! the Prince of Peace,
Lo! the Son of God is come!

138 *"Christ is born in Bethlehem."* Luke 2: 13, 14. **7s.**

1 Hark! the herald angels sing,
"Glory to the new-born King!
Peace on earth, and mercy mild;
God and sinners reconciled."

2 Joyful, all ye nations, rise;
Join the triumphs of the skies;
With th' angelic hosts proclaim,
"Christ is born in Bethlehem."

3 Hail, the heaven-born Prince of Peace!
Hail, the Sun of Righteousness!
Light and life to all he brings,
Ris'n with healing in his wings.

4 Let us then with angels sing,
"Glory to the new-born King!—
Peace on earth, and mercy mild;
God and sinners reconciled!"

139 *"The Heavenly theme."* **7s.**

1 Now begin the heavenly theme,
Sing aloud of Jesus' name;
Ye who his salvation prove,
Triumph in redeeming love.

NEW YEAR.

HORTON. 7s.

2 Mourning souls, dry up your tears,
Banish all your guilty fears;
See your guilt and curse remove,
Canceled by redeeming love.

3 Welcome, all by sin oppressed,
Welcome to his sacred rest:
Nothing brought him from above,
Nothing but redeeming love.

4 Hither, then, your music bring,
Strike aloud each joyful string:
Mortals, join the hosts above,
Join to praise redeeming love!

140 *New Year.* 7s.

1 While with ceaseless course the sun
Hasted through the former year,
Many souls their race have run,
Never more to meet us here.

2 Fix'd in an eternal state,
They have done with all below;
We a little longer wait,
But how little—none can know.

3 As the winged arrow flies,
Speedily the mark to find;
As the lightning from the skies,
Darts and leaves no trace behind:

4 Swiftly thus our fleeting days
Bear us down life's rapid stream;
Upwards, Lord, our spirits raise,
All below is but a dream.

5 Thanks for mercies past receive,
Pardon of our sins renew;
Teach us henceforth how to live,
With eternity in view.

6 Bless thy word to young and old,
Fill us with the Saviour's love;
And when life's short tale is told,
May we dwell with thee above.

141 *New Year.* 7s.

1 For thy mercy and thy grace,
Faithful through another year,
Hear our song of thankfulness,
Father and Redeemer! hear.

2 In our weakness and distress,
Rock of strength! be thou our stay;
In the pathless wilderness
Be our true and living way.

3 Who of us death's awful road
In the coming year shall tread?
With thy rod and staff, O God!
Comfort thou his dying head.

4 Keep us faithful, keep us pure,
Keep us evermore thine own;
Help, oh help us to endure;
Fit us for the promised crown.

Doxology. 7s.

Praise the name of God most high,
Praise him, all below the sky,
Praise him, all ye heav'nly host,
Father, Son, and Holy Ghost.

ADVENT

AUTUMN. 8s & 7s. Double.

142 *Birth of Christ.—Luke 2: 14.* 8s & 7s.

1 Hark! what mean those holy voices,
Sweetly sounding through the skies!
Lo! the angelic host rejoices,
Heavenly hallelujahs rise.

2 Listen to the wondrous story
Which they chant in hymns of joy;
"Glory in the highest, glory!
Glory be to God most high!

3 Peace on earth, good will from heaven,
Reaching far as man is found;
Souls redeemed and sins forgiven,
Loud our golden harps shall sound.

4 Christ is born, the great Anointed,
Heaven and earth his praises sing;
Glad receive, whom God appointed,
For your Prophet, Priest, and King.

5 Hasten, mortals, to adore him,
Learn his name and taste his joy;
Till in heaven you sing before him,
Glory be to God most high!"

6 Let us learn the wondrous story
Of our great Redeemer's birth,
Spread the brightness of his glory,
Till it cover all the earth.

143 *"The Desire of all Nations."*
Hag. 2: 7. 8s & 7s.

1 Come, thou long-expected Jesus,
Born to set thy people free;
From our fears and sins release us;
Let us find our rest in thee.

2 Israel's strength and consolation,
Hope of all the earth thou art;
Dear desire of every nation,
Joy of every longing heart.

3 Born, thy people to deliver;
Born a child, and yet a king;
Born to reign in us forever,
Now thy gracious kingdom bring.

4 By thine own eternal Spirit,
Rule in all our hearts alone;
By thine all-sufficient merit,
Raise us to thy glorious throne.

144 *"Over all, God blessed forever."*
Rom. 9: 5. 8s & 7s.

1 Crown his head with endless blessing,
Who, in God the Father's name,
With compassions never ceasing,
Comes salvation to proclaim.

2 Lo! Jehovah, we adore thee;
Thee, our Saviour; thee, our God!
From his throne his beams of glory
Shine through all the world abroad.

3 Jesus, thee our Saviour hailing
Thee, our God, in praise we own;
Highest honors, never failing,
Rise eternal round thy throne.

4 Now, ye saints, his power confessing,
In your grateful strains adore;
For his mercy, never ceasing,
Flows, and flows for evermore.

CHRISTMAS AND SECOND ADVENT.

VESPERS. 8s & 7s.

145 *"Being the brightness of his glory."—Heb. 1: 3.* 8s & 7s.

1 Brightness of the Father's glory,
Shall thy praise unuttered lie?
Break, my tongue, such guilty silence;
Sing the Lord who came to die.

2 Did archangels sing thy coming?
Did the shepherds learn their lays?
Shame would cover me, ungrateful,
Should my tongue refuse to praise.

3 From the highest throne in glory
To the cross of deepest woe,
All to ransom guilty captives!
Flow, my praise, forever flow.

4 Re-ascend, immortal Saviour!
Leave thy footstool, take thy throne:
Thence return, and reign forever;
Be the kingdom all thine own.

146 *"And the Light shineth in darkness."—John 1: 9.* 8s & 7s.

1 Light of those whose dreary dwelling
Borders on the shades of death!
Rise on us, thyself revealing,
Rise and chase the clouds beneath.

2 Thou, of heaven and earth Creator!
In our deepest darkness rise;
Scatter all the night of nature;
Pour the day upon our eyes.

3 Still we wait for thine appearing;
Life and joy thy beams impart,
Chasing all our fears, and cheering
Every poor, benighted heart.

4 By thine all-sufficient merit,
Every burdened soul release;
Every weary, wandering spirit
Guide into thy perfect peace.

Second Advent.

147 Joel 2: 1. 8s & 7s.

1 Hark! an awful voice is sounding,
"Christ is nigh!" it seems to say;
"Cast away the dreams of darkness,
O ye children of the day!"

2 Startled at the solemn warning,
Let the earth-bound soul arise;
Christ, her Sun, all sloth dispelling,
Shines upon the morning skies.

3 Lo, the Lamb, so long expected,
Comes with pardon down from heaven;
Let us haste, with tears of sorrow,
One and all, to be forgiven.

4 So, when next he comes with glory,
Wrapping all the earth in fear,
With His mercy He may shield us,
And with words of love draw near.

5 Honor, glory, virtue, merit,
To the Father and the Son,
With the Everlasting Spirit,
While eternal ages run.

Doxology. 8s & 7s.

Praise the God of our salvation;
Praise the Father's boundless love·
Praise the Lamb, our expiation;
Praise the Spirit from above.

CHRISTMAS AND

STIRLING. L. M.

148 *Luke 2: 11.* **L. M.**

1 When Jordan hushed his waters still,
And silence slept on Zion's hill,
When Bethlehem's shepherds through the night,
Watched o'er their flocks by starry light—

2 Hark! from the midnight hills around,
A voice of more than mortal sound,
In distant hallelujahs stole,
Wild murmuring o'er the raptured soul.

3 On wheels of light, on wings of flame,
The glorious hosts of Zion came;
High heaven with songs of triumph rung,
While thus they struck their harps and sung:

4 "O Zion, lift thy raptured eye;
The long-expected hour is nigh;
The joys of nature rise again;
The Prince of Salem comes to reign.

5 "See, Mercy, from her golden urn,
Pours a rich stream to them that mourn;
Behold, she binds, with tender care,
The bleeding bosom of despair.

6 "He comes to cheer the trembling heart;
Bids Satan and his host depart;
Again the day-star gilds the gloom,
Again the bowers of Eden bloom."

149 *The Star of Bethlehem.* **L. M.**
Matth. 2: 9.

1 When marshaled on the nightly plain,
The glittering host bestud the sky,
One star alone, of all the train,
Can fix the sinner's wandering eye.

2 Hark! hark! to God the chorus breaks,
From every host, from every gem;
But one alone, the Saviour speaks:
It is the Star of Bethlehem.

3 Once on the raging seas I rode:
The storm was loud, the night was dark;
The ocean yawned, and rudely blowed
The wind that tossed my foundering bark.

4 Deep horror then my vitals froze;
Death-struck I ceased the tide to stem;
When suddenly a star arose!
It was the star of Bethlehem.

5 It was my guide, my light, my all;
It bade my dark forebodings cease;
And thro' the storm, and danger's thrall,
It led me to the port of peace.

6 Now safely moored, my perils o'er,
I'll sing, first in night's diadem,
For ever and for evermore,
The Star—the Star of Bethlehem!

150 *A Hymn of the Reformation on* **L. M.**
the Birth of Christ.

1 All praise to thee, eternal Lord!
Clothed in a garb of flesh and blood;
Choosing a manger for thy throne,
While worlds on worlds are thine alone.

2 Once did the skies before thee bow;
A virgin's arms contain thee now:
Angels, who did in thee rejoice,
Now listen for thine infant voice.

NEW YEAR.

LAMBIC. L. M. G. KINGSLEY.

3 A little child, thou art our guest,
That weary ones in thee may rest;
Forlorn and lowly is thy birth,
That we may rise to heaven from earth.

4 Thou comest in the darksome night
To make us children of the light,—
To make us, in the realms divine,
Like thine own angels round thee shine.

5 All this for us thy love hath done,
By this to thee our love is won:
For this we tune our cheerful lays,
And shout our thanks in ceaseless praise.

151 *New Year.* **L. M.**

1 Our Helper, God! we bless thy name,
The same thy power, thy grace the same;
The tokens of thy loving care
Open and crown and close the year.

2 Amid ten thousand snares we stand,
Supported by thy guardian hand;
And see, when we survey our ways,
Ten thousand monuments of praise.

3 Thus far thine arm hath led us on;
Thus far we make thy mercy known;
And, while we tread this desert land,
New mercies shall new songs demand.

4 Our grateful souls on Jordan's shore
Shall raise one sacred pillar more;
Then bear, in thy bright courts above,
Inscriptions of immortal love.

152 *New Year.* **L. M.**

1 Great God, we sing that mighty hand,
By which supported, still we stand;
The op'ning year thy mercy shows,
Let mercy crown it till it close.

2 By day, by night, at home, abroad,
Still we are guarded by our God,
By his incessant bounty fed,
By his unerring counsel led.

3 With grateful hearts the past we own;
The future, all to us unknown,
We to thy guardian care commit,
And peaceful leave before thy feet.

4 In scenes exalted or depress'd,
Be thou our joy, and thou our rest;
Thy goodness all our hope shall raise,
Ador'd through all our changing days.

5 When death shall interrupt these songs,
And seal in silence mortal tongues,
Our Helper, God, in whom we trust,
In better worlds, our souls shall boast.

Doxology. **L. M.**

To God the Father, God the Son,
And God the Spirit, three in one,
Be honor, praise, and glory given,
By all on earth, and all in heaven.

CHRISTMAS, EPIPHANY

LENOX. H. M.

153 *"Good tidings of great joy."* Luke 2: 13, 14.

1 Hark! hark! the notes of joy
Roll o'er the heavenly plains,
And seraphs find employ
For their sublimest strains:
Some new delight in heaven is known;
Loud sound the harps around the throne.

2 Hark! hark! the sound draws nigh,—
The joyful host descends;
Jesus forsakes the sky,
To earth his footsteps bends;
He comes to bless our fallen race;
He comes with messages of grace.

3 Bear, bear the tidings round!
Let every mortal know
What love in God is found,
What pity he can show:
Ye winds that blow, ye waves that roll,
Bear the glad news from pole to pole.

4 Strike, strike the harps again,
To great Immanuel's name!
Arise, ye sons of men,
And all his grace proclaim:
Angels and men, wake every string,
'Tis God the Saviour's praise we sing!

H. M. 154 *The Year of Jubilee.*—Luke 4: 19. **H. M.**

1 Blow ye the trumpet, blow,
The gladly solemn sound!
Let all the nations know,
To earth's remotest bound:
The year of jubilee has come;
Return, ye ransomed sinners, home.

2 Jesus, our great High Priest,
Hath full atonement made:
Ye weary spirits, rest;
Ye mournful souls, be glad:
The year of jubilee is come;
Return, ye ransomed sinners, home.

3 Exalt the Lamb of God,
The sin-atoning Lamb;
Redemption in his blood
To all the world proclaim:
The year of jubilee is come;
Return, ye ransomed sinners, home.

4 The Gospel trumpet hear,—
The news of heavenly grace;
And, saved from earth, appear
Before your Saviour's face:
The year of jubilee is come;
Return, ye ransomed sinners, home.

LORD'S DAY, &c.

LISCHER. H. M.

155 *Communion of Saints.*
"*One Lord, one faith, one baptism.*"—Eph. 4: 5. H. M.

1 One sole baptismal sign,
One Lord, below, above,
One faith, one hope divine,
One only watchword—Love:
From different temples though it rise,
One song ascendeth to the skies.

2 Our sacrifice is one;
One Priest before the throne;
The slain, the risen Son,
Redeemer, Lord alone!
And sighs from contrite hearts that spring,
Our chief, our choicest offering.

3 Head of thy Church beneath!
The catholic, the true,
On all her members breathe;
Her broken frame renew!
Then shall thy perfect will be done
When Christians love and live as one.

156 *Lord's Day.* H. M.

1 Welcome, delightful morn,
Thou day of sacred rest!
I hail thy kind return;—
Lord, make these moments blest:
From the low train of mortal toys,
I soar to reach immortal joys.

2 Now may the King descend
And fill his throne of grace;
Thy scepter, Lord, extend,
While saints address thy face:
Let sinners feel thy quickening word,
And learn to know and fear the Lord.

3 Descend, celestial Dove,
With all thy quickening powers;
Disclose a Saviour's love,
And bless the sacred hours:
Then shall my soul new life obtain,
Nor Sabbaths be enjoyed in vain.

157 *Laying of a Corner-Stone.*
"*Christ is our Corner-stone.*"
Eph. 2: 20. H. M.

1 Christ is our corner-stone;
On him alone we build;
With his true saints alone
The courts of heaven are filled:
On his great love | Of present grace
Our hopes we place, | And joys above.

2 Oh, then, with hymns of praise
These hallowed courts shall ring!
Our voices we will raise,
The Three in One to sing;
And thus proclaim | Both loud and long,
In joyful song, | That glorious Name.

3 Here, gracious God, do thou
For evermore draw nigh;
Accept each faithful vow,
And mark each suppliant sigh:
In copious shower, | Each holy day,
On all who pray, | Thy blessings pour.

4 Here may we gain from heaven
The grace which we implore,
And may that grace, once given,
Be with us evermore,—
Until that day | To endless rest
When all the blest | Are called away.

EPIPHANY, LENT, AND

MISSIONARY CHANT. L. M.

158 *"He shall have dominion from sea to sea."—Psalm 72.* **L. M.**

1 Jesus shall reign where'er the sun
Does his successive journeys run;
His kingdom stretch from shore to shore,
Till moons shall wax and wane no more.

2 People and realms of every tongue
Dwell on his love with sweetest song;
And infant voices shall proclaim
Their early blessings on his name.

3 Blessings abound where'er he reigns;
The prisoner leaps to loose his chains;
The weary find eternal rest,
And all the sons of want are blest.

4 Let every creature rise and bring
Peculiar honors to our King:
Angels descend with songs again,
And earth repeat the loud Amen!

159 *Reign of the Messiah.—Isa. 60.* **L. M.**

1 Rise, crowned with light; great Salem, rise!
Exalt thy head, and lift thine eyes;
See a long race thy courts adorn,
Of sons and daughters yet unborn.

2 See nations at thy gates attend,
And lowly in thy temple bend;
See crowds on every side arise,
Eager to mount above the skies.

3 See heaven its portals wide display,
And pour on thee a flood of day!
Thy day shall shine forever bright,
For God himself shall be thy light.

4 What though the skies in smoke decay,
Rocks fall, and mountains melt away!
Fixed is his word, his power remains:
Thy glorious King, Messiah, reigns!

160 *"Is there no Physician there?"—Jer. 8: 22.* **L. M.**

1 Why droops my soul, with grief oppressed?
Whence these wild tumults in my breast?
Is there no balm to heal my wound?
No kind physician to be found?

2 Raise to the cross thy weeping eyes;
Behold, the Prince of glory dies!
He dies extended on the tree,
Thence sheds a sovereign balm for thee.

3 Dear Saviour! at thy feet I lie,
Here to receive a cure, or die;
But grace forbids that painful fear—
Oh, boundless grace! it triumphs here

4 Expand, my soul, with holy joy;
Hosannas be thy blest employ,
Salvation thy eternal theme,—
And swell the song with Jesus' name!

161 *Gethsemane.* **L. M.**

1 'Tis midnight, and, on Olive's brow,
The star is dimmed that lately shone;
'Tis midnight; in the garden now
The suffering Saviour prays alone.

2 'Tis midnight; and, from all removed,
The Saviour wrestles lone with fears;
Ev'n that disciple whom he loved
Heeds not his Master's grief and tears.

3 'Tis midnight; and, for others' guilt,
The Man of sorrows weeps in blood;
Yet he, who hath in anguish knelt,
Is not forsaken by his God.

4 'Tis midnight,—and from ether-plains
Is borne the song that angels know:
Unheard by mortals are the strains
That sweetly soothe the Saviour's woe.

PASSION WEEK.

WARD. L. M.

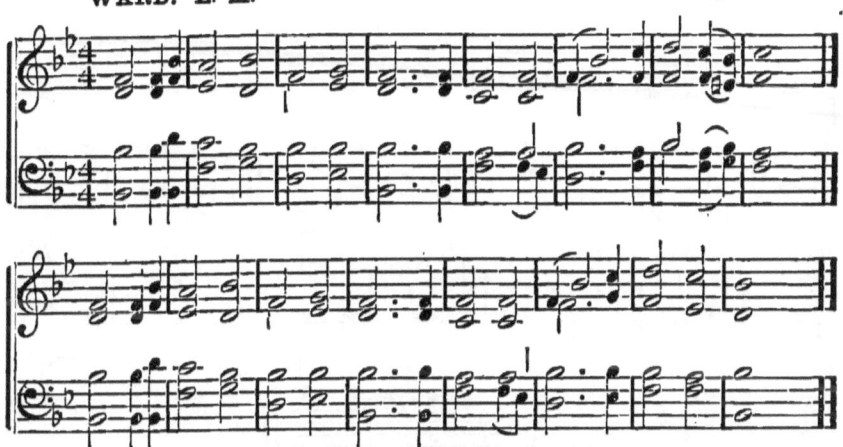

162 *"It is finished."* —John 19: 30.   L. M.

1 "'Tis finished!"—so the Saviour cried
And meekly bowed his head, and died:
"'Tis finished!"—yes, the race is run,
The battle fought, the victory won.

2 "'Tis finished!"—all that heaven foretold
By prophets in the days of old;
And truths are opened to our view,
That kings and prophets never knew.

3 "'Tis finished!"—Son of God, thy power
Hath triumphed in this awful hour;
And yet, our eyes with sorrow see
That life to us was death to thee.

4 "'Tis finished!"—let the joyful sound
Be heard through all the nations round;
"'Tis finished!"—let the echo fly
Thro' heaven and hell, thro' earth and sky.

163 *The Song of Songs.*—Rev. 5: 9-13.   L. M.

1 Come, let us sing the song of songs—
The saints in heaven began the strain—
The homage which to Christ belongs:
"Worthy the Lamb, for he was slain!"

2 Slain to redeem us by his blood,
To cleanse from every sinful stain,
And make us kings and priests to God—
"Worthy the Lamb, for he was slain!"

3 To him who suffered on the tree,
Our souls, at his soul's price, to gain,
Blessing, and praise, and glory be:
"Worthy the Lamb, for he was slain!"

4 To him, enthroned by filial right,
All power in heaven and earth proclaim,
Honor, and majesty, and might:
"Worthy the Lamb, for he was slain!"

5 Long as we live, and when we die,
And while in heaven with him we reign;
This song our song of songs shall be:
"Worthy the Lamb, for he was slain!"

164 *Crucifixion to the world by the cross of Christ.*—Gal. 6: 14.   L. M.

1 When I survey the wondrous cross
On which the Prince of Glory died,
My richest gain I count but loss,
And pour contempt on all my pride.

2 Forbid it, Lord, that I should boast,
Save in the cross of Christ, my God;
All the vain things that charm me most,
I sacrifice them to thy blood.

3 See, from his head, his hands, his feet,
Sorrow and love flow mingled down;
Did e'er such love and sorrow meet,
Or thorns compose a Saviour's crown?

4 Were the whole realm of nature mine,
That were a tribute far too small;
Love so amazing, so divine,
Demands my life, my soul, my all.

Doxology.   L. M.

To God the Father, God the Son,
And God the Spirit, Three in One,
Be honor, praise, and glory given,
By all on earth and all in heaven.

EPIPHANY, LENT, AND

WEBB. 7s & 6s. Double.

165   *"All nations shall be blest in Him."* — Psalm 72.   7s & 6s.

1 Hail to the Lord's Anointed,
Great David's greater Son!
Hail, in the time appointed,
His reign on earth begun!
He comes to break oppression,
To set the captive free;
To take away transgression,
And rule in equity.

2 He shall come down like showers
Upon the fruitful earth;
And love, joy, hope, like flowers,
Spring in his path to birth;
Before him, on the mountains,
Shall Peace, the herald, go;
And Righteousness, in fountains,
From hill to valley flow.

3 Kings shall fall down before him,
And gold and incense bring;
All nations shall adore him,
His praise all people sing:
For he shall have dominion
O'er river, sea, and shore,
Far as the eagle's pinion,
Or dove's light wing can soar.

166   John 19: 2.   7s & 6s.

1 O sacred Head, now wounded,
With grief and shame weighed down,
Now scornfully surrounded
With thorns, thine only crown;
O sacred Head, what glory,
What bliss, till now was thine!
Yet though despised and gory,
I joy to call thee mine.

2 What thou, my Lord, hast suffered
Was all for sinners' gain;
Mine, mine was the transgression,
But thine the deadly pain;
Lo, here I fall, my Saviour!
'Tis I deserve thy place;
Look on me with thy favor,
Vouchsafe to me thy grace.

3 What language shall I borrow
To thank thee, dearest Friend,
For this thy dying sorrow,
Thy pity without end?
Oh, make me thine forever;
And should I fainting be,
Lord, let me never, never
Outlive my love to thee!

4 Be near me when I'm dying:
Oh, show thy cross to me!
And for my succor flying,
Come, Lord, and set me free!
These eyes, new faith receiving,
From Jesus shall not move;
For he who dies believing,
Dies safely, through thy love.

PASSION WEEK.

CRUCIFIX. 7s & 6s. D.

167 *Heb. 2: 9.*   **7s & 6s.**

1 Lord Jesus, by Thy Passion,
To Thee I make my prayer;
Thou who in mercy smitest,
Have mercy, Lord, and spare:
O wash me in the fountain
That floweth from Thy side;
O clothe me in the raiment
Thy Blood hath purified.

2 O hold Thou up my goings,
And lead from strength to strength,
That unto Thee in Zion
I may appear at length:
O make my spirit worthy
To join that ransomed throng;
O teach my lips to utter
That everlasting song.

3 O give that last, best blessing
That even saints can know,
To follow in Thy footsteps
Wherever Thou dost go.
Not wisdom, might, or glory,
I ask to win above;
I ask for Thee, Thee only,
O Thou Eternal Love!

168 *"He hath borne our griefs, and carried our sorrows.—Is. 53: 4.* **7s & 6s.**

1 I lay my sins on Jesus,
The spotless Lamb of God;
He bears them all, and frees us
From the accursed load:
I bring my guilt to Jesus,
To wash my crimson stains
White in his blood most precious,
Till not a stain remains.

2 I lay my wants on Jesus;
All fullness dwells in him;
He heals all my diseases,
He doth my soul redeem:
I lay my griefs on Jesus,
My burdens and my cares,
He from them all releases,
He all my sorrow shares.

3 I rest my soul on Jesus,
This weary soul of mine;
His right hand me embraces,
I on his breast recline.
I love the name of Jesus,
Immanuel, Christ, the Lord;
Like fragrance on the breezes,
His name abroad is poured.

4 I long to be like Jesus,
Meek, loving, lowly, mild;
I long to be like Jesus,
The Father's holy child:
I long to be with Jesus
Amid the heavenly throng,
To sing with saints his praises,
To learn the angels' song.

FOUNTAIN. C. M.

169 *There is a fountain filled with blood. Zech. 14: 1.*   C. M.

1 There is a fountain filled with blood,
Drawn from Immanuel's veins;
And sinners, plunged beneath that flood,
Lose all their guilty stains.

2 The dying thief rejoiced to see
That fountain in his day;
And there may I, though vile as he,
Wash all my sins away.

3 Dear dying Lamb! thy precious blood
Shall never lose its power,
Till all the ransomed church of God
Are saved, to sin no more.

4 Since first, by faith, I saw the stream
Thy flowing wounds supply,
Redeeming love has been my theme,
And shall be, till I die.

5 And when this feeble, stammering tongue
Lies silent in the grave,
Then, in a nobler, sweeter song,
I'll sing thy power to save.

170 *Matth. 27: 45.*   C. M.

1 Alas! and did my Saviour bleed,
And did my Sov'reign die?
Would he devote that sacred head
For such a worm as I?

2 Was it for crimes that I had done,
He groan'd upon the tree?
Amazing pity! grace unknown!
And love beyond degree!

3 Well might the sun in darkness hide,
And shut his glories in,
When God the mighty Maker died
For man the creature's sin.

4 Thus might I hide my blushing face,
While his dear cross appears,
Dissolve my heart in thankfulness,
And melt my eyes to tears.

5 But drops of grief can ne'er repay
The debt of love I owe:
Here, Lord, I give myself away;
'Tis all that I can do.

171 *"Turn Thee unto me, and have mercy upon me."*   C. M.

1 O thou, whose tender mercy hears
Contrition's humble sigh;
Whose hand indulgent wipes the tears
From sorrow's weeping eye;

2 See, Lord, before thy throne of grace,
A wretched wanderer mourn:
Hast thou not bid me seek thy face?
Hast thou not said — "Return"?

3 And shall my guilty fears prevail
To drive me from thy feet?
Oh, let not this dear refuge fail,
This only safe retreat!

4 Absent from thee, my Guide! my Light!
Without one cheering ray,
Through dangers, fears, and gloomy night,
How desolate my way!

PASSION WEEK.

REITER. C. M. GEO. KINGSLEY.

5 Oh, shine on this benighted heart,
With beams of mercy shine!
And let thy healing voice impart
A taste of joy divine.

172 *Restoring grace. Jer. 3: 22.* **C. M.**

1 How oft, alas! this wretched heart
Has wander'd from the Lord!
How oft my roving thoughts depart,
Forgetful of his word.

2 Yet sov'reign mercy calls, "Return;"
Dear Lord, and may I come!
My vile ingratitude I mourn;
Oh take the wand'rer home!

3 And canst thou, wilt thou yet forgive,
And bid my crimes remove?
And shall a pardon'd rebel live
To speak thy wondrous love?

4 Almighty grace, thy healing pow'r,
How glorious, how divine!
That can to life and bliss restore
So vile a heart as mine.

5 Thy pard'ning love, so free, so sweet,
Dear Saviour, I adore;
Oh keep me at thy sacred feet,
And let me rove no more.

173 *The Safe Retreat. Ps. 145: 18.* **C. M.**

1 Dear Father, to thy mercy-seat
My soul for shelter flies:
'T is here I find a safe retreat
When storms and tempests rise.

2 My cheerful hope can never die,
If thou, my God, art near;
Thy grace can raise my comforts high,
And banish every fear.

3 My great Protector, and my Lord,
Thy constant aid impart;
Oh, let thy kind, thy gracious word
Sustain my trembling heart!

4 Oh, never let my soul remove
From this divine retreat!
Still let me trust thy power and love,
And dwell beneath thy feet.

174 *Matt. 26: 41.* **C. M.**

1 Alas! what hourly dangers rise,
What snares beset my way!
To heaven, oh, let me lift mine eyes,
And hourly watch and pray.

2 How oft my mournful thoughts complain,
And melt in flowing tears!
I strive against my foes in vain,
I sink amid my fears.

3 O Lord! increase my faith and hope
When foes and fears prevail,
And bear my fainting spirit up,
Or soon my strength will fail.

4 Oh, keep me in thy heavenly way,
And bid the tempter flee,
And never, never let me stray
From happiness and thee.

LENT, AND

AUTUMN. 8s & 7s. Double.

175 *Gazing on the Cross.* 8s & 7s.
Matt. 27: 36.

1 Sweet the moments, rich in blessing
Which before the cross I spend;
Life and health, and peace possessing
From the sinner's dying friend.

2 Here I'll sit, forever viewing
Mercy's streams, in streams of blood;
Precious drops my soul bedewing
Plead and claim my peace with God.

3 Here it is I find my heaven,
While upon the Lamb I gaze;
Here I see my sins forgiven,
Lost in wonder, love, and praise.

4 May I still enjoy this feeling,
In all need to Jesus go;
Prove his blood each day more healing,
And himself more deeply know.

176 *Prayer for Deliverance from Evil.* 8s & 7s.

1 Suff'ring Son of Man, be near me,
All my suff'rings to sustain,
By thy sorer griefs to cheer me,
By thy more than mortal pain.

2 By thy fainting in the garden,
By thy bloody sweat, I pray,
Write upon my heart the pardon;
Take my sins and fears away.

3 By the travail of thy spirit,
By thine outcry on the tree,
By thine agonizing merit,
In my pangs, remember me!

4 By thy death I now implore thee,
Lord! my dying soul befriend;
Make me lovingly adore thee,
Make me faithful to the end.

177 *Glorying in the cross.* 8s & 7s.
Gal. 6: 14.

1 In the cross of Christ I glory,
Towering o'er the wrecks of time;
All the light of sacred story
Gathers round its head sublime.

2 When the woes of life o'ertake me,
Hopes deceive, and fears annoy,
Never shall the cross forsake me:
Lo! it glows with peace and joy.

3 Bane and blessing, pain and pleasure,
By the cross are sanctified;
Peace is there, that knows no measure,
Joys that through all time abide.

4 In the cross of Christ I glory,
Towering o'er the wrecks of time;
All the light of sacred story
Gathers round its head sublime.

178 *Psalm 103: 13.* 8s & 7s.

1 Jesus, full of all compassion,
Hear Thy humble suppliant's cry;
Let me know Thy great salvation;
See, I languish, faint, and die;

2 Guilty, but with heart relenting,
Overwhelmed with helpless grief,
Prostrate at Thy feet, repenting,
Send, oh, send me quick relief.

PASSION WEEK.

VESPER HYMN. 8s & 7s.

3 Whither should a wretch be flying,
But to Him who comfort gives?
Whither, from the dread of dying,
But to Him who ever lives?

4 Saved! the deed shall spread new glory
Through the shining realms above;
Angels sing the pleasing story,
All enraptured with Thy love.

5 God of God, the One-Begotten,
Light of Light, Immanuel,
In whose Body, joined together,
All the saints forever dwell,

6 Pour upon us of Thy fulness,
That we may for evermore
God the Father, God the Son, and
God the Holy Ghost adore.

179   *John 14: 13.*   **8s & 7s.**

1 Humbly now, with deep contrition,
We Thy mercy, Lord, entreat,
Now, as mourning, weeping, kneeling,
We bow down before Thy feet.

2 Father, in the day of anguish,
And of darkness, and of shame,
Cling we to that precious promise
Made to us in Jesus' name.

3 For His sake, our great Redeemer,
Through His death of wondrous love,
Dare we to approach the footstool
Of Thy mighty throne above:

4 Aye, through Him who bore in sorrow,
Bore in want, in woe, and strife,
This same weight of human weakness,
This same weary human life.

5 Through His Name, and by His merits,
Whom we worship and adore,
For His blessed sake, we pray Thee,
Hear us, spare us evermore.

6 By His hour of mortal weakness,
Give Thine erring children strength,
That they bear the burden bravely,
That they win the crown at length.

180   *(Closing Hymn.)*   **8s & 7s.**

1 May the grace of Christ the Saviour,
And the Father's boundless love,
With the Holy Spirit's favor,
Rest upon us from above.

2 Thus may we abide in union
With each other and the Lord,
And possess, in sweet communion,
Joys which earth can not afford.

Doxology.   **8s & 7s.**

Praise the God of our salvation,
Praise the Fathers's boundless love;
Praise the Lamb, our expiation;
Praise the Spirit from above:
Praise the Fountain of salvation,
Him by whom our spirits live;
Undivided adoration
To the one Jehovah give!

BOYLSTON. S. M.

181 *Behold the Lamb of God.*
John 1: 29. S. M.

1 Not all the blood of beasts,
On Jewish altars slain,
Could give the guilty conscience peace,
Or wash away the stain.

2 But Christ, the heavenly Lamb,
Takes all our sins away —
A sacrifice of nobler name,
And richer blood than they.

3 My faith would lay her hand
On that dear head of thine,
While like a penitent I stand,
And there confess my sin.

4 My soul looks back to see
The burdens thou didst bear.
When hanging on the cursed tree,
And hopes her guilt was there.

5 Believing, we rejoice
To see the curse remove;
We bless the Lamb with cheerful voice,
And sing his bleeding love.

182 *"My God, my God, why hast thou*
forsaken me."—Matt. 27: 46. S. M.

1 O'erwhelmed in depths of woe,
Upon the tree of scorn
Hangs the Redeemer of mankind,
With racking anguish torn.

2 Hark! with what awful cry
His spirit takes its flight;
That cry, it pierced His mother's heart,
And whelmed her soul in night.

3 Earth hears, and to its base
Rocks wildly to and fro;
Tombs burst; seas, rivers, mountains quake;
The veil is rent in two.

4 The sun withdraws his light,
The midday heavens grow pale,
The moon, the stars, the universe,
Their Maker's death bewail.

5 Shall man alone be mute?
Come, youth and hoary hairs,
Come, rich and poor, come, all mankind,
And bathe those feet in tears!

6 Come, fall before His cross
Who shed for us His blood;
Who died the Victim of pure love,
To make us sons of God.

183 *Compassion of Christ.*
Luke 19: 41. S. M.

1 Did Christ o'er sinners weep,
And shall our cheeks be dry?
Let floods of penitential grief
Burst forth from every eye.

2 The Son of God in tears
The wondering angels see!
Be thou astonished, O my soul!
He shed those tears for thee.

3 He wept that we might weep;
Each sin demands a tear:
In heaven alone no sin is found,
And weeping is not there.

EASTER.

LABAN. S. M.

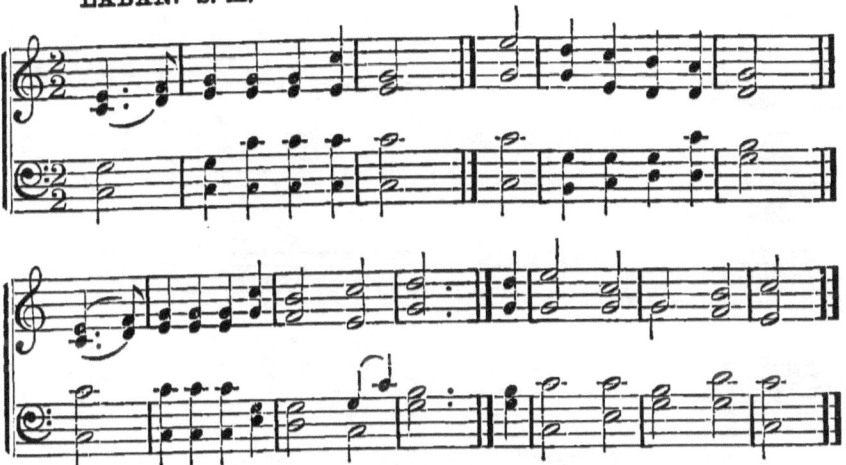

184 *The Fifty-third Chapter of Isaiah.* **S. M.**

1 Like sheep we went astray,
And broke the fold of God;
Each wandering in a different way,
But all the downward road.

2 How dreadful was the hour,
When God our wanderings laid,
And did at once his vengeance pour
Upon the Shepherd's head!

3 How glorious was the grace,
When Christ sustained the stroke!
His life and blood the Shepherd pays,
A ransom for the flock!

4 But God shall raise his head
O'er all the sons of men;
And make him see a numerous seed,
To recompense his pain.

5 "I'll give him," saith the Lord,
"A portion with the strong;
He shall possess a large reward,
And hold his honors long."

185 *"The Lord is risen indeed." John 24: 34.* **S. M.**

1 "The Lord is risen indeed:"
Now is his work performed;
Now is the mighty Captive freed,
And death our foe disarmed.

2 "The Lord is risen indeed:"
The Grave has lost his prey;
With him is risen the ransomed seed
To reign in endless day.

3 "The Lord is risen indeed:"
He lives, to die no more;
He lives, the sinner's cause to plead,
Whose curse and shame he bore.

4 "The Lord is risen indeed:"
Attending angels, hear;
Up to the courts of heaven, with speed,
The joyful tidings bear.

5 Then take your golden lyres,
And strike each cheerful chord;
Join all the bright celestial choirs,
To sing our risen Lord!

186 *New Year.* **S. M.**
"Our days are as an hand-breadth." Ps. 39: 5.

1 My few revolving years,
How swift they glide away!
How short the term of life appears,
When past—but as a day!—

2 A dark and cloudy day,
Made up of grief and sin;
A host of enemies without,
Of guilty fears within.

3 Lord, through another year,
If thou permit my stay,
With watchful care may I pursue
The true and living way!

Doxology. **S. M.**

Praise to the Father be;
Praise to His only Son;
Praise to the blessed Paraclete,
While endless ages run.

LENT, AND

LITANY. 7s. D.

187   *"Deep regret for follies past."*   Jer. 14: 20.

1 God of mercy! God of love!
Hear our sad, repentant song;
Sorrow dwells on every face,
Penitence on every tongue.

2 Deep regret for follies past,
Talents wasted, time misspent;
Hearts debased by wordly cares,
Thankless for the blessings lent;

3 Foolish fears and fond desires,
Vain regrets for things as vain;
Lips too seldom taught to praise,
Oft to murmur and complain;

4 These, and every secret fault,
Filled with grief and shame, we own:
Humbled at thy feet we lie,
Seeking pardon from thy throne.

188   *The penitential plea.*

1 Saviour, when in dust to thee
Low we bend the adoring knee;
When repentant to the skies
Scarce we lift our weeping eyes;
Oh, by all the pains and woe
Suffered once for man below,
Bending from thy throne on high,
Hear our solemn Litany!

2 By thy helpless infant years;
By thy life of want and tears;

7s. By thy days of sore distress
In the lonely wilderness;
By the dread mysterious hour
Of the insulting tempter's power:
Turn, oh turn a favoring eye;
Hear our solemn Litany!

3 By the sacred griefs that wept
O'er the grave where Lazarus slept;
By the boding tears that flowed
Over Salem's loved abode;
By the anguished sigh that told
Treachery lurked within thy fold;
From thy seat above the sky,
Hear our solemn Litany!

4 By thine hour of dire despair;
By thine agony of prayer;
By the cross, the nail, the thorn,
Piercing spear and torturing scorn;
By the gloom that veiled the skies
7s. O'er the dreadful sacrifice;
Listen to our humble cry,
Hear our solemn Litany!

5 By thy deep expiring groan;
By the sad sepulchral stone;
By the vault, whose dark abode
Held in vain the rising God;
Oh, from earth to heaven restored,
Mighty reascended Lord,
Listen, listen to the cry
Of our solemn Litany!

PASSION WEEK.

COMFORT. 7s. D.

189 *1 Tim. 1: 15.*

1 Sovereign Ruler, Lord of all!
Prostrate at thy feet we fall;
Hear, oh, hear our earnest cry!
Frown not, lest we faint and die.

2 Vilest of the sons of men,
Chief of sinners, we have been;
Oft have sinned before thy face;
Trampled on thy richest grace.

3 Justly might the fatal dart
Pierce our guilty, broken heart;
Justly might thy righteous breath
Doom us to eternal death.

4 Jesus! save our dying soul;
Make our broken spirit whole:
Humbled in the dust we lie,
Saviour! leave us not to die.

190 *John 19: 30.*

1 "It is finished!" shall we raise
Songs of sorrow, or of praise?
Mourn to see the Saviour die,
Or proclaim his victory?

2 If of Calvary we tell,
How can songs of triumph swell?
If of man redeemed from woe,
How shall notes of mourning flow?

7s. 3 Ours the guilt which pierced his side,
Ours the sin for which he died;
But the blood which flowed that day
Washed our sin and guilt away.

4 Lamb of God! thy death hath given
Pardon, peace, and hope of heaven:
"It is finished!" let us raise
Songs of thankfulness and praise.

191 *Gethsemane.* 7s.

1 Surely Christ thy griefs has borne;
Weeping soul, no longer mourn:
View him bleeding on the tree,
Pouring out his life for thee.

2 Weary sinner, keep thine eyes
On the atoning sacrifice;
There the incarnate Deity
Numbered with transgressors see.

3 Cast thy guilty soul on him,
Find him mighty to redeem;
At his feet thy burden lay,
Look thy doubts and cares away.

4 Lord, thine arm must be revealed,
Ere I can by faith be healed;
Since I scarce can look to thee,
Cast a gracious eye on me.

FEDERAL STREET. L. M.

192   *"O death, where is thy sting?"*   **L. M.**
            Luke 24: 46.

1 He dies! the Friend of sinners dies!
Lo! Salem's daughters weep around:
A solemn darkness vails the skies;
A sudden trembling shakes the ground.

2 Here's love and grief beyond degree:
The Lord of glory dies for men!
But, lo! what sudden joys we see,—
Jesus, the dead, revives again!

3 The rising God forsakes the tomb;
Up to his Father's court he flies:
Cherubic legions guard him home,
And shout him welcome to the skies.

4 Break off your tears, ye saints and tell
How high our great Deliverer reigns;
Sing how he spoiled the hosts of hell,
And led the tyrant Death in chains.

5 Say, "Live forever, glorious King,
Born to redeem and strong to save!
Where now, O Death, where is thy sting?
And where thy vict'ry, boasting Grave?"

193   *Isa 63: 3.*   **L. M.**

1 O Saviour, who for man hast trod
The winepress of the wrath of God,
Ascend, and claim again on high,
Thy glory left for us to die.

2 A radiant cloud is now thy seat,
And earth lies stretched beneath thy feet;
Ten thousand thousands round thee sing,
And share the triumph of their King.

3 The angel-host enraptured waits:
"Lift up your heads, eternal gates!"
O God-and-Man! the Father's Throne
Is now for evermore thine own.

4 Our great High-Priest and Shepherd, thou
Within the veil art entered now,
To offer there thy precious Blood
Once poured on earth a cleansing flood.

5 And thence the Church, thy chosen Bride,
With countless gifts of grace supplied,
Through all her members draws from thee
Her hidden life of sanctity.

6 O Christ, our Lord, of thy dear care
Thy lowly members heavenward bear;
Be ours with thee to suffer pain,
With thee for evermore to reign.

194   *The King of Glory.*   **L. M.**
            Psalm 24.

1 Our Lord is risen from the dead;
Our Jesus is gone up on high;
The powers of hell are captive led,
Dragged to the portals of the sky.

2 There his triumphal chariot waits,
And angels chant the solemn lay:
"Lift up your heads, ye heavenly gates!
Ye everlasting doors! give way."

3 "Loose all your bars of massy light,
And wide unfold th' ethereal scene;
He claims these mansions as his right;
Receive the King of glory in."

PENTECOST.

FOREST. L. M.

4 "Who is the King of glory?—who?"
"The Lord, that all our foes o'ercame,
The world, sin, death, and hell o'erthrew;
And Jesus is the Conqueror's name."

5 Lo! his triumphal chariot waits,
And angels chant the solemn lay:
"Lift up your heads, ye heavenly gates!
Ye everlasting doors! give way."

6 "Who is the King of glory?—who?"
"The Lord, of glorious power possessed:
The King of saints and angels too:
God over all, for ever blessed."

195 *"The Lord, He is the King of Glory."—Psalm 24.* **L. M**

1 Lift up your heads, ye gates! and wide
Your everlasting doors display;
Ye angel-guards, like flames divide,
And give the King of glory way.

2 Who is the King of glory?—He,
The Lord, omnipotent to save;
Whose own right arm, in victory,
Led captive Death, and spoiled the grave.

3 Lift up your heads, ye gates! and high
Your everlasting portals heave;
Welcome the King of glory nigh:
Him must the heaven of heavens receive.

4 Who is the King of glory—who?
The Lord of hosts; behold his name:
The kingdom, power, and honor due,
Yield him, ye saints, with glad acclaim!

196 *Prayer for the Guidance of the Spirit.* **L. M.**

1 Come, gracious Spirit, heavenly Dove,
With light and comfort from above;
Be thou our guardian, thou our guide,
O'er every thought and step preside.

2 The light of truth to us display,
And make us know and choose thy way;
Plant holy fear in every heart,
That we from God may ne'er depart.

3 Lead us to holiness—the road
Which we must take to dwell with God;
Lead us to Christ, the living way,
Nor let us from his pastures stray.

4 Lead us to God, our final rest,
To be with him for ever blest;
Lead us to heaven, its bliss to share—
Fullness of joy for ever there!

197 *Acts 2.* **L. M.**

1 Spirit of mercy, truth, and love,
Oh shed Thine influence from above!
And still through endless time convey
The wonders of this sacred day.

2 In every clime, by every tongue,
Be God's surpassing glory sung;
Let all the listening earth be taught
The wonders by our Saviour wrought.

3 Unfailing Comfort, Heavenly Guide,
Still in our longing hearts abide;
Still let mankind Thy blessings prove,
Spirit of mercy, truth and love.

HENRY. C. M.

198 *Luke 24: 34.* C. M.

1 The morning purples all the sky,
The air with praises rings,
Defeated hell stands sullen by,
The world exulting sings:

2 While He, the King all strong to save,
Rends the dark doors away,
And through the breaches of the grave
Strides forth into the day.

3 Death's captive, in his gloomy prison
Fast fettered He has lain;
But He has mastered death, is risen,
And death wears now the chain.

4 The shining angels cry, "Away
With grief; no spices bring;
Not tears, but songs, this joyful day,
Should greet the rising King!"

5 That thou our Paschal Lamb may'st be,
And endless joy begin,
Jesus, Deliverer, set us free
From the dread death of sin.

6 Glory to God! our glad lips cry;
All praise and worship be
On earth, in heaven, to God most High,
For Christ's great victory!

199 *1 Cor. 15: 53.* C. M.

1 O love! which lightens all distress,
Love, death cannot destroy;
O grave! whose very emptiness
To faith is full of joy!

2 Let but that Love our hearts supply
From heaven's exhaustless spring,
Then grave, where is thy victory?
And death, where is thy sting?

200 *Redemption finished.* C. M.

1 Triumphant, Christ ascends on high,
The glorious work complete,
Sin, death, and hell, low vanquished lie,
Beneath his awful feet.

2 There, with eternal glory crowned,
The Lord, the Conqueror, reigns;
His praise the heavenly choirs resound
In their immortal strains.

3 Amid the splendors of his throne,
Unchanging love appears;
The names he purchased for his own,
Still on his heart he bears.

4 Oh! the rich depths of love divine!
Of bliss a boundless store!
Dear Saviour, let me call thee mine;
I can not wish for more.

5 On thee alone my hope relies;
Beneath thy cross I fall,—
My Lord, my life, my sacrifice,
My Saviour, and my all!

201 *"Lift up your heads, O ye gates."* *Psalm 24.* C. M.

1 Lift up your heads, eternal gates!
Unfold, to entertain
The King of glory; see! he comes
With his celestial train.

ASCENSION.

NEWBOLD. C. M.

2 Who is the King of glory?—who?
The Lord, for strength renowned;
In battle mighty; o'er his foes
Eternal victor crowned.

3 Lift up your heads, ye gates! unfold,
In state to entertain
The King of glory; see! he comes
With all his shining train.

4 Who is the King of glory—who?
The Lord of hosts renowned;
Of glory he alone is King,
Who is with glory crowned.

202   *Acts 1: 9, 19.*   **C. M.**

1 O! for a shout of sacred joy
To God, the sovereign King:
Let all the lands their tongues employ,
And hymns of triumph sing.

2 Jesus, our God, ascends on high;
His heavenly guards around
Attend him rising through the sky,
With trumpets' joyful sound.

3 While angels shout and praise their King,
Let mortals learn their strains;
Let all the earth his honor sing;—
O'er all the earth he reigns.

4 Rehearse his praise, with awe profound!
Let knowledge lead the song;
Nor mock him with a solemn sound
Upon a thoughtless tongue.

203   *Heb 2: 9.*   **C. M.**

1 The head, that once was crowned with thorns,
Is crowned with glory now;
A royal diadem adorns
The mighty Victor's brow.

2 The highest place that heaven affords
Is his—is his by right,—
The King of kings, and Lord of lords,
And heaven's eternal Light.

3 The joy of all who dwell above,
The joy of all below,
To whom he manifests his love,
And grants his name to know.

4 To them the cross, with all its shame,
With all its grace, is given;
Their name, an everlasting name
Their joy, the joy of heaven.

5 They suffer with their Lord below,
They reign with him above,
Their profit and their joy to know
The mystery of his love.

6 The cross he bore is life and health,
Though shame and death to him;
His people's hope, his people's wealth,
Their everlasting theme.

Doxology.   **C. M.**

Let God the Father, and the Son,
And Spirit, be adored,
Where there are works to make Him known,
Or saints to love the Lord.

77

EASTER, AND

HEROLD. 7s.

204 *An ancient Hymn of the Resurrection.*

1 Jesus Christ is risen to-day—
Our triumphant holy day—
Who did once, upon the cross,
Suffer to redeem our loss.

2 Hymns of praise then let us sing
Unto Christ, our heavenly King;
Who endured the cross and grave,
Sinners to redeem and save.

3 But the pain which he endured
Our salvation hath procured;
Honor, then, to him, and praise,
Rising on this Day of days!

205 *"Christ, the first-fruits." Luke 24 : 34.*

1 Christ, the Lord is risen to-day!
Sons of men and angels say:
Raise your joys and triumphs high;
Sing, ye heavens! and earth, reply!

2 Love's redeeming work is done,
Fought the fight, the battle won:
Lo! our sun's eclipse is o'er;
Lo! he sets in blood no more.

3 Vain the stone, the watch, the seal—
Christ hath burst the gates of hell:
Death in vain forbids his rise,
Christ hath opened paradise.

4 Lives again our glorious King!
Where, O Death, is now thy sting?
Once he died, our souls to save:
Where's thy vic'try, boasting Grave?

7s. 5 Soar we now where Christ hath led,
Foll'wing our exalted head:
Made like him, like him we rise,
Ours the cross, the grave, the skies!

206 *Matt. 28 : 2.* 7s.

1 Angels, roll the rock away!
Death, yield up thy mighty prey!
See, the Saviour leaves the tomb,
Glowing with immortal bloom.

2 Hark! the wondering angels raise
Louder notes of joyful praise;
Let the earth's remotest bound
Echo with the blissful sound.

7s. 3 Saints on earth, lift up your eyes;
Now to glory see Him rise
In long triumph through the sky,
Up to waiting worlds on high.

4 Heaven unfolds its portals wide;
Mighty Conqueror, through them ride!
King of glory, mount Thy throne!
Boundless empire is Thine own.

5 Powers of heaven, seraphic choirs,
Sing and sweep your golden lyres;
Sons of men, in humbler strain
Sing your mighty Saviour's reign.

6 Every note with wonder swell,
Sin o'erthrown, and captive hell!
Where, O death, is now thy sting?
Where thy terrors, vanquished king?

PENTECOST.

SEELYE. 7s.

207   *Matt. 28: 6.*

1 Morning breaks upon the tomb;
Jesus scatters all its gloom;
Day of triumph! through the skies
See the glorious Saviour rise!

2 Christian, dry your flowing tears;
Chase those unbelieving fears;
Look on His deserted grave;
Doubt no more His power to save.

3 Ye, who are of death afraid,
Triumph in the scattered shade;
Drive your anxious cares away,
See the place where Jesus lay.

4 Lo! the rising sun appears,
Shedding radiance o'er the spheres;
Lo! returning beams of light
Chase the terrors of the night.

208   *"Holy Spirit, all Divine!"*   7s.

1 Holy Ghost, with light divine,
Shine upon this heart of mine!
Chase the shades of night away,
Turn my darkness into day.

2 Holy Ghost, with power divine,
Cleanse this guilty heart of mine;
Long hath sin, without control,
Held dominion o'er my soul.

3 Holy Ghost, with joy divine,
Cheer this saddened heart of mine;
Bid my many woes depart,
Heal my wounded, bleeding heart!

7s. 4 Holy Spirit, all Divine!
Dwell within this heart of mine;
Cast down every idol-throne;
Reign supreme, and reign alone!

209   *The Spirit's influence sought.*   7s.

1 Gracious Spirit, love divine!
Let thy light within me shine;
All my guilty fears remove,
Fill me full of heav'n and love.

2 Speak thy pard'ning grace to me,
Set the burden'd sinner free;
Lead me to the Lamb of God,
Wash me in his precious blood.

3 Life and peace to me impart,
Seal salvation on my heart;
Breathe thyself into my breast,
Earnest of immortal rest.

7s. 4 Let me never from thee stray,
Keep me in the narrow way;
Fill my soul with joy divine,
Keep me, Lord, for ever thine.

210   *1 Cor. 3: 16.*   7s.

1 Come, divine and peaceful Guest,
Enter each devoted breast;
Holy Ghost, our hearts inspire,
Kindle there the Gospel fire.

2 Bid our sin and sorrow cease;
Fill us with thy heavenly peace;
Joy divine we then shall prove,
Light of truth—and fire of love.

PENTECOST.

DOWNS. C. M.

211   *John 16: 7.*   C. M.

1 Come, Holy Spirit, heav'nly Dove,
With all thy quick'ning pow'rs,
Kindle a flame of sacred love
In these cold hearts of ours.

2 Look how we grovel here below,
Fond of these trifling toys;
Our souls can neither fly nor go,
To reach eternal joys.

3 In vain we tune our formal songs,
In vain we strive to rise;
Hosannas languish on our tongues,
And our devotion dies.

4 Dear Lord! and shall we ever live
At this poor, dying rate?
Our love so faint, so cold to thee,
And thine to us so great?

5 Come, Holy Spirit, heavn'ly Dove,
With all thy quick'ning pow'rs,
Come, shed abroad a Saviour's love,
And that shall kindle ours.

212 *Prayer for the witness of the Spirit.*   C. M.
       2 Cor. 1: 22.

1 Why should the children of a King
Go mourning all their days?
Great Comforter! descend and bring
Some tokens of thy grace.

2 Dost thou not dwell in all thy saints,
And seal them heirs of heaven?
When wilt thou banish my complaints,
And show my sins forgiven?

3 Assure my conscience of her part
In my Redeemer's blood;
And bear thy witness with my heart,
That I am born of God.

4 Thou art the earnest of his love,
The pledge of joys to come;
And thy soft wings, celestial Dove,
Will safe convey me home.

213   *1 Cor. 2: 10.*   C. M.

1 Spirit Divine! attend our prayer,
And make our hearts thy home;
Descend with all thy gracious power:
Come, Holy Spirit, come!

2 Come as the light: to us reveal
Our sinfulness and woe;
And lead us in those paths of life
Where all the righteous go.

3 Come as the fire, and purge our hearts,
Like sacrificial flame:
Let our whole soul an off'ring be
To our Redeemer's name.

4 Come as the dew, and sweetly bless
This consecrated hour;
May barrenness rejoice to own
Thy fertilizing power.

5 Come as the wind, with rushing sound,
With Pentecostal grace;
And make the great salvation known,
Wide as the human race.

PENTECOST.

BOARDMAN. C. M.

6 Spirit Divine, attend our prayer,
And make our hearts thy home;
Descend with all thy gracious power:
Come, Holy Spirit, come!

214   *John* 16: 7.   C. M.

1 Let songs of praises fill the sky!
Christ, our ascended Lord,
Sends down His Spirit from on high,
According to His word.

2 The Spirit, by His heavenly breath,
New life creates within;
He quickens sinners from their death
Of trespasses and sin.

3 The things of Christ the Spirit takes,
And to our hearts reveals;
Our bodies He His temple makes,
And our redemption seals.

4 Come, Holy Spirit, from above,
With Thy celestial fire;
Come, and with flames of zeal and love
Our hearts and tongues inspire!

215   *Rom.* 5: 5.   C. M.

1 O Holy Spirit, Fount of Love,
Blest Source of gifts divine,
Kindle, we pray Thee, from above,
The inmost souls of Thine.

2 Bond of the sacred Trinity,
Knit Thou our hearts in one,
To know the blessed unity
Of Father and of Son!

3 Shed in each faithful heart abroad
Love that doth all excel;
That God in us and we in God
For evermore may dwell.

4 O blessed Comforter, to Thee,
With the Eternal Son,
And with the Father, glory be,
While endless ages run.

216   *"Teach me the way of thy statutes."*   C. M.
Psalm 119.

1 O that the Lord would guide my ways
To keep his statutes still!
O that my God would grant me grace
To know and do his will!

2 Oh, send thy Spirit down, to write
Thy law upon my heart;
Nor let my tongue indulge deceit,
Nor act the liar's part.

3 Order my footsteps by thy word,
And make my heart sincere;
Let sin have no dominion, Lord,
But keep my conscience clear.

4 Make me to walk in thy commands—
'Tis a delightful road;
Nor let my head nor heart nor hands
Offend against my God.

Doxology.   C. M.

To praise the Father and the Son,
And Spirit all divine,
The One in Three, and Three in One,
Let saints and angels join.

DENNIS. S. M.

217 *John 14: 26.*

1 Come, Holy Spirit! come;
Let thy bright beams arise;
Dispel the sorrow from our minds,
The darkness from our eyes.

2 Convince us of our sin;
Then lead to Jesus' blood,
And to our wondering view reveal
The mercies of our God.

3 Revive our drooping faith,
Our doubts and fears remove,
And kindle in our breasts the flame
Of never-dying love.

4 'Tis thine to cleanse the heart,
To sanctify the soul,
To pour fresh life in every part,
And new-create the whole.

5 Come, Holy Spirit! come;
Our minds from bondage free;
Then shall we know and praise and love
The Father, Son and thee.

218 *"I love thy kingdom, Lord."*—Ps.137. S.M.

1 I love thy kingdom, Lord,—
The house of thine abode,
The church our blest Redeemer saved
With his own precious blood.

2 I love thy Church, O God!
Her walls before thee stand,
Dear as the apple of thine eye,
And graven on thy hand.

S. M.

3 For her my tears shall fall,
For her my prayers ascend;
To her my cares and toils be given,
Till toils and cares shall end.

4 Beyond my highest joy
I prize her heavenly ways,
Her sweet communion, solemn vows,
Her hymns of love and praise.

5 Jesus, thou Friend divine,
Our Saviour and our King,
Thy hand from every snare and foe
Shall great deliverance bring.

6 Sure as thy truth shall last,
To Zion shall be given
The brightest glories earth can yield,
And brighter bliss of heaven.

219 *The Ark of God.* S. M.

1 Like Noah's weary dove
That soared the earth around,
But not a resting-place above
The cheerless waters found,

2 Oh, cease, my wandering soul,
On restless wing to roam;
All the wide world, to either pole,
Has not for thee a home.

3 Behold the ark of God,
Behold the open door;
Hasten to gain that dear abode,
And rove, my soul, no more.

PENTECOST.

BOARDMAN. C. M.

6 Spirit Divine, attend our prayer,
And make our hearts thy home;
Descend with all thy gracious power:
Come, Holy Spirit, come!

214   *John 16: 7.*   **C. M.**

1 Let songs of praises fill the sky!
Christ, our ascended Lord,
Sends down His Spirit from on high,
According to His word.

2 The Spirit, by His heavenly breath,
New life creates within;
He quickens sinners from their death
Of trespasses and sin.

3 The things of Christ the Spirit takes,
And to our hearts reveals;
Our bodies He His temple makes,
And our redemption seals.

4 Come, Holy Spirit, from above,
With Thy celestial fire;
Come, and with flames of zeal and love
Our hearts and tongues inspire!

215   *Rom. 5: 5.*   **C. M.**

1 O Holy Spirit, Fount of Love,
Blest Source of gifts divine,
Kindle, we pray Thee, from above,
The inmost souls of Thine.

2 Bond of the sacred Trinity,
Knit Thou our hearts in one,
To know the blessed unity
Of Father and of Son!

3 Shed in each faithful heart abroad
Love that doth all excel;
That God in us and we in God
For evermore may dwell.

4 O blessed Comforter, to Thee,
With the Eternal Son,
And with the Father, glory be,
While endless ages run.

216   *"Teach me the way of thy statutes." Psalm 119.*   **C. M.**

1 O that the Lord would guide my ways
To keep his statutes still!
O that my God would grant me grace
To know and do his will!

2 Oh, send thy Spirit down, to write
Thy law upon my heart;
Nor let my tongue indulge deceit,
Nor act the liar's part.

3 Order my footsteps by thy word,
And make my heart sincere;
Let sin have no dominion, Lord,
But keep my conscience clear.

4 Make me to walk in thy commands—
'Tis a delightful road;
Nor let my head nor heart nor hands
Offend against my God.

Doxology.   **C. M.**

To praise the Father and the Son,
And Spirit all divine,
The One in Three, and Three in One,
Let saints and angels join.

PENTECOST, THE CHURCH,

DENNIS. S. M.

217 *John 14: 26.* S. M.

1 Come, Holy Spirit! come;
Let thy bright beams arise;
Dispel the sorrow from our minds,
The darkness from our eyes.

2 Convince us of our sin;
Then lead to Jesus' blood,
And to our wondering view reveal
The mercies of our God.

3 Revive our drooping faith,
Our doubts and fears remove,
And kindle in our breasts the flame
Of never-dying love.

4 'Tis thine to cleanse the heart,
To sanctify the soul,
To pour fresh life in every part,
And new-create the whole.

5 Come, Holy Spirit! come;
Our minds from bondage free;
Then shall we know and praise and love
The Father, Son and thee.

218 *"I love thy kingdom, Lord."—Ps. 137.* S.M.

1 I love thy kingdom, Lord,—
The house of thine abode,
The church our blest Redeemer saved
With his own precious blood.

2 I love thy Church, O God!
Her walls before thee stand,
Dear as the apple of thine eye,
And graven on thy hand.

3 For her my tears shall fall,
For her my prayers ascend;
To her my cares and toils be given,
Till toils and cares shall end.

4 Beyond my highest joy
I prize her heavenly ways,
Her sweet communion, solemn vows,
Her hymns of love and praise.

5 Jesus, thou Friend divine,
Our Saviour and our King,
Thy hand from every snare and foe
Shall great deliverance bring.

6 Sure as thy truth shall last,
To Zion shall be given
The brightest glories earth can yield,
And brighter bliss of heaven.

219 *The Ark of God.* S. M.

1 Like Noah's weary dove
That soared the earth around,
But not a resting-place above
The cheerless waters found,

2 Oh, cease, my wandering soul,
On restless wing to roam;
All the wide world, to either pole,
Has not for thee a home.

3 Behold the ark of God,
Behold the open door;
Hasten to gain that dear abode,
And rove, my soul, no more.

THE COMMUNION OF SAINTS.

FRANKLIN SQUARE. S. M.

4 There safe thou shalt abide,
There sweet shall be thy rest,
And every longing satisfied,
With full salvation blessed.

220 Ps. 63: 2. **S. M.**

1 How charming is the place
Where my Redeemer God
Unveils the beauties of his face,
And sheds his love abroad!

2 Not the fair palaces
To which the great resort
Are once to be compared with this,
Where Jesus holds his court.

3 Here, on the mercy-seat,
With radiant glory crowned,
Our joyful eyes behold him sit
And smile on all around.

4 To him their prayers and cries
Each humble soul presents;
He listens to their broken sighs,
And grants them all their wants.

5 To them his sovereign will
He graciously imparts,
And in return accepts, with smiles,
The tribute of their hearts.

6 Give me, O Lord! a place
Within thy blest abode,
Among the children of thy grace,
The servants of my God.

221 *Christian Fellowsh'p.* Rom. 12: 5. **S. M.**

1 Blest be the tie that binds
Our hearts in Christian love:
The fellowship of kindred minds
Is like to that above.

2 Before our Father's throne
We pour our ardent prayers;
Our fears, our hopes, our aims are one,
Our comforts and our cares.

3 We share our mutual woes,
Our mutual burdens bear:
And often for each other flows
The sympathizing tear.

4 When we asunder part,
It gives us inward pain;
But we shall still be joined in heart,
And hope to meet again.

5 This glorious hope revives
Our courage by the way;
While each in expectation lives,
And longs to see the day.

6 From sorrow, toil, and pain,
And sin, we shall be free,
And perfect love and friendship reign
Through all eternity.

Doxology. **S. M.**

The Father and the Son,
And Spirit we adore;
We praise, we bless, we worship thee,
Both now and evermore!

ASCENSION, TRINITY,

OLIVET. 6s & 4s.

222 *"That at the name of Jesus every knee should bow."*

1 Let us awake our joys;
Strike up with cheerful voice:
Each creature, sing:
Angels! begin the song;
Mortals! the strain prolong,
In accents sweet and strong,
"Jesus is King!"

2 Proclaim abroad his name;
Tell of his matchless fame;
What wonders done!
Above, beneath, around,
Let all the earth resound,
Till heaven's high arch rebound,
"Vict'ry is won!"

3 He vanquished sin and hell,
And our last foe will quell:
Mourners, rejoice!
His dying love adore;
Praise him, now raised in power:
Praise him for evermore,
With joyful voice.

4 All hail the glorious day,
When, through the heavenly way,
Lo, he shall come!
While they who pierced him wail,
His promise shall not fail;
Saints, see your King prevail:
Great Saviour, come!

223 *"To Thee, great One in Three."* **6s & 4s.**

1 Come, thou almighty King,
Help us thy name to sing,

6s & 4s. Help us to praise!
Father all glorious.
O'er all victorious,
Come and reign over us,
Ancient of days.

2 Jesus, our Lord, descend;
From all our foes defend,
Nor let us fall:
Let thine almighty aid
Our sure defense be made,
Our souls on thee be stayed:
Lord, hear our call!

3 Come, thou incarnate Word,
Gird on thy mighty sword;
Our prayer attend:
Come, and thy people bless,
And give thy word success:
Spirit of holiness,
On us descend.

4 Come, holy Comforter,
Thy sacred witness bear,
In this glad hour:
Thou, who almighty art,
Now rule in every heart,
And ne'er from us depart,
Spirit of power.

5 To thee, great One in Three,
The highest praises be,
Hence evermore!
Thy sovereign majesty
May we in glory see,
And to eternity
Love and adore!

MISSIONS, AND FAITH.

ITALIAN HYMN. 6s & 4s.

224 *Prayer to the Trinity for the World's Conversion.* 6s & 4s.

1 Thou, whose almighty word
Chaos and darkness heard,
And took their flight,
Hear us, we humbly pray,
And where the gospel day
Sheds not its glorious ray,
"Let there be light."

2 Thou, who didst come to bring,
On thy redeeming wing,
Healing and sight,
Health to the sick in mind,
Sight to the inly blind,
Oh, now to all mankind
"Let there be light."

3 Spirit of truth and love,
Life-giving, Holy Dove,
Speed forth thy flight;
Move on the waters' face,
Bearing the lamp of grace;
And in earth's darkest place
"Let there be light."

2 May thy rich grace impart
Strength to my fainting heart,—
My zeal inspire!
As thou hast died for me,
Oh, may my love to thee
Pure, warm, and changeless be—
A living fire!

3 While life's dark maze I tread,
And griefs around me spread,
Be thou my guide;
Bid darkness turn to day,
Wipe sorrow's tears away,
Nor let me ever stray
From thee aside.

4 When ends life's transient dream,
When death's cold, sullen stream
Shall o'er me roll,
Blest Saviour! then, in love,
Fear and distrust remove;
Oh, bear me safe above—
A ransomed soul!

225 *"My faith looks up to Thee."* 6s & 4s.

1 My faith looks up to thee,
Thou Lamb of Calvary,
Saviour Divine!
Now hear me while I pray;
Take all my guilt away;
Oh, let me, from this day,
Be wholly thine!

Doxology. 6s & 4s.

To God, the Father, Son,
And Spirit, Three in One,
All praise be given!
Crown him in every song;
To him your hearts belong;
Let all his praise prolong
On earth, in heaven!

TRINITY, THE CHURCH, AND

DUKE STREET. L. M.

6 *The Trinity.* **L. M.**

1 O holy, holy, holy Lord!
Bright in Thy deeds and in Thy name,
Forever be Thy name adored,
Thy glories let the world proclaim!

2 O Jesus, Lamb once crucified
To take our load of sins away,
Thine be the hymn that rolls its tide
Along the realms of upper day!

3 O Holy Spirit! from above,
In streams of light and glory given,
Thou source of ecstacy and love,
Thy praises ring through earth and heaven!

4 O God Triune! to Thee we owe
Our every thought, our every song;
And ever may Thy praises flow
From saint and seraph's burning tongue.

227 *Salvation sought from the Trinity.* **L. M.**

1 Father of heaven! whose love profound,
A ransom for our souls hath found,
Before thy throne we sinners bend:
To us thy pard'ning love extend.

2 Almighty Son! incarnate Word!
Our Prophet, Priest, Redeemer, Lord!
Before thy throne we sinners bend:
To us thy saving grace extend.

3 Eternal Spirit! by whose breath
The soul is raised from sin and death,
Before thy throne we sinners bend:
To us thy quick'ning power extend.

4 Jehovah! Father, Spirit, Son!
Mysterious Godhead! Three in One!
Before thy throne we sinners bend:
Grace, pardon, life, to us extend!

228 *"Awake! put on thy strength, O Zion."—Isaiah 52: 1.* **L. M.**

1 Triumphant Zion! lift thy head
From dust and darkness and the dead;
Though humbled long, awake at length,
And gird thee with thy Saviour's strength.

2 Put all thy beauteous garments on,
And let thy various charms be known:
Then, decked in robes of righteousness,
The world thy glories shall confess.

3 No more shall foes unclean invade,
And fill thy hallowed walls with dread;
No more shall hell's insulting host
Their vict'ry and thy sorrows boast.

4 God, from on high, thy groans will hear;
His hand thy ruins shall repair;
Nor will thy watchful Monarch cease
To guard thee in eternal peace.

229 *"Unto Thee shall all flesh come." Psalm 65.* **L. M.**

1 The praise of Zion waits for thee,
Great God! and praise becomes thy house;
There shall thy saints thy glory see,
And there perform their public vows.

2 O thou whose mercy bends the skies,
To save when humble sinners pray!
And lands to thee shall lift their eyes,
And grateful isles of every sea.

MISSIONS.

FEDERAL STREET. L. M.

3 Soon shall the flocking nations run
To Zion's hill, and own their Lord;
The rising and the setting sun
Shall see the Saviour's name adored.

230   *The Song of Triumph.*   L. M.

1 Soon may the last glad song arise
Through all the millions of the skies—
That song of triumph which records
That all the earth is now the Lord's!

2 Let thrones and powers and kingdoms be
Obedient, mighty God, to thee!
And, over land and stream and main,
Wave thou the scepter of thy reign!

3 Oh, let that glorious anthem swell,
Let host to host the triumph tell,
That not one rebel heart remains,
But over all the Saviour reigns!

231   Isa. 51: 9.   L. M.

1 Arm of the Lord, awake, awake!
Put on Thy strength, the nations shake,
And let the world adoring see
Triumphs of mercy wrought by Thee!

2 Say to the heathen, from Thy throne,
"I am Jehovah, God alone;"
Thy voice their idols shall confound,
And cast their altars to the ground.

3 Almighty God, Thy grace proclaim
In every land, of every name;
Let adverse powers before Thee fall,
And crown the Saviour, Lord of all!

232   *"The world shall hear Thy voice."*   L. M.
Ps. 105: 13.

1 Sovereign of worlds! display thy power;
Be this thy Zion's favored hour;
Bid the bright morning Star arise,
And point the nations to the skies.

2 Set up thy throne where Satan reigns,—
On Afric's shore, on India's plains,
On wilds and continents unknown,—
And make the nations all thine own.

3 Speak! and the world shall hear thy voice;
Speak! and the desert shall rejoice;
Scatter the gloom of heathen night,
And bid all nations hail the light.

233   Matt. 9: 38.   L. M.

1 Lord of the harvest! bend thine ear,
For Zion's heritage appear;
Oh, send forth laborers filled with zeal
Swift to obey their Master's will.

2 Our lifted eyes, O Lord! behold
The ripening harvest tinged with gold;
Wide fields are opening to our view;
The work is great, the laborers few.

3 Under the guidance of thy hand
May Zion's sons to every land
Go forth, to bless the dying race,
As heralds of redeeming grace.

4 Bid all their hearts with ardor glow
The Saviour's dying love to show,
And spread the gospel's joyful sound
Far as the race of man is found.

TRINITY, SECOND ADVENT.

SICILIAN HYMN. 8s, 7s & 4s.

234 *The Trinity.* 8s, 7s & 4s.

1 Glory be to God the Father!
Glory be to God the Son!
Glory be to God the Spirit!
Great Jehovah, Three in One:
   Glory, Glory,
While eternal ages run!

2 Glory be to Him who loved us,
Washed us from each spot and stain;
Glory be to Him who bought us,
Made us kings with Him to reign:
   Glory, Glory,
To the Lamb that once was slain!

3 Glory to the King of angels!
Glory to the Church's King!
Glory to the King of nations!
Heaven and earth your praises bring:
   Glory, Glory,
To the King of glory bring!

4 Glory, blessing, praise eternal!
Thus the choir of angels sings;
Honor, riches, power, dominion!
Thus its praise creation brings:
   Glory, Glory,
Glory to the King of kings!

235 *Second Advent.*
Matt. 25:31. 8s, 7s & 4s.

1 Lo! He comes, with clouds descending,
Once for favored sinners slain;
Thousand thousand saints attending

Swell the triumph of His train:
   Hallelujah!
Jesus comes, He comes to reign.

2 Every eye shall now behold Him
Robed in dreadful majesty;
Those who set at naught, and sold Him,
Pierced and nailed Him to the tree,
   Deeply wailing,
Shall the true Messiah see.

3 Every island, sea, and mountain,
Heaven and earth, shall flee away;
All who hate Him must, confounded,
Hear the trump proclaim the day;
   Come to judgment!
Come to judgment! come away!

4 Answer Thine own Bride and Spirit;
Hasten, Lord, and quickly come!
The new heaven and earth to inherit,
Take Thy pining exiles home!
   All creation
Travails, groans, and bids Thee come!

5 Yea, amen! let all adore Thee,
High on Thine eternal throne!
Saviour, take the power and glory,
Claim the kingdom for Thine own!
   Oh, come quickly!
Hallelujah! come, Lord, come!

236 *Second Advent.*
Matt. 25:34. 8s, 7s & 4s.

1 Day of Judgment, day of wonders!
Hark! the trumpet's awful sound,

CHRISTIAN WARFARE, AND DISMISSAL.

ZION. 8s, 7s & 4s.

Louder than a thousand thunders,
Shakes the vast creation round:
  How the summons
Will the sinner's heart confound!

2 See the Judge, our nature wearing,
Clothed in majesty divine!
Ye, who long for His appearing,
Then shall say, This God is mine!
  Gracious Saviour,
Own me in that day for Thine.

3 At His call, the dead awaken,
Rise to life from earth and sea;
All the powers of nature, shaken
By His look, prepare to flee:
  Careless sinner,
What will then become of thee?

4 But to those who have confessed,
Loved and served the Lord below,
He will say,—"Come near, ye blessed!
See the kingdom I bestow:
  You forever
Shall My love and glory know."

237   *The Pilgrim's Prayer.*   8s, 7s & 4s.
      Ex. 14: 19.

1 Guide me, O thou great Jehovah,
Pilgrim through this barren land;
I am weak, but thou art mighty;
Hold me with thy powerful hand:
  Bread of heaven!
Feed me till I want no more.

2 Open thou the crystal fountain,
Whence the healing streams do flow;
Let the fiery, cloudy pillar
Lead me all my journey through:
  Strong Deliverer!
Be thou still my strength and shield.

3 When I tread the verge of Jordan,
Bid my anxious fears subside;
Death of death! and hell's Destruction!
Land me safe on Canaan's side:
  Songs of praises
I will ever give to thee.

238   Phil. 1: 11.   8s, 7s & 4s.

1 Lord! dismiss us with thy blessing,
Fill our hearts with joy and peace;
Let us each, thy love possessing,
Triumph in redeeming grace;
  Oh! refresh us,
Traveling through this wilderness.

2 Thanks we give and adoration,
For thy Gospel's joyful sound;
May the fruits of thy salvation
In our hearts and lives abound;
  May thy presence
With us, evermore, be found.

3 So, whene'er the signal's given,
Us from earth to call away,
Borne on angels' wings to heaven,
Glad the summons to obey,
  We shall surely
Reign with Christ in endless day.

THE CHURCH, AND

BALERMA. C. M.

239   *Dan. 2: 44.*   **C. M.**

1 O, where are kings and empires now
Of old that went and came?
But, Lord! thy church is praying yet,
A thousand years the same.

2 We mark her goodly battlements
And her foundations strong;
We hear within the solemn voice
Of her unending song.

3 For not like kingdoms of the world
Thy holy church, O God!
Though earthquake shocks are threatening her,
And tempests are abroad,

4 Unshaken as eternal hills,
Immovable she stands,
A mountain that shall fill the earth,
A house not made by hands.

240   *Ps. 132: 8.*   **C. M.**

1 Arise, O King of grace! arise,
And enter to thy rest;
Lo! thy church waits with longing eyes,
Thus to be owned and blest.

2 Enter with all thy glorious train,
Thy Spirit and thy word;
All that the ark did once contain
Could no such grace afford.

3 Here, mighty God! accept our vows;
Here let thy praise be spread;
Bless the provisions of thy house,
And fill thy poor with bread.

4 Here let the Son of David reign,
Let God's Anointed shine;
Justice and truth his court maintain
With love and power divine.

5 Here let him hold a lasting throne;
And as his kingdom grows,
Fresh honors shall adorn his crown,
And shame confound his foes.

241   *Ps. 27.*   **C. M.**

1 The Lord of glory is my light,
And my salvation too;
God is my strength, nor will I fear
What all my foes can do.

2 One privilege my heart desires;
Oh, grant me an abode
Among the churches of thy saints,
The temples of my God.

3 There shall I offer my requests,
And see thy beauty still,
Shall hear thy messages of love,
And there inquire thy will.

4 When troubles rise and storms appear,
There may his children hide;
God has a strong pavilion where
He makes my soul abide.

5 Now shall my head be lifted high
Above my foes around,
And songs of joy and victory
Within thy temple sound.

THE COMMUNION OF SAINTS.

CAMBRIDGE. C. M.

242 *Blessedness of the Communion of Saints. 1 Cor. 12: 27.* **C. M.**

1 Happy the souls to Jesus joined,
And saved by grace alone:
Walking in all his ways, they find
Their heaven on earth begun.

2 The church triumphant in thy love,—
Their mighty joys we know:
They sing the Lamb in hymns above,
And we, in hymns below.

3 Thee in thy glorious realm, they praise
And bow before thy throne:
We, in the kingdom of thy grace;—
The kingdoms are but one.

4 The holy to the holiest leads;
From thence our spirits rise:
And he that in thy statutes treads
Shall meet thee in the skies.

243 *The Communion of Saints.* **C. M.**

1 Come let us join our friends above
That have obtained the prize;
And on the eagle wings of love,
To joys celestial rise.

2 Let all the saints terrestrial sing
With those to glory gone;
For all the servants of our King,
In heaven and earth, are one.

3 One family, we dwell in Him,
One church above, beneath,
Though now divided by the stream,
The narrow stream of death.

4 One army of the living God,
To his command we bow;
Part of His host have crossed the flood,
And part are crossing now.

5 Ten thousand to their endless home
This solemn moment fly;
And we are to the margin come,
And we expect to die.

6 His militant, embodied host,
With wishful looks we stand,
And long to see that happy coast,
And reach the heavenly land.

244 *Heb. 11: 13.* **C. M.**

1 Glory to God! whose witness-train,
Those heroes bold in faith,
Could smile on poverty and pain,
And triumph e'en in death.

2 God whom we serve, our God, can save,
Can damp the scorching flame,
Can build an ark, can smooth the wave,
For such as love His name.

3 Lord, if Thine arm support us still
With its eternal strength,
We shall o'ercome the mightiest ill,
And conquerors prove at length.

Doxology. **C. M.**

The Father's Name we loudly raise,
The Son we all adore,
The Holy Ghost, One God, we praise,
Both now and evermore.

THE CHURCH — THE COMMUNION OF SAINTS, AND

ST. THOMAS. S. M.

245 *"The mountain of His holiness."* Psalm 48. **S. M.**

1 Great is the Lord our God,
And let his praise be great;
He makes his churches his abode,
His most delightful seat.

2 These temples of his grace—
How beautiful they stand!
The honors of our native place,
And bulwarks of our land.

3 In Zion God is known
A refuge in distress;
How bright has his salvation shone
Through all her palaces!

4 Oft have our fathers told,
Our eyes have often seen,
How well our God secures the fold
Where his own sheep have been.

5 In every new distress
We'll to his house repair,
We'll think upon his wondrous grace,
And seek deliverance there.

246 *Blessings of Christian Unity.* Psalm 133. **S. M.**

1 Blest are the sons of peace
Whose hearts and hopes are one;
Whose kind designs to serve and please
Through all their actions run.

2 Blest is the pious house
Where zeal and friendship meet:
Their songs of praise, their mingled vows
Make their communion sweet.

3 From those celestial springs
Such streams of pleasure flow,
As no increase of riches brings,
Nor honors can bestow.

4 Thus on the heavenly hills
The saints are blest above;
Where joy, like morning dew, distills,
And all the air is love!

247 *"Thou shalt arise, and have mercy upon Zion."* **S. M.**

1 O Lord our God! arise;
The cause of truth maintain;
And wide o'er all the peopled world
Extend her blessed reign.

2 Thou Prince of life! arise,
Nor let thy glory cease;
Far spread the conquests of thy grace,
And bless the earth with peace.

3 Thou Holy Ghost! arise,—
Extend thy healing wing,
And o'er a dark and ruined world,
Let light and order spring.

4 O all ye nations! rise,—
To God the Saviour sing;
From shore to shore, from earth to heaven
Let echoing anthems ring!

248 *"How beautiful upon the mountains!"—Isaiah 52: 7.* **S. M.**

1 How beauteous are their feet
Who stand on Zion's hill!
Who bring salvation on their tongues,
And words of peace reveal.

MISSIONS.

BADEA. S. M.

2 How charming is their voice!
How sweet the tidings are! —
"Zion, behold thy Saviour King!
He reigns and triumphs here."

3 How happy are our ears,
That hear this joyful sound,
Which kings and prophets waited for,
And sought, but never found!

4 How blessed are our eyes,
That see this heavenly light!
Prophets and kings desired it long,
But died without the sight.

5 The watchmen join their voice,
And tuneful notes employ;
Jerusalem breaks forth in songs,
And deserts learn the joy.

6 The Lord makes bare his arm
Through all the earth abroad :
Let every nation now behold
Their Saviour and their God.

249 *Matt.* 6: 10. S. M.

1 Come, kingdom of our God,
Sweet reign of light and love!
Shed peace, and hope, and joy abroad,
And wisdom from above.

2 Over our spirits first
Extend thy healing reign;
There raise and quench the sacred thirst
That never pains again.

3 Come, kingdom of our God,
And make the broad earth thine;
Stretch o'er her lands and isles the rod
That flowers with grace divine.

4 Soon may all tribes be blest
With fruit from life's glad tree;
And in its shade like brothers rest,
Sons of one family.

250 *Num.* 14: 21. S. M.

1 O God of sovereign grace,
We bow before Thy throne,
And plead, for all the human race,
The merits of Thy Son.

2 Spread through the earth, O Lord,
The knowledge of Thy ways;
And let all lands with joy record
The great Redeemer's praise.

251 *Psalm* 72. S. M.

1 Now living waters flow
To cheer the humble soul;
From sea to sea those waters go,
And spread from pole to pole.

2 Now righteousness shall spring,
And grow on earth again;
Jehovah-Jesus be our King,
And o'er the nations reign!

3 Jesus shall rule alone,
The world shall hear His word;
By one blest name shall He be known,
The universal Lord.

Doxology. S. M.

To God, the Father, Son,
And Spirit, glory be,
As was, and is, and shall remain
Through all eternity.

MISSIONS.

DEDHAM. C. M.

252 *"They come, they come—thine exiled bands."—Isa 52.* **C. M.**

1 Daughter of Zion! from the dust
Exalt thy fallen head;
Again in thy Redeemer trust:
He calls thee from the dead.

2 Awake, awake! put on thy strength,
Thy beautiful array;
The day of freedom dawns at length,
The Lord's appointed day.

3 Rebuild thy walls, thy bounds enlarge,
And send thy heralds forth;
Say to the south, "Give up thy charge,"
And keep not back, O north!

4 They come, they come!—thine exiled bands,
Where'er they rest or roam,
Have heard thy voice in distant lands,
And hasten to their home.

5 Thus, though the universe shall burn,
And God his works destroy,
With songs thy ransomed shall return,
And everlasting joy.

253 *Ps. 96.* **C. M.**

1 Shine, mighty God! on Zion shine
With beams of heavenly grace;
Reveal thy power through all our coasts,
And show thy smiling face.

2 When shall thy name from shore to shore
Sound all the earth abroad,
And distant nations know and love
Their Saviour and their God?

3 Sing to the Lord, ye distant lands!
Sing loud with solemn voice;
Let every tongue exalt his praise,
And every heart rejoice.

4 He, the great Lord, the sovereign Judge,
That sits enthroned above,
In wisdom rules the worlds he made,
And bids them taste his love.

254 *Ps. 72.* **C. M.**

1 Light of the lonely pilgrim's heart!
Star of the coming day!
Arise, and with thy morning beams
Chase all our griefs away.

2 Come, blessed Lord! let every shore
And answering island sing
The praises of thy royal name,
And own thee as their King.

3 Bid the whole earth, responsive now
To the bright world above,
Break forth in sweetest strains of joy
In memory of thy love.

4 Jesus! thy fair creation groans,
The air, the earth, the sea,
In unison with all our hearts,
And calls aloud for thee.

5 Thine was the cross, with all its fruits
Of grace and peace divine;
Be thine the crown of glory now
The palm of victory thine.

INSTALLATION AND PRAYER.

MANOAH. C. M.

255 *Ps. 72.*

1 Jesus, immortal King! arise,
Rise and assert thy sway,
Till earth, subdued, its tribute bring,
And distant lands obey.

2 Ride forth, victorious Conqueror! ride,
Till all thy foes submit,
And all the powers of hell resign
Their trophies at thy feet.

3 Send forth thy word, and let it fly
This spacious earth around,
Till every soul beneath the sun
Shall hear the joyful sound.

4 From sea to sea, from shore to shore,
May Jesus be adored,
And earth, with all her millions, shout
Hosannas to the Lord.

256 *(Installation of Elders and Deacons.)* C. M.

1 Father of mercies! condescend
To hear our fervent prayer,
While these our brethren we commend
To Thy paternal care.

2 Before them set an open door;
Their various efforts bless;
On them Thy Holy Spirit pour,
And crown them with success.

3 Endow them with a heavenly mind;
Supply their every need;
Make them in spirit meek, resigned,
But bold in word and deed.

C. M.

4 In every tempting, trying hour,
Uphold them by Thy grace,
And guard them by Thy mighty power,
Till they shall end their race.

257 *What is Prayer?* C. M.

1 Prayer is the soul's sincere desire,
Uttered or unexpressed;
The motion of a hidden fire
That trembles in the breast.

2 Prayer is the burden of a sigh,
The falling of a tear,
The upward glancing of an eye,
When none but God is near.

3 Prayer is the simplest form of speech
That infant lips can try;
Prayer the sublimest strains that reach
The Majesty on high.

4 Prayer is the contrite sinner's voice,
Returning from his ways:
While angels in their songs rejoice,
And cry, "Behold, he prays!"

5 Prayer is the Christian's vital breath,
The Christian's native air,
His watchword at the gates of death:
He enters heaven with prayer.

6 O thou by whom we come to God,
The Life, the Truth, the Way!
The path of prayer thyself hast trod;
Lord! teach us how to pray.

MISSIONARY HYMN. 7s & 6s.

258 *"Waft, waft, ye winds, his story."* 7s & 6s.

1 From Greenland's icy mountains,
From India's coral strand,
Where Afric's sunny fountains
Roll down their golden sand,—
From many an ancient river,
From many a palmy plain,
They call us to deliver
Their land from error's chain.

2 What though the spicy breezes
Blow soft o'er Ceylon's isle;
Though every prospect pleases,
And only man is vile;
In vain with lavish kindness
The gifts of God are strown;
The heathen, in his blindness,
Bows down to wood and stone!

3 Shall we, whose souls are lighted
With wisdom from on high,—
Shall we to men benighted
The lamp of life deny?
Salvation, oh, salvation!
The joyful sound proclaim,
Till earth's remotest nation
Has learned Messiah's name.

4 Waft, waft, ye winds, his story,
And you, ye waters, roll,
Till, like a sea of glory,
It spreads from pole to pole;
Till o'er our ransomed nature
The Lamb for sinners slain,
Redeemer, King, Creator,
In bliss returns to reign!

259 *The gospel banner.—Ps. 60: 4.* 7s & 6s.

1 Now be the gospel banner
In ev'ry land unfurl'd,
And be the shout hosanna
Re-echoed through the world;
Till ev'ry isle and nation,
Till ev'ry tribe and tongue
Receive the great salvation,
And join the happy throng.

2 Yes, thou shalt reign for ever,
O Jesus, King of kings,
Thy light, thy love, thy favor,
Each ransom'd captive sings;
The isles for thee are waiting,
The deserts learn thy praise,
The hills and valleys greeting,
The song responsive raise.

LORD'S SUPPER.

YARMOUTH. 7s & 6s.

1. Stand up!—stand up for Jesus! Ye soldiers of the cross; Lift high his royal banner, It must not suffer loss: From vict'ry un-to vict'ry His army shall he lead, Till every foe is vanquished, Till every foe is vanquished, Till every foe is vanquished, And Christ is Lord indeed.

260 *"Stand, therefore, having your loins girt adout." Eph. 6: 13.* 7s & 6s.

2 Stand up!—stand up for Jesus!
The trumpet call obey;
Forth to the mighty conflict,
In this his glorious day :
"Ye that are men, now serve him,"
Against unnumbered foes ;
Your courage rise with danger,
And strength to strength oppose.

3 Stand up!—stand up for Jesus!
Stand in his strength alone ;
The arm of flesh will fail you—
Ye dare not trust your own :
Put on the gospel armor,
And, watching unto prayer,
Where duty calls or danger,
Be never wanting there!

4 Stand up!—stand up for Jesus!
The strife will not be long ;
This day the noise of battle,
The next the victor's song :
To him that overcometh,
A crown of life shall be ;
He with the King of Glory
Shall reign eternally !

261 *An ancient Sacramental Hymn.* 7s & 6s.

1 O Bread to pilgrims given,
O Food that angels eat,
O Manna sent from heaven,
For heaven-born natures meet !
Give us, for thee long pining,
To eat till richly filled ;
Till, earth's delights resigning,
Our every wish is stilled !

2 O Water, life-bestowing,
From out the Saviour's heart,
A fountain purely flowing,
A fount of love thou art !
Oh let us, freely tasting,
Our burning thirst assuage !
Thy sweetness, never wasting,
Avails from age to age.

3 Jesus, this feast receiving,
We thee unseen adore ;
Thy faithful word believing,
We take—and doubt no more ;
Give us, thou true and loving,
On earth to live in thee ;
Then, death the vail removing,
Thy glorious face to see !

BAPTISM, COVENANT RELATION, AND

SHIRLAND. S. M.

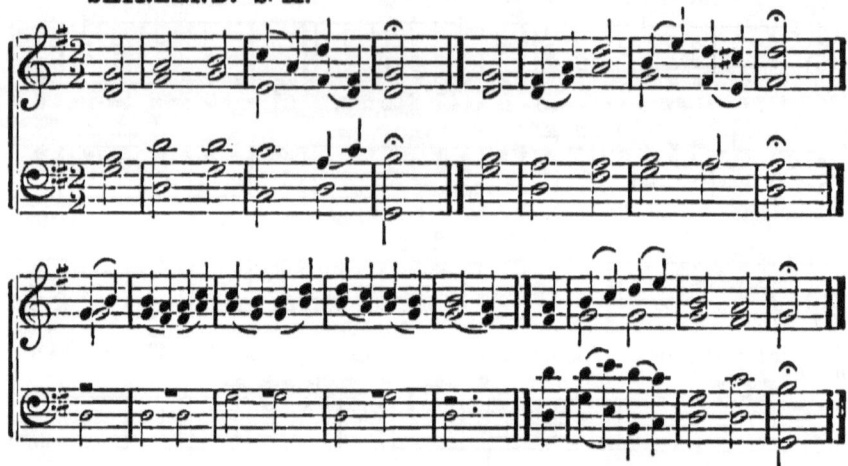

262 *Matt. 19: 14.* S. M.

1 The Saviour kindly calls
Our children to His breast;
He folds them in His gracious arms,
Himself declares them blest.

2 "Let them approach," He cries,
"Nor scorn their humble claim;
The heirs of heaven are such as these,
For such as these I came."

3 With joy we bring them, Lord,
Devoting them to Thee,
Imploring that as we are Thine,
Thine may our offspring be.

263 *"Children in the Covenant."* S. M.
Acts 2: 39.

1 Lord, what our ears have heard
Our eyes delighted trace,
Thy love in long succession shown,
To every faithful race.

2 Our children Thou dost claim,
O Lord, our God, as Thine:
Ten thousand blessings to Thy name
For goodness so divine!

3 Thy covenant may they keep,
And bless the happy bands,
Which, closer still, engage their hearts
To honor thy commands.

4 Thee let the fathers own,
Thee let the sons adore,
Joined to the Lord in solemn vows
To be forgot no more.

5 How great Thy mercies, Lord!
How plenteous is Thy grace,
Which, in the promise of Thy love,
Includes our rising race.

6 Our offspring, still Thy care,
Shall own their fathers' God,
To latest times Thy blessings share,
And sound Thy praise abroad.

264 *Heb. 8: 10.* S. M.

1 O God of Abraham, hear
The parents' humble cry;
In covenant mercy now appear,
While in the dust we lie.

2 These children of our love,
In mercy Thou hast given,
That we through grace may faithful prove
In training them for heaven.

3 Oh grant Thy Spirit, Lord,
Their hearts to sanctify;
Remember now Thy gracious word,
Our hopes on Thee rely.

4 Draw forth the melting tear,
The penitential sigh;
Inspire their hearts with faith sincere,
And fix their hopes on high.

5 These children now are Thine,
We give them back to Thee;
Oh lead them by Thy grace divine,
Along the heavenly way.

LORD'S SUPPER.

FERGUSON. S. M.

265 *Mark 10: 14.* S. M.

1 Thou God of sovereign grace,
In mercy now appear;
We long to see thy smiling face,
And feel that thou art near.

2 Receive these lambs to-day,
O Shepherd of the flock,
And wash the stains of guilt away
Beside the smitten Rock.

3 To-day in love descend;
Oh, come, this precious hour;
In mercy now their spirits bend
By thy resistless power.

4 Low bending at thy feet,
Our offspring we resign:
Thine arm is strong, thy love is great,
And high thy glories shine.

266 *Ps. 144: 12.* S. M.

1 Great God, now condescend
To bless our rising race;
Soon may their willing spirits bend,
The subjects of thy grace.

2 Oh, what a pure delight
Their happiness to see;
Our warmest wishes all unite,
To lead their souls to thee.

3 Now bless, thou God of love,
This ordinance divine;

Send thy good Spirit from above,
And make these children thine.

267 *Cant. 2: 4.* S. M.

1 Jesus, we thus obey
Thy last and kindest word,
And in Thine own appointed way
We come to meet Thee, Lord.

2 Thus we remember Thee,
And take this bread and wine
As Thine own dying legacy,
And our redemption's sign.

3 Thy presence makes the feast;
Now let our spirits feel
The glory not to be expressed,
The joy unspeakable.

4 With high and heavenly bliss
Thou dost our spirits cheer;
Thy house of banqueting is this,
And Thou hast brought us here.

6 Now let our souls be fed
With manna from above,
And over us Thy banner spread
Of everlasting love.

Doxology. S. M.

Praise to the Father be;
Praise to His Only Son;
Praise to the blessed Paraclete,
While endless ages run.

BAPTISM, CONFIRMATION, CORNER-STONE

WARWICK. C. M.

268 *"Suffer them to come unto Me."* Matt. 19: 14. **C. M.**

1 See Israel's gentle Shepherd stand
With all-engaging charms;
Hark, how he calls the tender lambs,
And folds them in his arms!

2 "Permit them to approach," he cries,
"Nor scorn their humble name;
For 't was to bless such souls as these,
The Lord of angels came.

3 We bring them, Lord, in thankful bands,
And yield them up to thee;
Joyful that we ourselves are thine,—
Thine let our offspring be.

269 *"And forbid them not."* Matt. 19: 14. **C. M.**

1 O, wondrous is thy mercy, Lord!
We hear thy word of grace,
"Forbid them not,"—oh, rich the word
That calls our infant race!

2 Our infant race we bring to thee:
Receive them as thine own!
Now and forever may they be
Thine wholly, thine alone.

270 John 10: 14. **C. M.**

1 Shepherd of Israel! from above
Thy feeble flock behold,
And let them never lose thy love,
Nor wander from thy fold.

2 Thou wilt not cast thy lambs away;
Thy hand is ever near

To guide them, lest they go astray,
And keep them safe from fear.

3 Thy tender care supports the weak,
And will not let them fall;
Then teach us, Lord! thy praise to speak
And on thy name to call.

4 We want thy help, for we are frail;
Thy light, for we are blind;
Let grace o'er all our doubts prevail,
To prove that thou art kind.

5 Teach us the things we ought to know,
And may we find them true,
And still in stature as we grow
Increase in wisdom too.

6 Guide us through life; and when at last
We enter into rest
Thy tender arms around us cast,
And fold us to thy breast.

271 *"I am the vine, ye are the branches."* **C. M.**

1 Planted in Christ, the living vine,
This day, with one accord,
Ourselves, with humble faith and joy,
We yield to thee, O Lord!

2 Joined in one body may we be:
One inward life partake;
One be our heart, one heavenly hope
In every bosom wake.

3 In prayer, in effort, tears, and toils,
One wisdom be our guide;
Taught by one Spirit from above,
In thee may we abide.

AND CONSECRATION OF A CHURCH.

VALENTIA. C. M.

4 Then, when among the saints in light
Our joyful spirits shine,
Shall anthems of immortal praise,
O Lamb of God, be thine!

272 *"A good profession before many witnesses."—1 Tim. 6:12.* **C. M.**

1 Witness, ye men and angels, now
Before the Lord we speak;
To him we make our solemn vow,
A vow we dare not break:—

2 That, long as life itself shall last,
Ourselves to Christ we yield;
Nor from his cause will we depart,
Or ever quit the field.

3 We trust not in our native strength,
But on his grace rely,
That with returning wants the Lord
Will all our need supply.

4 Oh, guide our doubtful feet aright,
And keep us in thy ways:
And, while we turn our vows to prayers,
Turn thou our prayers to praise!

273 *Christ the foundation of his Church.—Ps. 118.* **C. M.**

1 Behold the sure foundation Stone
Which God in Zion lays,
To build our heav'nly hopes upon,
And his eternal praise.

2 Chosen of God, to sinners dear,
How glorious is thy name!
Saints trust their whole salvation here,
Nor shall they suffer shame.

3 The foolish builders, scribe and priest,
Reject it with disdain;
Yet on this rock the church shall rest,
And envy rage in vain.

4 What though the gates of hell withstood,
Yet must this building rise;
'Tis thine own work, Almighty God,
And wondrous in our eyes.

274 *"Thou and the ark of thy strength."* **C. M.**

1 O thou, whose own vast temple stands,
Built over earth and sea,
Accept the walls that human hands
Have raised to worship thee!

2 Lord, from thine inmost glory send,
Within these courts to bide,
The peace that dwelleth without end
Serenely by thy side!

3 May erring minds that worship here
Be taught the better way;
And they who mourn, and they who fear
Be strengthened as they pray.

4 May faith grow firm, and love grow warm,
And pure devotion rise,
While round these hallowed walls the storm
Of earth-born passion dies.

Doxology. **C. M.**

To Father, Son and Holy Ghost,
One God, whom we adore,
Be glory as it was, is now,
And shall be evermore!

CONFIRMATION — ORDINATION.

HAPPY DAY. L. M.

1. O happy day, that seals my choice
On thee, my Savior and my God!
Well may this glowing heart rejoice,
And tell its raptures all abroad.

Chorus.
Happy day, happy day, When Jesus washed my sins away!
He taught me how to watch and pray,
And live rejoicing ev'ry day.

275 *Confirmation.*—Isa 49: 8. L. M.

2 O happy bond! that seals my vows
To him who merits all my love;
Let cheerful anthems fill his house,
While to his sacred throne I move.

3 'T is done, the great transaction's done;
Deign, gracious Lord, to make me thine;
Help me, through grace, to follow on,
Glad to confess thy voice divine.

4 Here rest my oft-divided heart,
Fix'd on thy God, thy Savior, rest;
Who with the world would grieve to part,
When call'd on angel's food to feast?

5 High heav'n that hears the solemn vow,
That vow renew'd shall daily hear,
Till in life's latest hour I bow,
And bless in death a bond so dear.

276 *"Lord, I am Thine, entirely Thine."*—1 Cor. 6: 20. L. M.

1 Lord, I am thine, entirely thine,
Purchased and saved by blood divine,
With full consent I thine would be,
And own thy sovereign right in me.

2 Here, O my Lord, my soul, my all,
I yield to thee beyond recall;
Accept thine own,—so long withheld,
Accept what I so freely yield.

3 Grant one poor sinner more a place
Among the children of thy grace;
A wretched sinner lost to God,
But ransomed by Immanuel's blood.

4 The vow is past beyond repeal;
Now will I set the solemn seal:
Thine would I live, thine would I die,
Be thine through all eternity.

277 *"Go, preach My Gospel."* Mark 16: 15-20. L. M.

1 "Go, preach my gospel," saith the Lord;
"Bid the whole earth my grace receive;
He shall be saved who trusts my word;
And they condemned who disbelieve.

2 "I'll make your great commission known,
And ye shall prove my gospel true
By all the works that I have done,
By all the wonders ye shall do.

3 "Teach all the nations my commands;
I'm with you till the world shall end;
All power is trusted in my hands;
I can destroy, and I defend."

4 He spake, and light shone round his head;
On a bright cloud to heaven he rode;
They to the farthest nations spread
The grace of their ascended God.

CORNER-STONE — CONSECRATION.

MENDON. L. M.

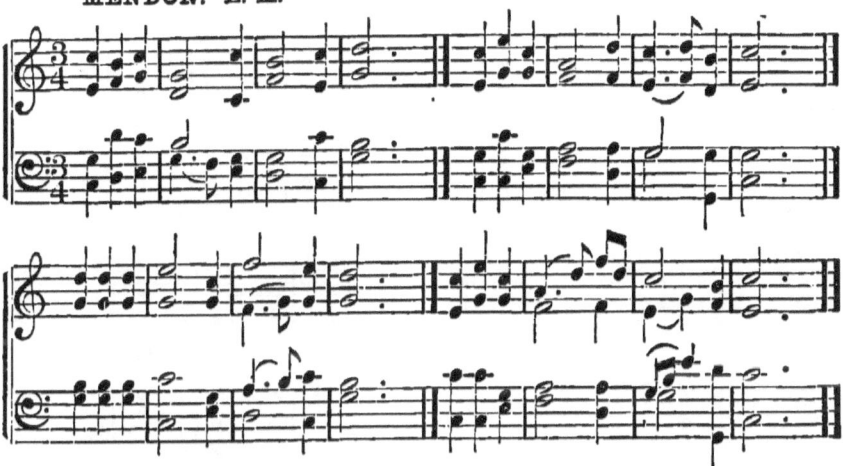

278   *"Go ye into all the world." Mark 16: 15.*   **L. M.**

1 Ye Christian heralds! go proclaim
Salvation through Immanuel's name;
To distant climes the tidings bear,
And plant the rose of Sharon there.

2 He'll shield you with a wall of fire,
With flaming zeal your breasts inspire,
Bid raging winds their fury cease,
And hush the tempest into peace.

3 And when our labors all are o'er,
Then we shall meet to part no more,—
Meet with the blood-bought throng, to fall,
And crown our Jesus—Lord of all!

279   *(Laying of a Corner-stone.)*   **L. M.**

1 O Lord of hosts, whose glory fills
The bounds of the eternal hills,
And yet vouchsafes, in Christian lands,
To dwell in temples made with hands!

2 Oh, grant that we who here to-day
Rejoicing this foundation lay
May be in very deed thine own,
Built on the precious Corner-stone.

3 Endue the creatures with thy grace,
That shall adorn thy dwelling-place;
The beauty of the oak and pine,
The gold and silver, make them thine.

4 To thee they all pertain; to thee
The treasures of the earth and sea;
And when we bring them to thy throne,
We but present thee with thine own.

5 The heads that guide endue with skill,
The hands that work preserve from ill,
That we who these foundations lay
May raise the top-stone in its day.

6 Both now and ever, Lord! protect
The temple of thine own elect;
Be thou in them and they in thee,
O ever-blessed Trinity!

280   *Solomon's Prayer. 2 Chron. 6.*   **L. M.**

1 When in these courts we seek thy face,
And dying sinners pray to live,
Hear thou, in heaven, thy dwelling-place,
And when thou hearest, Lord! forgive.

2 When here thy messengers proclaim
The blessed gospel of thy Son,
Still by the power of his great name
Be mighty signs and wonders done.

3 Hosanna!—to their heavenly King
When children's voices raise that song—
Hosanna!—let their angels sing,
And heaven with earth the strain prolong,

4 But will, indeed, Jehovah deign
Here to abide, no transient guest?
Here will the world's Redeemer reign,
And here the Holy Spirit rest?

5 That glory never hence depart!
Yet choose not, Lord, this house alone:
Thy kingdom come to every heart;
In every bosom fix thy throne.

PLEYEL'S HYMN. 7s.

281   1 Cor. 5: 7.

1 At the Lamb's high feast we sing
Praise to our victorious king,
Who hath washed us in the tide
Flowing from his pierced side.

2 Praise we him whose love divine
Gives his sacred blood for wine,
Gives his body for the feast,
Christ the Victim, Christ the Priest.

3 Where the paschal blood is poured,
Death's dark angel sheathes his sword;
Israel's hosts triumphant go
Through the wave that drowns the foe.

4 Praise we Christ, whose blood we shed,
Paschal Victim, paschal Bread;
With sincerity and love
Eat we manna from above.

5 Mighty Victim from the sky!
Hell's fierce powers beneath thee lie;
Thou hast conquered in the fight,
Thou hast brought us life and light.

6 Hymns of glory and of praise,
Risen Lord! to thee we raise;
Holy Father! praise to thee
With the Spirit ever be.

282   John 17: 9.

1 Thine forever! God of love,
Hear us from Thy throne above;
Thine forever may we be,
Here and in eternity.

7s.

2 Thine forever! Lord of life,
Shield us through the earthly strife;
Thou, the Life, the Truth, the Way,
Guide us to the realms of day.

3 Thine forever! oh, how blest
They who find in Thee their rest;
Saviour, Guardian, heavenly Friend,
Oh, defend us to the end.

4 Thine forever! Saviour keep
These Thy frail and trembling sheep;
Safe alone beneath Thy care,
Let us all Thy goodness share.

5 Thine forever! Thou our Guide,
All our wants by Thee supplied,
All our sins by Thee forgiven,
Lead us, Lord, from earth to heaven.

283   Matt. 26: 26.   7s.

1 Bread of heaven! on thee we feed,
For thy flesh is meat indeed;
Ever may our souls be fed
With this true and living bread.

2 Vine of heaven! thy blood supplies
This blest cup of sacrifice;
'Tis thy wounds our healing give,
To thy cross we look and live.

3 Day by day, with strength supplied
Through the life of him who died,
Lord of life! oh let us be
Rooted, grafted, built, in thee.

BURIAL.

HENDON. 7s.

284 *"None but Christ."* 7s.

1 Jesus, all-atoning Lamb,
Thine, and only thine, I am:
Take my body, spirit, soul;
Only thou possess the whole.

2 Thou my one thing needful be;
Let me ever cleave to thee;
Let me choose the better part:
Let me give thee all my heart.

3 Whom have I on earth below?
Thee, and only thee, I know:
Whom have I in heaven but thee?
Thou art all in all to me.

285 *John 10: 11.*

1 Jesus, Shepherd of the sheep,
Thou Thy flock in safety keep!
Living Bread, Thy life supply,
Strengthen us, or else we die!

2 Thou who feedest us below,
Source of all we have or know,
Bring us to the feast of love,
With Thy saints and Thee above!

286 *Peace through the Blood of Christ.*
Heb. 13: 20, 21.

1 Now may he, who from the dead
Brought the Shepherd of the Sheep,
Jesus Christ, our King and Head,
All our souls in safety keep!

2 May he teach us to fulfill
What is pleasing in his sight;
Perfect us in all his will,
And preserve us day and night!

3 Great Redeemer! thee we praise, 7s.
Who the covenant sealed with blood;
While our hearts and voices raise
Loud thanksgiving unto God.

287 *Heb. 7: 24.* 7s.

1 When our heads are bowed with woe,
When our bitter tears o'erflow,
When we mourn the lost, the dear,
Jesus, Son of Mary! hear.

2 Thou our throbbing flesh hast worn,
Thou our mortal griefs hast borne,
Thou hast shed the human tear;
Jesus, Son of Mary! hear. 7s.

3 When the solemn death-bell tolls
For our own departing souls,
When our final doom is near,
Jesus, Son of Mary! hear.

4 Thou hast bowed the dying head,
Thou the blood of life hast shed,
Thou hast filled a mortal bier;
Jesus, Son of Mary! hear. 7s.

5 When the heart is sad within
With the thought of all its sin,
When the spirit shrinks with fear,
Jesus, Son of Mary! hear.

6 Thou the shame, the grief, hast known,
Though the sins were not thine own;
Thou hast deigned their load to bear;
Jesus, Son of Mary! hear.

LORD'S SUPPER.

HOWARD. C. M.

288 *"The voice of many angels."* C. M.
Rev. 5: 12.

1 Come, let us join our cheerful songs
With angels round the throne;
Ten thousand thousand are their tongues,
But all their joys are one.

2 "Worthy the Lamb that died," they cry,
"To be exalted thus!"
"Worthy the Lamb!" our lips reply,
"For he was slain for us."

3 Jesus is worthy to receive
Honor and power divine;
And blessings more than we can give,
Be, Lord, for ever thine!

4 Let all that dwell above the sky,
And air, and earth, and seas,
Conspire to lift thy glories high,
And speak thine endless praise.

5 The whole creation join in one,
To bless the sacred name
Of him who sits upon the throne,
And to adore the Lamb!

289 *"The Saviour died for me."* C. M.

1 Prepare us, Lord, to view thy cross,
Who all our griefs hast borne;
To look on thee, whom we have pierced—
To look on thee, and mourn.

2 While thus we mourn, we would rejoice,
And, as thy cross we see,
Let each exclaim in faith and hope—
"The Saviour died for me!"

290 *"This do in remembrance of Me."* C. M.
Luke 22: 19.

1 According to thy gracious word,
In meek humility,
This will I do, my dying Lord!
I will remember thee.

2 Thy body, broken for my sake,
My bread from heaven shall be;
Thy testamental cup I take,
And thus remember thee.

3 Gethsemane can I forget?
Or there thy conflict see,
Thine agony and bloody sweat—
And not remember thee?

4 When to the cross I turn my eyes,
And rest on Calvary,
O Lamb of God! my Sacrifice,
I must remember thee!

5 Remember thee, and all thy pains,
And all thy love to me—
Yea, while a breath, a pulse remains
Will I remember thee!

6 And when these failing lips grow dumb,
And mind and memory flee,
When thou shalt in thy kingdom come,
Jesus, remember me!

291   1 Cor. 10: 16.   C. M.

1 Jesus, at whose supreme command,
We now approach to God,
Before us in Thy vesture stand,
Thy vesture dipped in blood.

LORD'S SUPPER.

EVAN. C. M.

2 Obedient to Thy gracious word,
We break the hallowed bread,
Commemorate our dying Lord,
And trust on Thee to feed.

3 The cup of blessing, blest by Thee,
Let it Thy blood impart:
The bread Thy mystic body be,
And cheer each languid heart.

4 Now, Saviour, now Thyself reveal,
And make Thy nature known;
Affix Thy blessed Spirit's seal,
And stamp us for Thine own.

292 *Faith, hope and love.* C. M.

1 The blest memorials of thy grief,
The suff'rings of thy death,
We come, dear Saviour, to receive,
But would receive with *faith*.

2 The tokens sent us to relieve
Our spirits when they droop,
We come, dear Saviour, to receive,
But would receive with *hope*.

3 The pledges thou wast pleas'd to leave,
Our mournful minds to move,
We come, dear Saviour, to receive,
But would receive with *love*.

4 Here in obedience to thy word,
We take the bread and wine,
The utmost we can do, dear Lord,
For all beyond is thine.

5 Increase our faith, and hope, and love;
Lord, give us all that's good;
We would thy full salvation prove,
And share thy flesh and blood.

293 *Redemption by price and power.* C. M.

1 Jesus, with all thy saints above,
My tongue would bear her part;
Would sound aloud thy saving love,
And sing thy bleeding heart.

2 Bless'd be the Lamb, my dearest Lord,
Who bought me with his blood,
And quench'd his Father's flaming sword,
In his own vital flood.

3 All glory to the dying Lamb,
And never-ceasing praise,
While angels live to know his name,
Or saints to feel his grace.

294 *(After the Lord's Supper.)* C. M.

1 With humble faith, and thankful heart,
Lord, I accept Thy love:
'Tis a rich banquet I have had,
What will it be above!

2 Ye saints below, and hosts of heaven,
Join all your praising powers;
No theme is like redeeming love,
No Saviour is like ours.

3 Had I ten thousand hearts, dear Lord,
I'd give them all to Thee;
Had I ten thousand tongues, they all
Should join the harmony.

MEAR. C. M.

295 *"Our dwelling-place in all generations.—Psalm 90."* **C. M.**

1 O God, our help in ages past,
Our hope for years to come,
Our shelter from the stormy blast,
And our eternal home!

2 Under the shadow of thy throne,
Thy saints have dwelt secure;
Sufficient is thine arm alone,
And our defense is sure.

3 Before the hills in order stood,
Or earth received her frame,
From everlasting thou art God,
To endless years the same.

4 Thy word commands our flesh to dust:
"Return, ye sons of men;"
All nations rose from earth at first,
And turn to earth again.

5 Time, like an ever-rolling stream,
Bears all its sons away;
They fly, forgotten, as a dream
Dies at the opening day.

6 O God, our help in ages past,
Our hope for years to come,
Be thou our guard while troubles last,
And our eternal home!

296 *"Having a desire to depart, and to be with Christ."* **C. M.**

1 Why do we mourn departing friends,
Or shake at death's alarms?
'Tis but the voice that Jesus sends
To call them to his arms.

2 Why should we tremble to convey
Their bodies to the tomb?
There the dear flesh of Jesus lay,
There hopes unfading bloom.

3 The graves of all his saints he blessed,
And softened every bed;
Where should the dying members rest,
But with the dying Head?

4 Thence he arose, ascending high,
And showed our feet the way;
Up to the Lord our souls shall fly,
At the great rising day.

297 *Man is of few days and full of trouble.* **C. M.**

1 Few are thy days, and full of wo,
O man, of woman born!
Thy doom is written, "Dust thou art,
"To dust thou shalt return."

2 Behold the emblem of thy state,
In flow'rs that bloom and die,
Or in the shadow's fleeting form
That mocks the gazer's eye.

3 Determin'd are the days that fly
Successive o'er thy head;
The number'd hour is on the wing
That lays thee with the dead.

4 Great God! afflict not in thy wrath
The short allotted span,
That bounds the few and weary days
Of pilgrimage to man.

BURIAL.

DUNDEE. C. M.

298 *"And entered into rest."* **C. M.**

1 Why should our tears in sorrow flow,
When God recalls his own,
And bids them leave a world of woe
For an immortal crown?

2 Is not ev'n death a gain to those
Whose life to God is given?
Gladly to earth their eyes they close,
To open them in heaven.

3 Their toils are past, their work is done,
And they are fully blest:
They fought the fight, the victory won,
And entered into rest.

4 Then let our sorrows cease to flow;
God has recalled his own:
And let our hearts, in every woe,
Still say—"Thy will be done!"

299 *Blessed are the dead that die in the Lord.* **C. M.**

1 Hear what the voice from heav'n proclaims
For all the pious dead;
Sweet is the savor of their names,
And soft their sleeping bed.

2 They die in Jesus and are bless'd;
How kind their slumbers are!
From suff'rings and from sin releas'd,
And freed from ev'ry snare.

3 Far from this world of toil and strife,
They're present with the Lord;
The labors of their mortal life
End in a large reward.

300 *"He fell asleep."* **C. M.**

1 Behold the western evening light!
It melts in evening gloom:
So calmly Christians sink away,
Descending to the tomb.

2 The winds breathe low, the withering leaf
Scarce whispers from the tree:
So gently flows the parting breath,
When good men cease to be.

3 How beautiful on all the hills
The crimson light is shed!
'Tis like the peace the Christian gives
To mourners round his bed.

4 How mildly on the wandering cloud
The sunset beam is cast!
'Tis like the memory left behind,
When loved ones breathe their last.

5 And now above the dews of night
The rising star appears:
So faith springs in the heart of those
Whose eyes are bathed in tears.

6 But soon the morning's happier light
Its glory shall restore,
And eyelids that are sealed in death
Shall wake to close no more.

Doxology. **C. M.**

To Father, Son, and Holy Ghost,
The God whom we adore,
Be glory as it was, is now,
And shall be evermore.

OLMUTZ. S. M.

301 *"Let me die the death of the righteous."—Num. 23: 10.* S. M.

1 O for the death of those
Who slumber in the Lord!
Oh, be like theirs my last repose,
Like theirs my last reward!

2 Their bodies in the ground
In silent hope may lie,
Till the last trumpet's joyful sound
Shall call them to the sky.

3 Their ransomed spirits soar,
On wings of faith and love,
To meet the Saviour they adore,
And reign with him above.

4 With us their names shall live
Through long, succeeding years,
Embalmed with all our hearts can give,
Our praises and our tears.

5 O for the death of those
Who slumber in the Lord!
Oh, be like theirs my last repose,
Like theirs my last reward!

302 *"This mortal shall put on immortality."* S. M.

1 And must this body die?
This mortal frame decay?
And must these active limbs of mine
Lie moldering in the clay?

2 God, my Redeemer, lives
And ever from the skies
Looks down and watches all my dust,
Till he shall bid it rise.

3 Arrayed in glorious grace
Shall these vile bodies shine,
And every shape, and every face
Look heavenly and divine.

4 These lively hopes we owe
To Jesus' dying love;
We would adore his grace below,
And sing his power above.

5 Dear Lord! accept the praise
Of these our humble songs,
Till tunes of nobler sound we raise
With our immortal tongues.

303 *"Whoso believeth in Me shall never die."* S. M.

1 It is not death to die—
To leave this weary road,
And, 'mid the brotherhood on high,
To be at home with God.

2 It is not death to close
The eye long dimmed by tears,
And wake, in glorious repose
To spend eternal years.

3 It is not death to bear
The wrench that sets us free
From dungeon chain—to breathe the air
Of boundless liberty.

4 It is not death to fling
Aside this sinful dust,
And rise, on strong exulting wing,
To live among the just.

BURIAL.

DENNIS. S. M.

5 Jesus, thou Prince of life!
Thy chosen cannot die;
Like thee, they conquer in the strife,
To reign with thee on high.

304 *"As a father pitieth his children."* S. M.
Psalm 103.

1 The pity of the Lord
To those that fear his name,
Is such as tender parents feel;
He knows our feeble frame.

2 He knows we are but dust,
Scattered with every breath;
His anger, like a rising wind,
Can send us swift to death.

3 Our days are as the grass,
Or like the morning flower;
If one sharp blast sweep o'er the field,
It withers in an hour.

4 But thy compassions, Lord,
To endless years endure;
And children's children ever find
Thy words of promise sure.

305 *"Wait thou His time."—Ps. 30.* S. M.

1 Give to the winds thy fears;
Hope on, be not dismayed:
God hears thy sighs and counts thy tears;
God shall lift up thy head.

2 Through waves and clouds and storms,
He gently clears thy way;
Wait thou his time: the darkest night
Shall end in brightest day.

3 Far, far above thy thought
His counsel shall appear,
When fully he the work hath wrought,
That caused thy needless fear.

4 What though thou rulest not!
Yet heaven and earth and hell
Proclaim—God sitteth on the throne
And ruleth all things well.

306 *"The Rock that is higher than I."* S. M.
Psalm 61.

1 When, overwhelmed with grief,
My heart within me dies,
Helpless and far from all relief,
To heaven I lift mine eyes.

2 Oh, lead me to the Rock
That's high above my head!
And make the covert of thy wings
My shelter and my shade.

3 Within thy presence, Lord,
Forever I'll abide:
Thou art the tower of my defense,
The refuge where I hide.

4 Thou givest me the lot
Of those that fear thy name;
If endless life be their reward,
I shall possess the same.

Doxology. S. M.

To God, the Father, Son,
And Spirit, glory be,
As was, and is, and shall remain
Through all eternity.

BURIAL.

MIDDLETON. 8s & 7s. D.

307 *"And there shall be no more death."* **8s&7s.**

1 Cease, ye mourners; cease to languish
O'er the grave of those you love;
Pain and death and night and anguish
Enter not the world above.

2 While our silent steps are straying
Lonely through night's deepening shade,
Glory's brightest beams are playing
Round the happy Christian's head.

3 Light and peace at once deriving
From the hand of God most high,
In his glorious presence living,
They shall never, never die.

4 Now, ye mourners, cease to languish
O'er the grave of those you love;
Far removed from pain and anguish,
They are chanting hymns above.

308 *"Abide with us; for it is toward evening."—Luke 24: 29.* **8s&7s.**

1 Tarry with me, O my Saviour!
For the day is passing by;
See! the shades of evening gather,
And the night is drawing nigh.

2 Deeper, deeper grow the shadows,
Paler now the glowing west,
Swift the night of death advances;
Shall it be the night of rest?

3 Feeble, trembling, fainting, dying,
Lord, I cast myself on thee;
Tarry with me through the darkness;
While I sleep, still watch by me.

4 Tarry with me, O my Saviour!
Lay my head upon thy breast
Till the morning; then awake me—
Morning of eternal rest!

309 *The saints in glory.* **8s&7s.**

1 Hark! the sound of holy voices
Chanting at the crystal sea,
Hallelujah! Hallelujah!
Hallelujah! Lord, to Thee.

2 Multitudes which none can number,
Like the stars in glory stand,
Clothed in white apparel, holding
Victor-palms in every hand.

3 They have come from tribulation,
And have washed their robes in blood,
Washed them in the blood of Jesus;
Tried they were, and firm they stood.

4 Gladly, Lord, with Thee they suffered,
Gladly, Lord, with Thee they died;
And, by death, to life immortal
They were born, and glorified.

5 Now they reign in heavenly glory
Now they walk in golden light,
Now they drink, as from a river,
Holy bliss and infinite.

6 Love and peace they taste forever,
And all truth and knowledge see
In the beatific vision
Of the Blessed Trinity.

BURIAL.

MOUNT VERNON. 8s & 7s.

310   Ps. 18: 35.   8s & 7s.

1 Gently, Lord, oh, gently lead us
Through this lonely vale of tears;
Through the changes thou'st decreed us,
Till our last great change appears.

2 When temptation's darts assail us,
When in devious paths we stray,
Let thy goodness never fail us;
Lead us in thy perfect way.

3 In the hour of pain and anguish,
In the hour when death draws near,
Suffer not our hearts to languish,
Suffer not our souls to fear.

4 And, when mortal life is ended,
Bid us on thy bosom rest;
Till, by angel-bands attended,
We awake among the blest.

311   James 4: 14.   8s & 7s.

1 Every thing we love and cherish
Hastens onward to the grave;
Earthly joys and pleasures perish,
Time can nothing, nothing save.

2 All is fading, all is fleeing;
Earthly flames must cease to glow,
Earthly beings cease from being,
Earthly blossoms cease to blow.

3 Yet unchanged, while all decayeth,
Jesus lives, the first, the last,
Lean on me alone, he sayeth;
Hope and love and firmly trust.

4 Oh, abide, abide with Jesus,
Who himself forever lives,
Who from death eternal frees us,
And who life eternal gives!

312   "*Weep not: she is not dead, but sleepeth.*"   8s & 7s.

1 Sister, (or brother) thou wast mild and lovely,
Gentle as the summer breeze,
Pleasant as the air of evening,
When it floats among the trees.

2 Peaceful be thy silent slumber—
Peaceful in the grave so low:
Thou no more wilt join our number;
Thou no more our songs shalt know.

3 Dearest sister! (or brother) thou hast left us;
Here thy loss we deeply feel;
But 't is God that hath bereft us,
He can all our sorrows heal.

4 Yet again we hope to meet thee,
When the day of life is fled;
Then in heaven with joy to greet thee,
Where no farewell tear is shed!

Doxology.   8s & 7s.

Praise the God of our salvation,
Praise the Father's boundless love;
Praise the Lamb, our expiation;
Praise the Spirit from above;
Praise the Fountain of salvation,
Him by whom our spirits live;
Undivided adoration
To the one Jehovah give!

BURIAL.

REST. L. M.

313 *1 Thess. 4: 14.* L. M.

1 Asleep in Jesus! blessed sleep
From which none ever wakes to weep!
A calm and undisturbed repose
Unbroken by the last of foes!

2 Asleep in Jesus! oh, how sweet
To be for such a slumber meet!
With holy confidence to sing
That death has lost his venomed sting!

3 Asleep in Jesus! peaceful rest
Whose waking is supremely blest!
No fear, no woe, shall dim that hour
That manifests the Saviour's power.

4 Asleep in Jesus! oh, for me
May such a blissful refuge be:
Securely shall my ashes lie,
And wait the summons from on high.

5 Asleep in Jesus! far from thee
Thy kindred and their graves may be:
But there is still a blessed sleep
From which none ever wakes to weep.

314 *"Blessed—who die in the Lord."* L. M.
Rev. 14: 13.

1 How blest the righteous when he dies!
When sinks a weary soul to rest!
How mildly beam the closing eyes!
How gently heaves th' expiring breast!

2 So fades a summer cloud away;
So sinks the gale when storms are o'er;
So gently shuts the eye of day;
So dies a wave along the shore.

3 A holy quiet reigns around,
A calm which life nor death destroys;
And naught disturbs that peace profound
Which his unfettered soul enjoys.

4 Farewell, conflicting hopes and fears,
Where lights and shades alternate dwell;
How bright th' unchanging morn appears!
Farewell, inconstant world, farewell!

5 Life's labor done, as sinks the clay,
Light from its load the spirit flies,
While heaven and earth combine to say,
"How blest the righteous when he dies!"

315 *A funeral psalm.*
Man mortal, and God eternal. L. M.

1 Through every age, eternal God!
Thou art our rest, our safe abode;
High was thy throne ere heav'n was made,
Or earth thy humble footstool laid.

2 But man, weak man, is born to die,
Made up of guilt and vanity;
Thy dreadful sentence, Lord, was just,
"Return, ye sinners, to your dust."

3 A thousand of our years amount
Scarce to a day in thine account;
Like yesterday's departed light,
Or the last watch of ending night.

4 Death, like an overflowing stream,
Sweeps us away; our life's a dream;
An empty tale; a morning flow'r,
Cut down and wither'd in an hour.

BURIAL.

ORIEL. L. M., or 8s & 4s.

5 Teach us, O Lord, how frail is man,
And kindly lengthen out our span;
Till faith, and love, and piety
Fit us to die and dwell with thee.

316 *"So He giveth His beloved sleep."* **L. M.**

1 Why should we start, and fear to die!
What timorous worms we mortals are!
Death is the gate of endless joy,
And yet we dread to enter there.

2 The pains, the groans, and dying strife
Fright our approaching souls away
We still shrink back again to life,
Fond of our prison and our clay.

3 Oh, if my Lord would come and meet,
My soul should stretch her wings in haste,
Fly fearless through death's iron gate,
Nor feel the terrors as she passed!

4 Jesus can make a dying bed
Feel soft as downy pillows are,
While on his breast I lean my head,
And breathe my life out sweetly there!

317 *A funeral psalm. Mortality and Hope.* **L. M.**

1 Remember, Lord, our mortal state,
How frail our life, how short the date!
Where is the man that draws his breath
Safe from disease, secure from death?

2 Lord, while we see whole nations die,
Our flesh and sense repine and cry,
"Must death forever rage and reign?
"Or hast thou made mankind in vain?

3 "Where is thy promise to the just?
"Are not thy servants turn'd to dust?"
But faith forbids these mournful sighs,
And sees the sleeping dust arise.

4 That glorious hour, that dreadful day,
Wipes the reproach of saints away,
And clears the honor of thy word;
Awake, our souls, and bless the Lord.

318 *"It is even a vapor."* **L. M.**

1 How vain is all beneath the skies!
How transient every earthly bliss!
How slender all the fondest ties,
That bind us to a world like this!

2 The evening cloud, the morning dew,
The withering grass, the fading flower,
Of earthly hopes are emblems true—
The glory of a passing hour!

3 But though earth's fairest blossoms die,
And all beneath the skies is vain,
There is a land, whose confines lie
Beyond the reach of care and pain.

4 Then let the hope of joys to come
Dispel our cares, and chase our fears:
If God be ours, we're traveling home,
Though passing through a vale of tears.

Doxology. **S. M.**

To God the Father, God the Son,
And God the Spirit, Three in One,
Be honor, praise, and glory given,
By all on earth, and all in heaven!

BURIAL AND

EXPOSTULATION. 11s.

319 *"Earth to earth, ashes to ashes, dust to dust."* **11s.**

1 The things of the earth, in the earth let us lay,
   The ashes with ashes, the dust with the clay:
   But lift up the heart, and the eye, and the love,
   O lift up the soul to the regions above!

2 Since He, the Immortal, hath entered the gate,
   So too shall we mortals, or sooner or late:
   Then stand we on Christ; let us mark Him ascend,
   For His is the glory and life without end.

3 On earth with His own ones, the Giver of good,
   Bestowing His blessing, a little while stood:
   Now nothing can part us, nor distance, nor foes,
   For lo! He is with us, and who can oppose?

4 So, Lord, we commit this our *brother* to Thee,
   Whose body is dead, but whose spirit is free:
   We know that thro' grace, when our life here is done,
   We live still in Thee, and forever in one.

5 All glory to Thee, Father, Spirit, and Son,
   Who Three art in Person, in essence but One,
   In whom we have victory over the grave,
   Who lovest Thy people to pardon and save.

320 *Longing for Heaven.* **11s.**

1 I am weary of straying; oh fain would I rest
   In the far distant land of the pure and the blest,
   Where sin can no longer her blandishments spread,
   And tears and temptations forever have fled.

2 I am weary of loving what passes away;
   The sweetest, the dearest, alas, may not stay;
   I long for that land where these partings are o'er,
   And death and the tomb can divide hearts no more.

3 I am weary, my Saviour, of grieving Thy love;
   Oh, when shall I rest in Thy presence above?
   I am weary—but oh, let me never repine,
   While Thy word, and Thy love, and Thy promise are mine.

LONGING.

HOME. 11s.

Home.

321 11s.

1 'Mid scenes of confusion and creature complaints,
   How sweet to my soul is communion with saints,
   To find at the banquet of mercy there's room,
   And feel in the presence of Jesus at home,
       Home, home, sweet, sweet home.
       Prepare me, dear Saviour, for glory, my home.

2 Sweet bonds that unite all the children of peace!
   And thrice precious Jesus, whose love cannot cease!
   Though oft from thy presence in sadness I roam,
   I long to behold thee in glory at home.

3 Whate'er thou deniest, oh give me thy grace,
   The Spirit's sure witness, and smiles of thy face;
   Endue me with patience to wait at thy throne,
   And find, even now, a sweet foretaste of home.

322 *Job 7: 16.* 11s.

1 I would not live alway: I ask not to stay
   Where storm after storm rises dark o'er the way;
   The few lurid mornings that dawn on us here
   Are enough for life's woes, full enough for its cheer.

2 I would not live alway, thus fettered by sin,
   Temptation without and corruption within:
   E'en the rapture of pardon is mingled with fears,
   And the cup of thanksgiving with penitent tears.

3 I would not live alway; no, welcome the tomb;
   Since Jesus hath lain there, I dread not its gloom;
   There sweet be my rest, till he bid me arise
   To hail Him in triumph descending the skies.

4 Who, who would live alway, away from his God?
   Away from yon heaven, that blissful abode,
   Where the rivers of pleasure flow o'er the bright plains,
   And the noontide of glory eternally reigns:

5 Where the saints of all ages in harmony meet,
   Their Saviour and brethren transported to greet,
   While the anthems of rapture unceasingly roll,
   And the smile of the Lord is the feast of the soul.

THANKSGIVING, AND

NUREMBURG. 7s.

323 *"Sing unto Him a new song."* 7s.

1 Swell the anthem, raise the song;
Praises to our God belong;
Saints and angels! join to sing
Praises to the heavenly King.

2 Blessings from his liberal hand
Flow around this happy land:
Kept by him, no foes annoy;
Peace and freedom we enjoy.

3 Here, beneath a virtuous sway,
May we cheerfully obey;
Never feel oppression's rod,
Ever own and worship God.

4 Hark! the voice of nature sings
Praises to the King of kings;
Let us join the choral song,
And the grateful notes prolong.

324 *Ps. 106.*

1 Let us, with a gladsome mind,
Praise the Lord, for he is kind:
For his mercies shall endure
Ever faithful, ever sure.

2 Let us sound his name abroad,
For of gods he is the God:
For his mercies shall endure,
Ever faithful, ever sure.

3 He, with all-commanding might,
Filled the new-made world with light:
For his mercies shall endure,
Ever faithful, ever sure.

4 All things living he doth feed;
His full hand supplies their need;
For his mercies shall endure,
Ever faithful, ever sure.

5 He his chosen race did bless
In the wasteful wilderness:
For his mercies shall endure,
Ever faithful, ever sure.

6 He hath, with a piteous eye,
Looked upon our misery:
For his mercies shall endure,
Ever faithful, ever sure.

7 Let us then with gladsome mind,
Praise the Lord, for he is kind:
For his mercies shall endure,
Ever faithful, ever sure.

325 *"Lord, thou hast been favorable unto thy land."* 7s.

1 Praise to God, immortal praise,
For the love that crowns our days!
Bounteous source of every joy,
Let thy praise our tongues employ!

2 For the blessings of the field,
For the stores the gardens yield,
For the joy which harvests bring,
Grateful praises now we sing.

HARVEST.

DALLAS. 7s.

3 Clouds that drop refreshing dews;
Suns that genial heat diffuse;
Flocks that whiten all the plain;
Yellow sheaves of ripened grain;

4 All that Spring, with bounteous hand,
Scatters o'er the smiling land;
All that liberal Autumn pours
From her overflowing stores;

5 These, great God, to thee we owe,
Source whence all our blessings flow;
And, for these, our souls shall raise
Grateful vows, and solemn praise.

326   Psalm 136.   7s.

1 Praise, oh praise our God and King,
Hymns of adoration sing;
For His mercies still endure
Ever faithful, ever sure.

2 Praise Him that He made the sun
Day by day his course to run;
And the silver moon by night,
Shining with her gentle light.

3 Praise Him that He gave the rain
To mature the swelling grain;
And hath bid the fruitful field
Crops of precious increase yield.

4 Praise Him for our harvest-store,—
He hath filled the garner-floor,—
And for richer food than this,
Pledge of everlasting bliss.

327   Psalm 145.   7s.

1 Summer ended, harvest o'er,
Lord! to thee our song we pour,
For the valley's golden yield,
For the fruits of tree and field.

2 For the promise ever sure
That while heaven and earth endure
Seed-time, harvest, cold and heat
Shall their yearly round complete.

3 For the care which, while we slept,
Watch o'er field and furrow kept,
Watch o'er all the buried grain,
Soon to burst to life again.

4 When the reaping angels bring
Tares and wheat before the King,
Jesus! may we gathered be
In the heavenly barn to thee.

5 Then the angel-cry shall sound,
Praise the Lamb; the lost are found;
And the answering song shall be,
Alleluia, praise to thee—

6 Praise to thee, the toil is o'er;
Blight and curse shall be no more;
Lo! the mighty work is done:
Glory to the three in one.

Doxology.   7s.

Glory to our bounteous King!
Glory let Creation sing!
Glory to the Father, Son,
And blest Spirit, Three in One!

THANKSGIVING, AND

ROCKINGHAM. L. M.

328 *Thanksgiving.* L. M.
1 Let Sion praise the mighty God,
And make his honors known abroad,
For sweet the joy our songs to raise,
And glorious is the work of praise.

2 Our children live secure and blest;
Our shores have peace, our cities rest;
He feeds our sons with finest wheat,
And adds his blessings to their meat.

3 Through all our coasts his laws are shown,
His gospel through the nation known;
He hath not thus revealed his word
To every land; praise ye the Lord.

329 *Thanksgiving.* L. M.
1 Salvation doth to God belong,
His power and grace shall be our song;
From him alone all mercies flow,
His arm alone subdues the foe.

2 Then praise this God, who bows his ear,
Propitious to his people's prayer;
And though deliverance he may stay,
Yet answers still in his own day.

3 Oh, may this goodness lead our land,
Still saved by thine almighty hand,
The tribute of its love to bring
To thee, our Saviour and our King.

4 Till every public temple raise
A song of triumph to thy praise,
And every peaceful private home
To thee a temple shall become.

5 Still be it our supreme delight
To walk as in thy glorious sight,
Still in thy precepts and thy fear
Till life's last hour to persevere.

330 *Thanksgiving.* L. M.
1 Eternal Source of every joy,
Well may Thy praise our lips employ,
While in Thy temple we appear
To hail Thee, Sovereign of the year.

2 Wide as the wheels of nature roll,
Thy hand supports and guides the whole;
The sun is taught by Thee to rise,
And darkness when to veil the skies.

3 The flowery spring, at Thy command,
Perfumes the air and paints the land;
The summer rays with vigor shine
To raise the corn and cheer the vine.

4 Thy hand, in autumn, richly pours
Through all our coasts redundant stores;
And winters, softened by Thy care,
No more the face of horror wear.

5 Seasons, and months, and weeks, and days,
Demand successive songs of praise;
And be the grateful homage paid,
With morning light and evening shade.

FAST DAYS.

GRATITUDE. L. M.

6 Here in Thy house let incense rise,
And circling sabbaths bless our eyes;
Till to those lofty heights we soar,
Where days and years revolve no more.

7 That so with all our hearts may we
Once more with joy give thanks to thee,
And walk obedient to thy word,
And now and ever praise the Lord.

331 *Fast Day.* **L. M.**

1 When in our hour of utmost need
We know not where to look for aid,
When days and nights of anxious thought
Nor help nor counsel yet have brought;

2 Then this our comfort is alone,
That we may meet before thy throne,
And cry, O faithful God! to thee
For rescue from our misery;

3 To thee may raise our hearts and eyes,
Repenting sore with bitter sighs,
And seek thy pardon for our sin,
And respite from our griefs within.

4 For thou hast promised, graciously
To hear all those who cry to thee
Through him whose name alone is great,
Our Saviour and our advocate.

5 And thus we come, O God! to-day,
And all our woes before thee lay,
For tried, afflicted, lo! we stand,
Peril and foes on every hand.

6 Ah! hide not for our sins thy face;
Absolve us through thy boundless grace;
Be with us in our anguish still,
Free us at last from every ill.

332 *"Oh, spare our guilty country, spare."* **L. M.**

1 On thee, O Lord our God, we call,
Before thy throne devoutly fall;
Oh, whither should the helpless fly?
To whom but thee direct their cry?

2 Lord, we repent, we weep, we mourn,
To our forsaken God we turn;
Oh, spare our guilty country, spare
The church thine hand hath planted here!

3 We plead thy grace, indulgent God!
We plead thy Son's atoning blood;
We plead thy gracious promises;
And are they unavailing pleas?

4 These pleas, presented at thy throne,
Have brought ten thousand blessings down
On guilty lands in helpless woe:
Let them prevail to save us, too.

Doxology. **L. M.**

To God the Father, God the Son,
And God the Spirit, Three in One,
Be honor, praise, and glory given,
By all on earth, and all in heaven!

HARVEST, THANKSGIVING, AND

AMERICA. 6s & 4s.

333 *"The God of harvest praise."* 6s & 4s.

1 The God of harvest praise;
In loud thanksgiving raise
Hand, heart, and voice!
The valleys laugh and sing;
Forests and mountains ring;
The plains their tribute bring;
The streams rejoice.

2 Yea, bless his holy name,
And joyous thanks proclaim
Through all the earth;
To glory in your lot
Is comely; but be not
God's benefits forgot
Amid your mirth.

3 The God of harvest praise;
Hands, hearts, and voices raise,
With sweet accord;
From field to garner throng,
Bearing your sheaves along,
And in your harvest song
Bless ye the Lord.

334 *The Voice of National Joy.* 6s & 4s.

1 My country, 'tis of thee,
Sweet land of liberty,
Of thee I sing:
Land where my fathers died,
Land of the pilgrim's pride,
From every mountain side
Let freedom ring!

2 My native country, thee—
Land of the noble free—
Thy name I love:
I love thy rocks and rills,
Thy woods and templed hills,
My heart with rapture thrills
Like that above.

3 Let music swell the breeze,
And ring from all the trees
Sweet freedom's song!
Let mortal tongues awake;
Let all that breathe partake;
Let rocks their silence break—
The sound prolong!

4 Our fathers' God! to thee,
Author of liberty,
To thee we sing;
Long may our land be bright
With freedom's holy light;
Protect us by thy might,
Great God, our King!

335 *"God save the State!"* 6s & 4s.

1 God bless our native land!
Firm may she ever stand,
Through storm and night;
When the wild tempests rave,
Ruler of winds and wave,
Do thou our country save
By thy great might.

2 For her our prayer shall rise
To God, above the skies;
On him we wait:
Thou who art ever nigh,
Guarding with watchful eye,
To thee aloud we cry,
God save the State!

COMFORT IN AFFLICTIONS.

NEW HAVEN. 6s & 4s.

336 *"O God! be Thou my stay."* **6s & 4s**

1 Father, oh, hear me now!
Father, oh, hear me now!
Father divine!
Thou, only thou, canst see
The heart's deep agony;
Help me to say to thee
"Thy will, not mine!"

2 O God! be thou my stay,
O God! be thou my stay,
In this dark hour;
Kindly each sorrow hear,
Hush every troubled fear,
Then let me still revere,
Still own thy power.

3 In thee alone I trust,
In thee alone I trust,
Thou Holy One!
Humbly to thee I pray
That through each troubled day
Of life, I still may say,
"Thy will be done!"

337 *Ps. 37: 25.* **6s & 4s.**

1 Now I have found a Friend
Whose love shall never end;
Jesus is mine.
Though earthly joys decrease,
Though human friendships cease,
Now I have lasting peace;
Jesus is mine.

2 Though I grow poor and old,
He will my faith uphold;
Jesus is mine.
He shall my wants supply;
His precious blood is nigh,
Naught can my hope destroy;
Jesus is mine.

3 When earth shall pass away,
In the great judgment day,
Jesus is mine.
Oh, what a glorious thing
Then to behold my King,
On tuneful harps to sing,
Jesus is mine.

338 *"What have I done for Thee?"* **6s & 4s.**
Acts 9: 6.

1 O thou best gift of heaven!
Thou who thyself hast given,—
For thou hast died!
This thou hast done for me:
What have I done for thee,
Thou crucified?

2 I long to serve thee more;
Reveal an open door,
Saviour, to me:
Then, counting all but loss,
I'll glory in thy cross,
And follow thee.

3 Do thou but point the way,
And give me strength t' obey;
Thy will be mine:
Then can I think it joy
To suffer or to die,
Since I am thine.

INVITATION, AND

HEBRON. L. M.

339 *"Behold, I stand at the door, and knock."—Rev. 3: 20.* **L. M.**

1 Behold a Stranger at the door:
He gently knocks, has knocked before;
Has waited long, is waiting still:
You treat no other friend so ill.

2 Oh, lovely attitude! he stands
With melting heart and open hands:
Oh, matchless kindness! and he shows
This matchless kindness to his foes!

3 Rise, touched with gratitude divine,
Turn out his enemy and thine;
Turn out thy soul-enslaving sin,
And let the heavenly stranger in.

4 Oh, welcome him, the Prince of Peace!
Now may his gentle reign increase!
Throw wide the door, each willing mind;
And be his empire all mankind.

340 *"Fear not; I have redeemed thee." Matt. 11: 28.* **L. M.**

1 Come, weary souls, with sin distressed,
Come, and accept the promised rest;
The Saviour's gracious call obey,
And cast your gloomy fears away.

2 Oppressed with guilt,—a painful load,—
Oh, come and bow before your God!
Divine compassion, mighty love,
Will all the painful load remove.

3 Here mercy's boundless ocean flows,
To cleanse your guilt and heal your woes;
Pardon, and life, and endless peace—
How rich the gift! how free the grace!

4 Dear Saviour! let thy powerful love
Confirm our faith, our fears remove;
Oh, sweetly reign in every breast,
And guide us to eternal rest.

341 *No Hope in the Grave—Ps. 88.* **L. M.**

1 While life prolongs its precious light,
Mercy is found, and peace is given;
But soon, ah! soon, approaching night
Shall blot out every hope of heaven.

2 While God invites, how blest the day!
How sweet the gospel's charming sound!
Come, sinners, haste, oh, haste away,
While yet a pardoning God he's found.

3 Soon, borne on time's most rapid wing,
Shall death command you to the grave,
Before his bar your spirits bring,
And none be found to hear or save.

4 Now God invites—how blest the day!
How sweet the gospel's charming sound!
Come, sinners, haste, oh, haste away,
While yet a pardoning God is found.

342 *"God calling yet."* **L. M.**

1 God calling yet!—shall I not hear?
Earth's pleasures shall I still hold dear?
Shall life's swift passing years all fly,
And still my soul in slumbers lie?

2 God calling yet!—shall I not rise?
Can I his loving voice despise,
And basely his kind care repay?
He calls me still: can I delay?

CONVICTION OF SIN.

WELTON. L. M.

3 God calling yet!—and shall he knock,
And I my heart the closer lock?
He still is waiting to receive,
And shall I dare his Spirit grieve?

4 God calling yet!—and shall I give
No heed, but still in bondage live?
I wait, but he does not forsake;
He calls me still!—my heart, awake!

5 God calling yet!—I cannot stay;
My heart I yield without delay:
Vain world, farewell! from thee I part;
The voice of God hath reached my heart.

343 *"Come, ye heavy laden."*
Matth. 11: 28. **L. M.**

1 "Come hither, all ye weary souls;
Ye heavy-laden sinners, come!
I'll give you rest from all your toils,
And raise you to my heavenly home.

2 "They shall find rest who learn of me;
I'm of a meek and lowly mind;
But passion rages like the sea,
And pride is restless as the wind.

3 "Blest is the man whose shoulders take
My yoke, and bear it with delight:
My yoke is easy to his neck,
My grace shall make the burden light."

4 Jesus, we come at thy command;
With faith, and hope, and humble zeal,
Resign our spirits to thy hand,
To mold and guide us at thy will.

344 *Longing for Freedom from Sin.* **L. M.**

1 Jesus demands this heart of mine,
Demands my love, my joy, my care;
But ah! how dead to things divine,
How cold my best affections are!

2 'T is sin, alas! with dreadful power,
Divides my Saviour from my sight;
Oh, for one happy, cloudless hour
Of sacred freedom, sweet delight!

3 Lord! let thy love shine forth and raise
My captive powers from sin and death,
And fill my heart and life with praise,
And tune my last expiring breath.

345 *"Hide Thy face from my sins."*
Psalm 51. **L. M.**

1 Have mercy on me, O my God!
In loving kindness hear my prayer;
Withdraw the terror of thy rod;
Lord, in thy tender mercy, spare.

2 Offenses rise where'er I look,
But I confess their guilt to thee;
Blot my transgressions from thy book;
Wash me from all iniquity.

3 Not streaming blood nor cleansing fire
Thy seeming anger can appease;
Burnt offerings thou dost not require,
Or gladly I would render these.

4 The broken hearts in sacrifice,
Alone, with thine acceptance meet:
My heart, O God, do not despise,
Abased and contrite at thy feet.

INVITATIONS, AND

LITANY. 7s. D.

346   *Ezek.* 33: 11.   7s.

1 Sinners, turn, why will ye die?
God, your Maker, asks you why;
God, who did your being give,
Made you with Himself to live;
He the fatal cause demands,
Asks the work of His own hands;
Why, ye thankless creatures, why
Will ye cross His love, and die?

2 Sinners, turn, why will ye die?
God, your Saviour, asks you why;
God who did your souls retrieve,
Died Himself that ye might live:
Will you let Him die in vain?
Crucify your Lord again?
Why, ye ransomed sinners, why
Will you slight His grace, and die?

3 Sinners, turn, why will ye die?
God, the Spirit, asks you why;
He, who all your lives hath strove,
Wooed you to embrace His love:
Will you not His grace receive?
Will you still refuse to live?
Why, ye long-sought sinners, why
Will ye grieve your God, and die?

347   *The Voice of Jesus.*
         Matt. 11: 28—30.   7s.

1 Come, says Jesus' sacred voice,
Come, and make my paths your choice;
I will guide you to your home;
Weary wanderer, hither come!

2 Thou who, homeless and forlorn,
Long hast borne the proud world's scorn,
Long hast roamed the barren waste,
Weary wanderer, hither haste.

3 Ye who, tossed on beds of pain,
Seek for ease, but seek in vain;
Ye, by fiercer anguish torn,
In remorse for guilt who mourn:—

4 Hither come! for here is found
Balm that flows for every wound;
Peace that ever shall endure,
Rest eternal, sacred, sure.

348   *"Now is the day of salvation."*
         James 4: 13.   7s.

1 Haste, O sinner! now be wise;
Stay not for the morrow's sun:
Wisdom if you still despise,
Harder is it to be won.

2 Haste, and mercy now implore;
Stay not for the morrow's sun,
Lest thy season should be o'er
Ere the morrow is begun.

3 Haste, O sinner! now return;
Stay not for the morrow's sun,
Lest thy lamp should cease to burn
Ere salvation's work is done.

4 Lord! do thou the sinner turn—
Turn him from his fearful state;
Let him not thy counsel spurn,
Nor lament his choice too late!

PENITENCE.

MARTYN. 7s. Double.

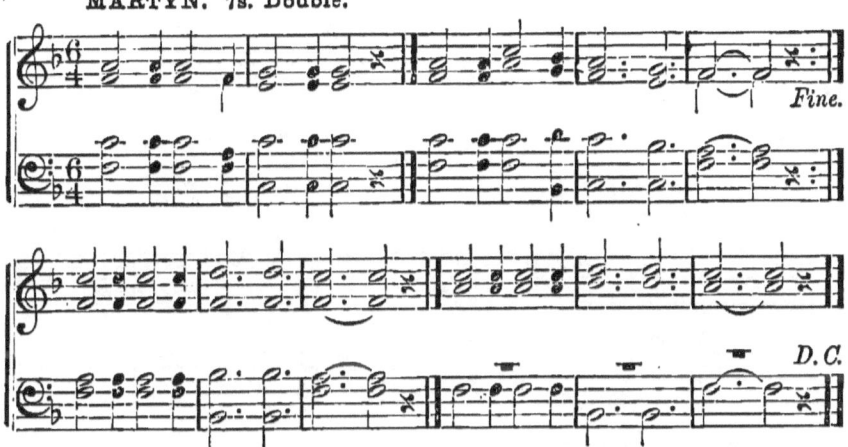

349 *Matt. 14: 30.*

1 Jesus, save my dying soul,
Make the broken spirit whole:
Humbled in the dust I lie;
Saviour, leave me not to die.

2 Jesus, full of every grace,
Now reveal Thy smiling face;
Grant the joy of sin forgiven,
Foretaste of the bliss of heaven.

3 All my guilt to Thee is known;
Thou art righteous, Thou alone;
All my help is from Thy cross,
All beside I count but loss.

4 Lord, in Thee I now believe;
Wilt Thou, wilt Thou not forgive?
Helpless at Thy feet I lie;
Saviour, leave me not to die!

350 *Mercy for the Chief of Sinners.* 7s.

1 Depth of mercy!—can there be
Mercy still reserved for me?
Can my God his wrath forbear?
Me, the chief of sinners, spare?

2 I have scorned the Son of God,
Trampled on his precious blood,
Would not hearken to his calls,
Grieved him by a thousand falls.

3 Lord, incline me to repent;
Let me now my fall lament—
Deeply my revolt deplore,
Weep, believe, and sin no more.

4 Still for me the Saviour stands,
Shows his wounds, and spreads his hands:
God is love! I know, I feel;
Jesus weeps, and loves me still.

351 *Confession.* 7s.

1 Oh these eyes, how dark and blind!
Oh this foolish, earthly mind!
Oh this froward, selfish will,
Which refuses to be still!

2 Oh these ever roaming eyes,
Upward that refuse to rise!
Oh these wayward feet of mine,
Found in every path but thine!

3 Oh this stubborn, prayerless knee,
Hands so seldom clasped to thee,
Longings of the soul that go,
Like the wild wind to and fro!

4 To and fro, without an aim,
Turning idly whence they came;
Bringing in no joy, no bliss,
Adding to my weariness.

5 Giver of the heavenly peace,
Bid, oh, bid these tumults cease;
Minister thy holy balm,
Fill me with thy Spirit's calm.

6 Thou, the Life, the Truth, the Way,
Leave me not in sin to stay;
Bearer of the sinner's guilt,
Lead me, lead me, as thou wilt!

INVITATION, AND

WOODSTOCK. C. M.

352 *The invitation of the Gospel.*   **C. M.**
Isa. 55: 1, 2.

1 Let every mortal ear attend,
And ev'ry heart rejoice;
The trumpet of the gospel sounds
With an inviting voice.

2 Ho! all ye hungry starving souls
That feed upon the wind,
And vainly strive with earthly toys
To fill an empty mind:

3 Eternal Wisdom has prepar'd
A soul-reviving feast,
And bids your longing appetites
The rich provision taste.

4 Ho! ye that pant for living streams,
And pine away and die;
Here you may quench your raging thirst
With springs that never dry.

5 Rivers of love and mercy here
In a rich ocean join;
Salvation in abundance flows,
Like floods of milk and wine.

6 The happy gates of gospel grace
Stand open night and day;
Lord, we are come to seek supplies,
And drive our wants away.

353   *The Resolve.—Est. 4: 16.*   **C. M.**

1 Come, humble sinner, in whose breast
A thousand thoughts revolve;
Come, with your guilt and fear *oppressed*
And make this last resolve:

2 "I'll go to Jesus, though my sin
High as the mountains rose;
I know his courts, I'll enter in,
Whatever may oppose.

3 "Prostrate I'll lie before his throne,
And there my guilt confess;
I'll tell him I'm a wretch undone,
Without his sovereign grace.

4 "I'll to the gracious King approach,
Whose scepter pardon gives;
Perhaps he may command my touch,
And then the suppliant lives.

5 "Perhaps he will admit my plea,
Perhaps will hear my prayer;
But if I perish, I will pray,
And perish only there.

6 "I can but perish if I go;
I am resolved to try;
For if I stay away I know
I must for ever die."

354   *Isa. 55: 7.*   **C. M.**

1 Return, O wanderer, now return,
And seek thy Father's face!
Those new desires, which in thee burn,
Were kindled by his grace.

2 Return, O wanderer, now return!
He hears thy humble sigh;
He sees thy softened spirit mourn,
When no one else is nigh,

PENITENCE.

FOUNTAIN. C. M.

3 Return, O wanderer, now return!
Thy Saviour bids thee live:
Go to his bleeding feet, and learn
How freely he'll forgive.

4 Return, O wanderer, now return,
And wipe the falling tear!
Thy Father calls — no longer mourn:
His love invites thee near.

355 *"He will abundantly pardon."* **C. M.**
Isaiah 55: 7, 8.

1 Sinners, the voice of God regard;
His mercy speaks to-day:
He calls you, by his sovereign word,
From sin's destructive way.

2 Why will you in the crooked ways
Of sin and folly go?
In pain you travel all your days,
To reap eternal woe!

3 But he that turns to God shall live,
Through his abounding grace;
His mercy will the guilt forgive
Of those who seek his face.

4 His love exceeds your highest thoughts;
He pardons like a God:
He will forgive your numerous faults
Through a Redeemer's blood.

356 *"Against Thee, Thee only, have I sinned."* **C. M.**

1 Prostrate, dear Jesus, at thy feet
A guilty rebel lies;
And upward to thy mercy-seat
Presumes to lift his eyes.

2 If tears of sorrow would suffice
To pay the debt I owe,
Tears should from both my weeping eyes
In ceaseless torrents flow.

3 But no such sacrifice I plead
To expiate my guilt;
No tears, but those which thou hast shed,
No blood, but thou hast spilt.

4 Think of thy sorrows, dearest Lord!
And all my sins forgive:
Justice will well approve the word
That bids the sinner live.

357 *"God be merciful to me a sinner."* **C. M.**

1 Lord, like the publican I stand,
And lift my heart to Thee;
Thy pardoning grace, O God, command;
Be merciful to me.

2 I smite upon my anxious breast,
O'erwhelmed with agony!
O save my soul by sin oppressed;
Be merciful to me.

3 My guilt, my shame, I all confess,
I have no hope nor plea
But Jesus' blood and righteousness;
Be merciful to me.

4 Here at Thy cross I still would wait,
Nor from its shelter flee,
Till Thou, O God, in mercy great,
Art merciful to me.

KENTUCKY. S. M.

358 *"Where shall rest be found?"* S. M.

1 O, where shall rest be found—
Rest for the weary soul?
'T were vain the ocean depths to sound,
Or pierce to either pole.

2 The world can never give
The bliss for which we sigh:
'Tis not the whole of life to live,
Nor all of death to die.

3 Beyond this vale of tears
There is a life above,
Unmeasured by the flight of years;
And all that life is love.

4 There is a death whose pang
Outlasts the fleeting breath:
Oh, what eternal horrors hang
Around the second death!

5 Lord God of truth and grace,
Teach us that death to shun;
Lest we be banished from thy face,
And evermore undone.

359 *"The Spirit and the Bride say, Come." Rev. 22: 17.* S. M.

1 The Spirit in our hearts,
Is whisp'ring, "Sinner, come;"
The bride, the church of Christ, proclaims
To all his children, "Come!"

2 Let him that heareth say
To all about him, "Come;"
Let him that thirsts for righteousness,
To Christ, the Fountain, come!

3 Yes, whosoever will,
Oh, let him freely come,
And freely drink the stream of life;
'T is Jesus bids him come.

4 Lo! Jesus, who invites,
Declares, "I quickly come;"
Lord, even so; we wait thine hour;
O blest Redeemer, come!

360 *2 Cor. 5: 21.* S. M.

1 How heavy is the night
That hangs upon our eyes,
Till Christ with his reviving light
Over our souls arise!

2 Our guilty spirits dread
To meet the wrath of Heaven;
But in His righteousness arrayed,
We see our sins forgiven.

3 The powers of hell agree
To hold our souls, in vain;
He sets the sons of bondage free,
And breaks the cursed chain.

4 Lord, we adore Thy ways
That bring us near to God;
Thy sovereign power, Thy healing grace,
And Thine atoning blood.

361 *Rest in God.—Gen 8: 9.* S. M.

1 Oh, cease, my wandering soul,
On restless wing to roam;
All this wide world, to either pole,
Hath not for thee a home.

CONVERSION.

THATCHER. S. M.

2 Behold the ark of God!
Behold the open door!
Oh, haste to gain that dear abode,
And rove, my soul, no more.

3 There safe thou shalt abide,
There sweet shall be thy rest,
And every longing satisfied,
With full salvation blest.

362   *"My soul, wait thou only upon God."*   S. M.

1 Thou Lord of all above,
And all below the sky,
Prostrate before thy feet I fall
And for thy mercy cry.

2 Forgive my follies past,
The crimes which I have done;
Bid a repenting sinner live,
Through thine incarnate Son.

3 Guilt, like a heavy load,
Upon my conscience lies;
To thee I make my sorrows known,
And lift my weeping eyes.

4 The burden which I feel,
Thou only canst remove;
Do thou display thy pard'ning grace,
And thine unbounded love.

5 One gracious look of thine
Will ease my troubled breast;
Oh, let me know my sins forgiven,
And I shall then be blest!

363   *Ezek.* 11: 19.   S. M.

1 Jesus, I come to Thee,
A sinner doomed to die;
My only refuge is Thy cross,
Here at Thy feet I lie.

2 Can mercy reach my case,
And all my sins remove?
Break, O my God, this heart of stone,
And melt it by Thy love.

3 Too long my soul has gone
Far from my God astray;
I've sported on the brink of hell,
In sin's delusive way.

4 But, Lord, my heart is fixed,
I hope in Thee alone;
Break off the chains of sin and death,
And bind me to Thy throne.

5 Thy blood can cleanse my heart,
Thy hand can wipe my tears;
Oh send Thy blessed Spirit down
To banish all my fears.

6 Then shall my soul arise,
From sin and Satan free;
Redeemed from hell and every foe,
I'll trust alone in Thee.

Doxology.   S. M.

To God, the Father, Son,
And Spirit, glory be,
As was, and is, and shall remain
Through all eternity!

PENITENCE, AND

WOODWORTH. L. M.

364 *"Just as I am."—John 1: 29.* L. M.

1 Just as I am, without one plea,
But that thy blood was shed for me,
And that thou bid'st me come to thee,
O Lamb of God, I come! I come!

2 Just as I am, and waiting not
To rid my soul of one dark blot,
To thee whose blood can cleanse each spot,
O Lamb of God, I come! I come!

3 Just as I am, though tossed about
With many a conflict, many a doubt,
Fightings within, and fears without,
O Lamb of God, I come! I come!

4 Just as I am—poor, wretched, blind;
Sight, riches, healing of the mind,
Yea, all I need, in thee to find,
O Lamb of God, I come! I come!

5 Just as I am—thou wilt receive,
Wilt welcome, pardon, cleanse, relieve,
Because thy promise I believe,
O Lamb of God, I come! I come!

6 Just as I am—thy love unknown
Hath broken every barrier down:
Now, to be thine, yea, thine alone,
O Lamb of God, I come! I come!

365 *Prayer of the Publican. Luke 18: 13.* L. M.

1 With broken heart and contrite sigh,
A trembling sinner, Lord, I cry;
Thy pardoning grace is rich and free:
O God, be merciful to me!

2 I smite upon my troubled breast,
With deep and conscious guilt oppressed;
Christ and his cross my only plea:
O God, be merciful to me!

3 Far off I stand with tearful eyes,
Nor dare uplift them to the skies;
But thou dost all my anguish see:
O God, be merciful to me!

4 Nor alms, nor deeds that I have done,
Can for a single sin atone;
To Calvary alone I flee:
O God, be merciful to me!

5 And when redeemed from sin and hell,
With all the ransomed throng I dwell,
My raptured song shall ever be,
God has been merciful to me!

366 *"Blot out my transgressions." Psalm 51.* L. M.

1 O thou that hear'st when sinners cry,
Though all my crimes before thee lie,
Behold me not with angry look,
But blot their mem'ry from thy book.

2 Create my nature pure within,
And form my soul averse to sin;
Let thy good Spirit ne'er depart,
Nor hide thy presence from my heart.

3 I cannot live without thy light,
Cast out and banished from thy sight;
Thy holy joys, my God, restore,
And guard me that I fall no more.

CONVERSION.

HALLET. L. M.   GEO. KINGSLEY.

4 Though I have grieved thy Spirit, Lord,
His help and comfort still afford;
And let a sinner seek thy throne,
To plead the merits of thy Son.

367   *"Show pity, Lord! O Lord, forgive." Psalm 51.*   **L. M.**

1 Show pity, Lord! O Lord, forgive;
Let a repenting rebel live;
Are not thy mercies large and free?
May not a sinner trust in thee?

2 My crimes are great, but ne'er surpass
The power and glory of thy grace:
Great God! thy nature hath no bound,
So let thy pard'ning love be found.

3 Oh, wash my soul from every sin,
And make my guilty conscience clean!
Here on my heart the burden lies,
And past offences pain mine eyes.

4 My lips with shame my sins confess,
Against thy law, against thy grace;
Lord, should thy judgment grow severe,
I am condemned, but thou art clear.

5 Should sudden vengeance seize my breath,
I must pronounce thee just in death;
And if my soul were sent to hell,
Thy righteous law approves it well.

6 Yet save a trembling sinner, Lord!
Whose hope, still hovering round thy word,
Would light on some sweet promise there,
Some sure support against despair.

368   *"Restore unto me the joy of Thy salvation." Psalm 51.*   **L. M.**

1 A broken heart, my God, my King,
Is all the sacrifice I bring;
The God of grace will ne'er despise
A broken heart for sacrifice.

2 My soul lies humbled in the dust,
And owns thy dreadful sentence just;
Look down, O Lord, with pitying eye,
And save the soul condemned to die.

3 Then will I teach the world thy ways:
Sinners shall learn thy sovereign grace;
I'll lead them to my Saviour's blood,
And they shall praise a pard'ning God.

369   *"Cast me not away from Thy presence." Psalm 51.*   **L. M.**

1 O turn, great Ruler of the skies!
Turn from my sin thy searching eyes;
Nor let th' offences of my hand
Within thy book recorded stand.

2 Give me a will to thine subdued,—
A conscience pure, a soul renewed;
Nor let me, wrapt in endless gloom,
An outcast from thy presence roam.

3 Oh, let thy Spirit to my heart
Once more its quickening aid impart;
My mind from every fear release,
And soothe my troubled thoughts to peace.

Doxology.   **L. M.**

To God the Father, God the Son,
And God the Spirit, three in one,
Be honor, praise and glory given
By all on earth and all in heaven.

PENITENCE, AND

NAOMI. C. M.

370 *"I heard the voice of Jesus."* C. M.

1 I heard the voice of Jesus say,
"Come unto me and rest;
Lay down, thou weary one, lay down
Thy head upon my breast:"

2 I came to Jesus as I was,
Weary, and worn, and sad;
I found in him a resting-place,
And he has made me glad.

3 I heard the voice of Jesus say,
"Behold, I freely give
The living water! thirsty one,
Stoop down, and drink, and live."

4 I came to Jesus, and I drank
Of that life-giving stream:
My thirst was quenched, my soul revived,
And now I live in him.

5 I heard the voice of Jesus say,
"I am this dark world's light:
Look unto me; thy morn shall rise,
And all thy day be bright."

6 I looked to Jesus and I found
In him my Star, my Sun;
And in that light of life I'll walk
Till all my journey's done.

371 Prov. 23 : 26. C. M.

1 Welcome, O Saviour! to my heart;
Possess thine humble throne;
Bid every rival hence depart,
And claim me for thine own.

2 The world and Satan I forsake—
To thee, I all resign;
My longing heart, O Jesus! take,
And fill with love divine.

3 Oh! may I never turn aside,
Nor from thy bosom flee;
Let nothing here my heart divide—
I give it all to thee.

372 *"Lord, remember me."* Luke 23 : 42. C. M.

1 O thou, from whom all goodness flows,
I lift my soul to thee;
In all my sorrows, conflicts, woes,
O Lord, remember me!

2 When on my aching, burdened heart
My sins lie heavily,
Thy pardon grant, new peace impart;
Then, Lord, remember me!

3 When trials sore obstruct my way,
And ills I cannot flee,
Oh, let my strength be as my day—
Dear Lord, remember me!

4 When in the solemn hour of death
I wait thy just decree;
Be this the prayer of my last breath:
Now, Lord, remember me!

5 And when before thy throne I stand,
And lift my soul to thee,
Then with the saints at thy right hand,
O Lord, remember me!

CONVERSION.

RHINE. C. M.

373 *Matt. 11: 28.* C. M.

1 Approach, my soul, the mercy-seat
Where Jesus answers prayer;
There humbly fall before His feet,
For none can perish there.

2 Thy promise is my only plea,
With this I venture nigh;
Thou callest burdened souls to Thee,
And such, O Lord, am I.

3 Bowed down beneath a load of sin,
By Satan sorely prest,
By war without, and fear within,
I come to Thee for rest.

4 Be Thou my Shield and Hiding-place,
That, sheltered near Thy side,
I may my fierce accuser face,
And tell him, Thou hast died.

5 Oh wondrous love, to bleed and die,
To bear the cross and shame,
That guilty sinners, such as I,
Might plead Thy gracious Name!

374 *Ps. 51: 10.* C. M.

1 O, for a heart to praise my God!
A heart from sin set free;
A heart that always feels thy blood,
So freely shed for me;

2 A heart resigned, submissive, meek,
My great Redeemer's throne,
Where only Christ is heard to speak,
Where Jesus reigns alone.

3 An humble, lowly, contrite heart,
Believing, true and clean;
Which neither life nor death can part
From him that dwells within!

4 A heart in every thought renewed,
And filled with love divine;
Perfect and right and pure and good,
A copy, Lord! of thine.

375 *"There is forgiveness with Thee." Psalm 130.* C. M.

1 Out of the deeps of long distress,
The borders of despair,
I sent my cries to seek thy grace,
My groans to move thine ear.

2 Great God! should thy severer eye,
And thine impartial hand,
Be strict to mark iniquity,
No mortal flesh could stand.

3 But there are pardons with my God,
For crimes of high degree;
Thy Son has bought them with his blood,
To draw us near to thee.

4 I wait for thy salvation, Lord;
With strong desires I wait:
My soul, invited by thy word,
Stands watching at thy gate.

5 In God the Lord let Israel trust;
O sinners, seek his face;
The Lord is good, as well as just,
And plenteous in his grace.

FAITH IN CHRIST.

ROCK OF AGES. 7s. 6 lines.

376 *"Rock of Ages."*—1 Cor. 10: 4.   7s.

1 Rock of ages, cleft for me!
Let me hide myself in thee;
Let the water and the blood
From thy riven side which flowed,
Be of sin the double cure;
Cleanse me from its guilt and power.

2 Not the labors of my hands
Can fulfill thy law's demands;
Could my zeal no respite know,
Could my tears for ever flow,
All for sin could not atone;
Thou must save, and thou alone.

3 Nothing in my hand I bring;
Simply to thy cross I cling;
Naked, come to thee for dress,
Helpless, look to thee for grace,
Foul, I to the fountain fly;
Wash me, Saviour! or I die.

4 Whilst I draw this fleeting breath,
When my eyelids close in death,
When I soar through worlds unknown,
See thee on thy judgment throne,
Rock of ages, cleft for me!
Let me hide myself in thee.

377   *Matt. 26: 20.*   7s.

1 Saviour of our ruined race,
Fountain of redeeming grace,
Let us now Thy fulness see,
While we here converse with Thee;
Hearken to our ardent prayer,
Let us all Thy blessing share.

2 Weak, unworthy, sinful, vile,
Yet we seek Thy heavenly smile;
Canst Thou all our sins forgive?
Dost Thou bid us look and live?
Lord, we wonder and adore!
Oh for grace to love Thee more.

378   *Phil. 3: 8.*   7s.

1 Blessed Saviour, Thee I love,
All my other joys above;
All my hopes in Thee abide,
Thou my Hope, and nought beside;
Ever let my glory be,
Only, only, only Thee.

2 Once again beside the cross,
All my gain I count but loss;
Earthly pleasures fade away;
Clouds they are that hide my day;
Hence, vain shadows! let me see
Jesus, crucified for me.

3 From beneath that thorny crown
Trickle drops of cleansing down;
Pardon from thy pierced hand
Now I take, while here I stand;
Only then I live to Thee,
When Thy wounded side I see.

4 Blessed Saviour, Thine am I,
Thine to live, and Thine to die;
Height or depth, or earthly power,
Ne'er shall hide my Saviour more:
Ever shall my glory be,
Only, only, only Thee!

PASSION-WEEK AND LORD'S DAY.

SABBATH. 7s. 6 lines.

379 *Our Example.* **7s.**

1 Go to dark Gethsemane,
Ye that feel the tempter's power;
Your Redeemer's conflict see,
Watch with him one bitter hour:
Turn not from his griefs away,
Learn of Jesus Christ to pray.

2 Follow to the judgment-hall,
View the Lord of life arraigned:
Oh the wormwood and the gall!
Oh the pangs his soul sustained!
Shun not suffering, shame, or loss;
Learn of him to bear the cross.

3 Calv'ry's mournful mountain climb;
There, adoring at his feet,
Mark that miracle of time,
God's own sacrifice complete:
"It is finished," hear him cry;
Learn of Jesus Christ to die.

4 Early hasten to the tomb
Where they laid his breathless clay:
All is solitude and gloom; —
Who hath taken him away?
Christ is ris'n! he meets our eyes:
Saviour, teach us so to rise.

380 *The Lord's Day.* **7s.**

1 Safely through another week
God has brought us on our way;
Let us now a blessing seek,
Waiting in his courts to-day:
Day of all the week the best,
Emblem of eternal rest.

2 While we pray for pard'ning grace,
Through the dear Redeemer's name,
Show thy reconciling face;
Take away our sin and shame:
From our worldly cares set free,
May we rest this day in thee.

3 Here we come, thy name to praise;
Let us feel thy presence near;
May thy glories meet our eyes,
While we in thy house appear:
Here afford us, Lord, a taste
Of our everlasting feast.

4 May the Gospel's joyful sound
Conquer sinners, comfort saints;
Make the fruits of grace abound;
Bring relief for all complaints:
Thus let all our Sabbaths prove,
Till we rest in thee above.

FAITH, ADOPTION, AND

ORTONVILLE. C. M.

381 *Prayer for strong Faith.* C. M.

1 O for a faith that will not shrink
Though pressed by every foe;
That will not tremble on the brink
Of any earthly woe!—

2 That will not murmur nor complain
Beneath the chastening rod,
But, in the hour of grief or pain,
Will lean upon its God;—

3 A faith that shines more bright and clear
When tempests rage without;
That, when in danger, knows no fear,
In darkness feels no doubt;—

4 A faith that keeps the narrow way
Till life's last hour is fled,
And with a pure and heavenly ray
Lights up a dying bed!

5 Lord, give us such a faith as this,
And then, whate'er may come,
We'll taste, ev'n here, the hallowed bliss
Of an eternal home.

382 *Faith of things unseen.* C. M.

1 Faith is the brightest evidence
Of things beyond our sight;
Breaks through the clouds of flesh and sense,
And dwells in heav'nly light.

2 It sets time past in present view,
Brings distant prospects home
Of things a thousand years ago,
Or thousand years to come.

3 By faith we know the worlds were made
By God's almighty word;
Abr'am to unknown countries led,
By faith obey'd the Lord.

4 He sought a city fair and high,
Built by th' eternal hands;
And faith assures us, though we die,
That heav'nly building stands.

383 2 Cor. 5: 7. C. M.

1 Faith adds new charms to earthly bliss,
And saves me from its snares,
Its aid in every duty brings,
And softens all my cares.

2 The wounded conscience knows its power
The healing balm to give;
That balm the saddest heart can cheer,
And make the dying live.

3 Wide it unveils celestial worlds,
Where deathless pleasures reign,
And bids me seek my portion there,
Nor bids me seek in vain;

4 Shows me the precious promise, sealed
With the Redeemer's blood,
And helps my feeble hope to rest
Upon a faithful God.

5 There, there unshaken would I rest
Till this vile body dies,
And then, on faith's triumphant wings,
At once to glory rise.

UNION WITH CHRIST.

MERTON. C. M.

384 *Abba, Father.* C. M.
1 Sov'reign of all the worlds on high,
  Allow my humble claim;
  Nor, while a worm would raise its head,
  Disdain a Father's name.

2 My Father, God! how sweet the sound!
  How tender, and how dear!
  Not all the harmony of heav'n
  Could so delight the ear.

3 Come, sacred Spirit, seal the name
  On my expanding heart,
  And show that in Jehovah's grace
  I share a filial part.

4 Cheer'd by a signal so divine,
  Unwav'ring I believe;
  And Abba, Father, humbly cry,
  Nor can the sign deceive.

385 *"Let me know my Father reigns."* C. M.
     Heb. 12: 7.
1 My God, my Father, blissful name!
  Oh, may I call thee mine?
  May I with sweet assurance claim
  A portion so divine?

2 Whate'er thy providence denies
  I calmly would resign;
  For thou art good and just and wise:
  Oh, bend my will to thine!

3 Whate'er thy sacred will ordains,
  Oh, give me strength to bear!
  And let me know my Father reigns,
  And trust his tender care.

4 Thy sovereign ways are all unknown
  To my weak, erring sight;
  Yet let my soul adoring own
  That all thy ways are right.

386 *One with Christ.—Rom.* 8: 38, 39. C. M.
1 Lord Jesus, are we one with thee?
  O height, O depth of love!
  With thee we died upon the tree;
  In thee we live above.

2 Such was thy grace, that for our sake
  Thou didst from heaven come down,
  Our mortal flesh and blood partake,
  In all our misery one.

3 Our sins, our guilt, in love divine,
  Were borne on earth by thee;
  The gall, the curse, the wrath were thine
  To set thy members free.

4 Ascended now in glory bright,
  Still one with us thou art;
  Nor life nor death nor depth nor height
  Thy saints and thee can part.

5 Soon, soon shall come that glorious day,
  When, seated on thy throne,
  Thou shalt to wondering worlds display
  That thou with us art one!

        Doxology.   C. M.
To praise the Father and the Son,
And Spirit All-Divine,
The One in Three, and Three in One,
Let saints and angels join.

FAITH AND

LAMBIE. L. M. G. KINGSLEY.

387   *2 Cor. 5: 7.*   **L. M.**

1 By faith in Christ I walk with God,
With heaven, my journey's end, in view;
Supported by his staff and rod,
My road is safe and pleasant too.

2 Though snares and dangers throng my path,
And earth and hell my course withstand,
I triumph over all by faith,
Guarded by his Almighty hand.

3 The wilderness affords no food,
But God for my support prepares,
Provides me every needful good,
And frees my soul from wants and cares.

4 With him sweet converse I maintain;
Great as he is, I dare be free;
I tell him all my grief and pain,
And he reveals his love to me.

5 Some cordial from his word he brings,
Whene'er my feeble spirit faints;
At once my soul revives and sings,
And yields no more to sad complaints.

6 I pity all that worldlings talk
Of pleasures that will quickly end;
Be this my choice, O Lord! to walk
With thee, my Guide, my Guard, my Friend.

388   *Heb. 11: 8.*   **L. M.**

1 As when the weary traveler gains
The height of some o'erlooking hill,
His heart revives, if o'er the plains
He sees his home, though distant still,—

2 So when the Christian pilgrim views,
By faith, his mansion in the skies,
The sight his fainting strength renews,
And wings his speed to reach the prize.

3 "'Tis there," he says, "I am to dwell
With Jesus in the realms of day:
Then shall I bid my cares farewell,
And he will wipe my tears away."

4 The best obedience of my hands
Dares not appear before thy throne;
But faith can answer thy demands
By pleading what my Lord has done.

389   *All things but loss for Christ.*
          Phil. 3: 7, 8.   **L. M.**

1 No more, my God, I boast no more
Of all the duties I have done;
I quit the hopes I held before,
To trust the merits of thy Son.

2 Now, for the love I bear his name,
What was my gain, I count my loss;
My former pride I call my shame,
And nail my glory to his cross.

3 Yes; and I must and will esteem
All things but loss for Jesus' sake;
Oh, may my soul be found in him,
And of his righteousness partake!

390   *"The faith of joys to come."*
          Heb. 11: 8.   **L. M.**

1 'Tis by the faith of joys to come
We walk thro' deserts dark as night;
Till we arrive at heaven, our home,
Faith is our guide, and faith our light.

JUSTIFICATION.

ORIEL. L. M., or 8s & 4s.

2 The want of sight she well supplies;
She makes the pearly gates appear;
Far into distant worlds she pries,
And brings eternal glories near.

3 Cheerful we tread the desert through,
While faith inspires a heavenly ray;
Though lions roar, and tempests blow,
And rocks and dangers fill the way.

391 *"It is God that justifieth."* L. M.
Rom. 8: 33—37.

1 Who shall the Lord's elect condemn?
'Tis God who justifies their souls;
And mercy, like a mighty stream,
O'er all their sins divinely rolls.

2 Who shall adjudge the saints to hell?
'Tis Christ who suffered in their stead;
And, the salvation to fulfill,
Behold him rising from the dead!

3 He lives! he lives! and sits above,
Forever interceding there:
Who shall divide us from his love,
Or what should tempt us to despair?

4 Shall persecution, or distress,
Famine, or sword, or nakedness?
He who hath loved us bears us through,
And makes us more than conquerors too.

5 Not all that men on earth can do,
Nor powers on high, nor powers below,
Shall cause his mercy to remove,
Or wean our hearts from Christ, our love.

392 Rom. 5: 9. L. M.

1 Jesus, thy Blood and Righteousness
My beauty are, my glorious dress;
'Midst flaming worlds, in these arrayed,
With joy shall I lift up my head.

2 Bold shall I stand in thy great day,
For who aught to my charge shall lay?
Fully absolved through these I am,
From sin and fear, from guilt and shame.

3 When from the dust of death I rise
To claim my mansion in the skies—
E'en then, this shall be all my plea:
Jesus hath lived, hath died for me.

4 Thus Abraham, the friend of God,
Thus all heaven's armies bought with blood,
Saviour of Sinners, thee proclaim;
Sinners, of whom the chief I am.

5 This spotless robe the same appears,
When ruined nature sinks in years;
No age can change its glorious hue,
The robe of Christ is ever new.

6 Oh, let the dead now hear thy voice!
Bid, Lord, thy mourning ones rejoice!
Their beauty this, their glorious dress,
Jesus, the Lord our Righteousness.

Doxology. L. M.

Praise God, from whom all blessings flow!
Praise him, all creatures here below!
Praise him above, ye heavenly host!
Praise Father, Son, and Holy Ghost!

ADOPTION, AND

DOVER. S. M.

393 *"That we should be called the sons of God."*—1 John 3: 1, 2. S. M.

1 Behold, what wondrous grace
The Father has bestowed
On sinners of a mortal race,
To call them sons of God!

2 Nor doth it yet appear
How great we must be made!
But when we see our Saviour here,
We shall be like our Head.

3 A hope so much divine
May trials well endure;
May purify our souls from sin,
As Christ, the Lord, is pure.

4 If in my Father's love
I share a filial part,
Send down thy Spirit, like a dove,
To rest upon my heart.

5 We would no longer lie
Like slaves beneath the throne;
Our faith shall "Abba, Father," cry,
And thou the kindred own.

394 *Eph.* 2: 8. S. M.

1 Grace! 'tis a charming sound,
Harmonious to the ear;
Heaven with the echo shall resound,
And all the earth shall hear.

2 Grace first contrived a way
To save rebellious man;
And all the steps that grace display,
Which drew the wondrous plan.

3 Grace taught my wandering feet
To tread the heavenly road;
And new supplies each hour I meet,
While pressing on to God.

4 Grace all the work shall crown,
Through everlasting days;
It lays in heaven the topmost stone,
And well deserves the praise.

395 *Weak believers encouraged.* S. M.

1 Your harps, ye trembling saints,
Down from the willows take;
Loud to the praise of Christ our Lord,
Bid ev'ry string awake.

2 Though in a foreign land,
We are not far from home;
And nearer to our house above
We ev'ry moment come.

3 His grace shall to the end
Stronger and brighter shine;
Nor present things, nor things to come
Shall quench the spark divine.

4 The time of love will come,
When we shall clearly see
Not only that he shed his blood,
But each shall say, "for me."

5 Tarry his leisure, then,
Wait the appointed hour;
Wait till the bridegroom of your souls
Reveals his love with pow'r.

UNION WITH CHRIST.

HAYDN. S. M.

396   *Gal. 2:20.*   **S. M.**

1 Jesus! I live to thee,
The loveliest and best;
My life in thee, thy life in me,
In thy blest love I rest.

2 Jesus! I die to thee
Whenever death shall come;
To die in thee is life to me
In my eternal home.

3 Whether to live or die,
I know not which is best;
To live in thee is bliss to me,
To die is endless rest.

4 Living or dying, Lord!
I ask but to be thine;
My life in thee, thy life in me,
Makes heaven for ever mine.

397   *"I in them, and Thou in me."*   **S. M.**

1 Dear Saviour! we are thine,
By everlasting bands;
Our hearts, our souls, we would resign
Entirely to thy hands.

2 To thee we still would cleave
With ever-growing zeal;
If millions tempt us Christ to leave,
Oh, let them ne'er prevail!

3 Thy Spirit shall unite
Our souls to thee, our Head;
Shall form in us thine image bright,
And teach thy paths to tread.

4 Death may our souls divide
From these abodes of clay;
But love shall keep us near thy side,
Through all the gloomy way.

5 Since Christ and we are one,
Why should we doubt or fear?
If he in heaven has fixed his throne,
He'll bring his members there.

398   *Jesus our Living Head.*   **S. M.**

1 Our heavenly Father calls,
And Christ invites us near;
With both, our friendship shall be sweet,
And our communion dear.

2 God pities all our griefs;
He pardons every day,—
Almighty to protect our souls,
And wise to guide our way.

3 How large his bounties are!
What various stores of good,
Diffused from our Redeemer's hand,
And purchased with his blood!

4 Jesus, our living Head!
We bless thy faithful care,—
Our Advocate before the throne,
And our Forerunner there.

5 Here fix, my roving heart;
Here wait, my warmest love;
Till the communion be complete,
In nobler scenes above.

Doxology.   **S. M.**

The Father and the Son,
And Spirit we adore;
We praise, we bless, we worship thee,
Both now and evermore!

HOPE AND TRUST IN GOD.

HENDON. 7s

399 *"By grace are ye saved, through faith."* 7s.

1 Joyful be the hours to-day;
Joyful let the season be;
Let us sing, for well we may:
Jesus! we will sing of thee.

2 Should thy people silent be,
Then the very stones would sing:
What a debt we owe to thee,
Thee, our Saviour, thee, our King!

3 Joyful are we now to own,
Rapture thrills us as we trace
All the deeds thy love hath done,
All the riches of thy grace.

4 'Tis thy grace alone can save;
Every blessing comes from thee—
All we have and hope to have,
All we are and hope to be.

5 Thine the Name to sinners dear!
Thine the Name all names before!
Blessed here and everywhere;
Blessed now and evermore!

400 *Confidence in God's Care. Psalm 23.* 7s.

1 To thy pastures fair and large,
Heavenly Shepherd, lead thy charge;
And my couch, with tend'rest care,
'Mid the springing grass prepare.

2 When I faint with summer's heat,
Thou shalt guide my weary feet
To the streams that, still and slow,
Through the verdant meadows flow.

3 Safe the dreary vale I tread,
By the shades of death o'erspread,
With thy rod and staff supplied—
This my guard, and that my guide.

4 Constant to my latest end,
Thou my footsteps shalt attend;
Thou shalt bid thy hallowed dome
Yield me an eternal home.

401 *"Let us not sleep, as do others."* 7s.

1 Sleep not, soldier of the Cross!
Foes are lurking all around;
Look not here to find repose:
This is but thy battle-ground.

2 Up! and take thy shield and sword;
Up! it is the call of heaven:
Shrink not faithless from thy Lord;
Nobly strive as he hath striven.

3 Break through all the force of ill;
Tread the might of passion down,—
Struggling onward, onward still,
To the conqu'ring Saviour's crown!

4 Through the midst of toil and pain,
Let this thought ne'er leave thy breast:
Every triumph thou dost gain
Makes more sweet thy coming rest.

402 *Onward go.* 7s.

1 Oft in danger, oft in woe,
Onward, Christian, onward go!
Fight the fight, maintain the strife,
Strengthened with the bread of life.

CHRISTIAN WARFARE AND PRAYER.

VON WEBER. 7s.

2 Onward, Christian, onward go!
Join the war and face the foe:
Will you flee in danger's hour?
Know you not your captain's power?

3 Let your drooping heart be glad;
March, in heavenly armor clad;
Fight! nor think the battle long;
Soon shall vict'ry tune your song.

4 Let not sorrow dim your eye;
Soon shall every tear be dry:
Let not fears your course impede;
Great your strength, if great your need.

5 Onward, then, to battle move!
More than conqu'ror you shall prove;
Though opposed by many a foe,
Christian soldier, onward go!

403   *Matt. 7: 7.*   7s.

1 Come, my soul, thy suit prepare,
Jesus loves to answer prayer;
He himself has bid thee pray,
Therefore will not say thee nay.

2 Thou art coming to a King,
Large petitions with thee bring;
For his grace and power are such,
None can ever ask too much.

3 With my burden I begin,
Lord, remove this load of sin;
Let thy blood, for sinners spilt,
Set my conscience free from guilt.

4 Lord, I come to thee for rest,
Take possession of my breast;
There thy blood-bought right maintain,
And without a rival reign.

5 While I am a pilgrim here,
Let thy love my spirit cheer;
As my Guide, my Guard, my Friend,
Lead me to my journey's end.

404   *Humble request.*   7s.

1 Lord, we come before thee now,
At thy feet we humbly bow;
O! do not our suit disdain;
Shall we seek thee, Lord, in vain?

2 In thine own appointed way,
Now we seek thee,—here we stay;
Lord, from hence we could not go,
Till a blessing thou bestow.

3 Send some message from thy word,
That may joy and peace afford;
Let thy spirit now impart
Full salvation to each heart.

4 Comfort those who weep and mourn,
Let the time of joy return;
Those who are cast down lift up,
Make them strong in faith and hope.

5 Grant that all may seek and find
Thee a God supremely kind;
Heal the sick, the captive free;
Let us all rejoice in thee.

ADOPTION, LONGING, THE CHURCH,

NETTLETON. 8 & 7s. Double.

405   *"Ye are the temple of the living God."*   8s & 7s.

1 Love divine, all love excelling,
Joy of heaven to earth come down!
Fix in us thy humble dwelling;
All thy faithful mercies crown:
Jesus! thou art all compassion;
Pure, unbounded love thou art:
Visit us with thy salvation;
Enter every longing heart.

2 Finish, Lord, thy new creation;
Pure and spotless may we be:
Let us see thy great salvation
Perfectly restored in thee:
Changed from glory into glory,
Till in heaven we take our place:
Till we cast our crowns before thee,
Lost in wonder, love, and praise.

406   *The Pilgrim's Prayer.*   8s & 7s.

1 Shepherd of thine Israel! lead us,
Pilgrims o'er this barren sand;
Thou who hast from bondage freed us,
Guard us by thine outstretched hand:
    Guide thy chosen
Safely to the promised land.

2 Feed us with the heavenly manna;
Fainting, may we feel thy might;
Go before us as our banner,
Cloud by day, and fire by night:
    Great Redeemer,
Shine around us;—thou art light.

3 When we come to death's dark river,
Bid the swelling stream divide;
Thou who canst our life deliver,
Bear us through the sundered tide:
    Praises, praises
Will we sing on Canaan's side.

407   1 Sam. 7: 12.   8s & 7s.

1 Come, thou fount of ev'ry blessing,
Tune my heart to sing thy grace;
Streams of mercy, never ceasing,
Call for songs of loudest praise.
Teach me some melodious sonnet,
Sung by flaming tongues above;
Praise the mount—I'm fixed upon it—
Mount of God's unchanging love.

2 Here I raise my Eben-Ezer,
Hither by thy help I'm come;
And I hope, by thy good pleasure,
Safely to arrive at home.
Jesus sought me when a stranger,
Wand'ring from the fold of God,
He to rescue me from danger,
Interpos'd with precious blood.

3 Oh! to grace how great a debtor,
Daily I'm constrain'd to be!
Let that grace now, like a fetter,
Bind my wand'ring heart to thee;
Prone to wander, Lord, I feel it—
Prone to leave the God I love;
Here's my heart—O take and seal it;
Seal it from thy courts above.

AND MISSIONS.

GREENVILLE. 8s, 7s & 4s.

408 *"Zion, city of our God."* 8s & 7s.
1 Glorious things of thee are spoken,
Zion, city of our God;
He whose word can ne'er be broken
Choose thee for his own abode.

2 Lord, thy Church is still thy dwelling,
Still is precious in thy sight;
Judah's temple far excelling,
Beaming with the Gospel's light.

3 On the Rock of Ages founded,
What can shake her sure repose?
With salvation's wall surrounded,
She can smile at all her foes.

4 Glorious things of thee are spoken,
Zion, city of our God;
He whose word can ne'er be broken
Chose thee for his own abode.

409 *"Thy kingdom come." Matt. 6:10.* 8s & 7s.
1 O'er the gloomy hills of darkness
Look, my soul! be still,—and gaze;
See the promises advancing
To a glorious day of grace:
    Blessed jubilee!
Let thy glorious morning dawn.

2 Let the dark, benighted pagan,
Let the rude barbarian see
That divine and glorious conquest,
Once obtained on Calvary:
    Let the Gospel
Loud resound, from pole to pole!

3 Kingdoms wide that sit in darkness—
Grant them, Lord, the glorious light;
Now from eastern coast to western
May the morning chase the night;
    Let redemption,
Freely purchased, win the day.

4 Fly abroad, thou mighty gospel!
Win and conquer,—never cease;
May thy lasting, wide dominions
Multiply and still increase:
    Sway thy scepter,
Saviour! all the world around.

Doxology. 8s & 7s.
Praise the God of our salvation,
Praise the Father's boundless love;
Praise the Lamb, our expiation;
Praise the Spirit from above:
Praise the Fountain of salvation,
Him by whom our spirits live;
Undivided adoration
To the one Jehovah give!

JOY, HOPE AND

RETREAT. L. M.

410   *"While I live will I praise the Lord."*   **L. M.**

1 God of my life! through all my days
My grateful powers shall sound thy praise;
The song shall wake with opening light,
And warble to the silent night.

2 When anxious care would break my rest,
And grief would tear my throbbing breast,
Thy tuneful praises raised on high,
Shall check the murmur and the sigh.

3 When death o'er nature shall prevail,
And all my powers of language fail,
Joy through my swimming eyes shall break,
And mean the thanks I cannot speak.

4 But, oh! when that last conflict's o'er,
And I am chained to flesh no more,
With what glad accents shall I rise
To join the music of the skies!

411   *"What sinners value, I resign." Psalm 17.*   **L. M.**

1 What sinners value, I resign;
Lord, 't is enough that thou art mine:
I shall behold thy blissful face,
And stand complete in righteousness.

2 This life's a dream, an empty show;
But the bright world to which I go
Hath joys substantial and sincere:
When shall I wake and find me there?

3 Oh, glorious hour! oh, blest abode!
I shall be near and like my God;
And flesh and sin no more control
The sacred pleasures of the soul.

4 My flesh shall slumber in the ground
Till the last trumpet's joyful sound;
Then burst the chains with sweet surprise,
And in my Saviour's image rise!

412   *Faith exemplified in the Life. Tit. 2 : 10—13.*   **L. M.**

1 So let our lips and lives express
The holy gospel we profess;
So let our works and virtues shine,
To prove the doctrine all divine.

2 Thus shall we best proclaim abroad
The honors of our Saviour God;
When his salvation reigns within,
And grace subdues the power of sin.

3 Our flesh and sense must be denied,
Passion and envy, lust and pride;
While justice, temperance, truth, and love,
Our inward piety approve.

4 Religion bears our spirits up,
While we expect that blessed hope,
The bright appearance of the Lord,—
And faith stands leaning on his word.

413   *Trust in Christ at the hour of death.*   **L. M.**

1 Jesus, in whom but thee above
Can I repose my trust, my love?
And shall an earthly object be
Loved in comparison with thee?

2 How soon, O Lord, will life decay!
How soon this world will pass away!
Ah! what can mortal friends avail,
When heart and strength and life shall fail!

3 Oh, then, be thou, my Saviour, nigh,
And I will triumph while I die;
My strength, my portion, is divine,
And Jesus is forever mine!

TRUST IN GOD.

HALLET. L. M. — Geo. Kingsley.

414 *Looking to God in Trouble.* L. M.

1 God of my life! to thee I call;
Afflicted, at thy feet I fall;
When high the water-floods prevail,
Leave not my trembling heart to fail.

2 Friend of the friendless and the faint,
Where should I lodge my deep complaint—
Where but with thee, whose open door
Invites the helpless and the poor?

3 Did ever mourner plead with thee,
And thou refuse that mourner's plea?
Doth not the word still fixed remain,
That none shall seek thy face in vain?

4 Poor though I am—despised, forgot,
Yet God, my God, forgets me not;
And he is safe, and must succeed,
For whom the Lord vouchsafes to plead.

415 *"I will praise thee forever because thou hast done it."* L. M.

1 Redeem'd from guilt, redeem'd from fears,
My soul enlarged and dried my tears,
What can I do, O Love divine,
What, to repay such gifts as thine?

2 What can I do, so poor, so weak,
But from Thy hands new blessings seek,
A heart to feel Thy mercies more,
A soul to know Thee, and adore?

O teach me at Thy feet to fall,
And yield Thee up myself, my all!

Before Thy saints my debts to own,
And live and die to Thee alone!

4 Thy Spirit, Lord, at large impart,
Expand and raise and fill my heart!
So may I hope my life shall be
Some faint return, O Lord, to Thee.

416 *"Search me, O God, and know my heart."* L. M.

1 O Thou, to whose all-searching sight,
The darkness shineth as the light,
Search, prove my heart, it pants for Thee;
Oh, burst these bonds and set it free!

2 Wash out its stains, refine its dross,
Nail my affections to the cross:
Hallow each thought, let all within
Be clean, as Thou, my Lord, art clean.

3 If in this darksome wild I stray
Be Thou my light, be Thou my Way;
No foes, no violence I fear,
No fraud, while Thou, my God, art near.

4 When rising floods my soul o'erflow,
When sinks my heart in waves of woe,
Jesus, Thy timely aid impart,
And raise my head and cheer my heart.

Doxology. L. M.

To Father, Son and Holy Ghost,
The God whom earth and heaven adore,
Be glory as it was of old,
Is now, and shall be evermore.

EVAN. C. M.

417 *Walking with God.* Gen. 5: 24. **C. M.**

1 O for a closer walk with God,
A calm and heav'nly frame,
A light to shine upon the road
That leads me to the Lamb!

2 Where is the blessedness I knew,
When first I saw the Lord?
Where is the soul-refreshing view
Of Jesus and his word?

3 What peaceful hours I then enjoy'd!
How sweet their mem'ry still!
But now I find an aching void
The world can never fill.

4 Return, O holy Dove! return,
Sweet messenger of rest!
I hate the sins that made thee mourn,
And drove thee from my breast.

5 The dearest idol I have known,
Whate'er that idol be,
Help me to tear it from thy throne,
And worship only thee.

6 So shall my walk be close with God,
Calm and serene my frame;
So purer light shall mark the ro
That leads me to the Lamb.

418 *"In my Father's house are many mansions."* **C. M.**

1 When I can read my title clear
To mansions in the skies,
I bid farewell to every fear,
And wipe my weeping eyes.

2 Should earth against my soul engage,
And hellish darts be hurled,
Then I can smile at Satan's rage,
And face a frowning world.

3 Let cares like a wild deluge come,
And storms of sorrow fall;
May I but safely reach my home,
My God, my heaven, my all,—

4 There shall I bathe my weary soul
In seas of heavenly rest,
And not a wave of trouble roll
Across my peaceful breast.

419 *The happiness of a Christian.* **C. M.**

1 O happy soul that lives on high!
While men lie grov'ling here,
His hopes are fix'd above the sky,
And faith forbids his fear.

2 His conscience knows no secret stings,
While grace and joy combine
To form a life, whose holy springs
Are hidden and divine.

3 He waits in secret on his God,
His God in secret sees;
Let earth be all in arms abroad,
He dwells in heav'nly peace.

4 His pleasures rise from things unseen,
Beyond this world and time,
Where neither eyes nor ears have been,
Nor thoughts of mortals climb.

5 He looks to heav'n's eternal hill,
To meet that glorious day,
When Christ his promise shall fulfill,
And call his soul away.

TRUST IN GOD.

BERNARD. C. M.

420 *Resting in God.* **C. M.**

1 Whilst thee I seek, protecting Power!
Be my vain wishes stilled;
And may this consecrated honr
With better hopes be filled!

2 Thy love the power of thought bestowed;
To thee my thoughts would soar;
Thy mercy o'er my life has flowed;
That mercy I adore.

3 In every joy that crowns my days,
In every pain I bear,
My heart shall find delight in praise,
Or seek relief in prayer.

4 When gladness wings my favored hour,
Thy love my thoughts shall fill;
Resigned, when storms of sorrow lower,
My soul shall meet thy will.

5 My lifted eye, without a tear,
The gathering storm shall see:
My steadfast heart shall know no fear;
That heart will rest on thee.

421 *Living to God.* **C. M.**

1 O thou, the Lord and Life of those
Who rest their hope in Thee;
Whose love, from everlasting woes,
Hath set Thy people free;

2 Thine agony and death display
The curse our guilt should bear;
Thy resurrection points the way
To bliss that we may share.

3 To thee, O Lord, we lift our heart,
Thy mercy we implore;
Help us to choose the better part,
And go, and sin no more.

4 Help us the Saviour to confess,
In whom our life to see;
And oh! may fruits of holiness
Prove that we live to Thee,

422 *"Walk in the light."*—1 John 1: 7. **C. M.**

1 Walk in the light! so shalt thou know
That fellowship of love
His Spirit only can bestow,
Who reigns in light above.

2 Walk in the light; and thou shalt own
Thy darkness passed away,
Because that light on thee hath shone
In which is perfect day.

3 Walk in the light! and ev'n the tomb
No fearful shade shall wear:
Glory shall chase away its gloom,
For Christ hath conquered there!

4 Walk in the light! and thine shall be
A path, though thorny, bright;
For God, by grace, shall dwell in thee,
And God himself is light!

Doxology. **C. M.**

To Father, Son, and Holy Ghost,
One God, whom we adore,
Be glory as it was, is now,
And shall be evermore.

JOY, HOPE, AND

WOODLAND. C. M.

423 *"Dear Refuge of my weary soul."* **C. M.**

1 Dear Refuge of my weary soul,
On thee, when sorrows rise—
On thee, when waves of trouble roll,
My fainting hope relies.

2 To thee I tell each rising grief,
For thou alone canst heal;
Thy word can bring a sweet relief
For every pain I feel.

3 Hast thou not bid me seek thy face?
And shall I seek in vain?
And can the ear of sovereign grace
Be deaf when I complain?

4 No; still the ear of sovereign grace
Attends the mourner's prayer;
Oh, may I ever find access
To breathe my sorrows there!

5 Thy mercy-seat is open still;
Here let my soul retreat,
With humble hope attend thy will,
And wait beneath thy feet.

424 *"Lord, I believe; help Thou mine unbelief."—Mark 9: 24.* **C. M.**

1 Lord, I believe; thy power I own,
Thy word I would obey;
I wander comfortless and lone,
When from thy truth I stray.

2 Lord, I believe; but gloomy fears
Sometimes bedim my sight;
I look to thee with prayers and tears,
And cry for strength and light.

3 Lord, I believe; but oft I know,
My faith is cold and weak;
My weakness strengthen, and bestow
The confidence I seek!

4 Yes! I believe; and only thou
Canst give my soul relief;
Lord! to thy truth my spirit bow;
"Help thou mine unbelief!"

425 *"Secure from every foe."* **C. M.**

1 Grant me within thy courts a place,
Among thy saints a seat,
For ever to behold thy face,
And worship at thy feet;

2 In thy pavilion to abide
When storms of trouble blow,
And in thy tabernacle hide,
Secure from every foe.

3 Then leave me not when griefs assail
And earthly comforts flee;
When father, mother, kindred, fail,
My God! remember me.

4 Wait on the Lord, with courage wait;
My soul, disdain to fear;
The righteous Judge is at the gate,
And thy redemption near.

426 *"Victory through our Lord Jesus Christ."—1 Cor. 15: 55.* **C. M.**

1 O for an overcoming faith
To cheer my dying hours!
To triumph o'er the monster, Death,
And all his frightful powers.

TRUST IN GOD.

COWPER. C. M.

2 Joyful, with all the strength I have,
My quiv'ring lips should sing, }
"Where is thy boasted vict'ry, Grave?
And where the monster's sting?"

3 If sin be pardoned, I'm secure;
Death hath no sting beside:
The law gives sin its damning power,
But Christ, my ransom, died.

4 Now to the God of victory
Immortal thanks be paid,
Who makes us conqu'rors while we die,
Through Christ, our living Head!

427   1 Cor. 6: 20.   C. M.

1 And must I part with all I have,
My dearest Lord, for thee?
It is but right, since thou hast done
Much more than this for me.

2 Ten thousand worlds, ten thousand lives,
How worthless they appear,
Compared with thee, supremely good,
Divinely bright and fair!

3 Saviour of souls, while I from thee
A single smile obtain,
Though destitute of all things else,
I'll glory in my gain.

428   "Trusting all in God."   C. M.

1 Father of love, our Guide and Friend,
Oh lead us gently on,
Until life's trial time shall end,
And heavenly peace be won!

2 We know not what the path may be
As yet by us untrod;
But we can trust our all to Thee,
Our Father and our God!

429   "Under the shadow of the Almighty."—Psalm 34.   C. M.

1 Through all the changing scenes of life,
In trouble and in joy,
The praises of my God shall still
My heart and tongue employ.

2 Of his deliverance I will boast,
Till all who are distressed
From my example comfort take,
And charm their griefs to rest.

3 Oh, magnify the Lord with me,
With me exalt his name!
When in distress to him I called,
He to my rescue came.

4 The hosts of God encamp around
The dwellings of the just;
Deliverance he affords to all
Who on his succor trust.

5 Oh, make but trial of his love:
Experience will decide
How blest are they, and only they,
Who in his truth confide.

6 Fear him, ye saints, and ye will then
Have nothing else to fear;
Make ye his service your delight,
He'll make your wants his care.

Doxology.   C. M.

Let God the Father and the Son,
And Spirit be adored,
Where there are works to make him known,
Or saints to love the Lord.

THE CHRISTIAN WARFARE.

ORTONVILLE. C. M.

430 *"Am I a soldier of the Cross."*
2 Tim. 2: 3.   C. M.

1 Am I a soldier of the cross,
A follower of the Lamb?
And shall I fear to own his cause,
Or blush to speak his name?

2 Must I be carried to the skies
On flowery beds of ease,
While others fought to win the prize,
And sailed through bloody seas?

3 Are there no foes for me to face?
Must I not stem the flood?
Is this vile world a friend to grace,
To help me on to God?

4 Sure I must fight if I would reign;
Increase my courage, Lord!
I'll bear the toil, endure the pain,
Supported by thy word.

5 Thy saints, in all this glorious war,
Shall conquer, though they die;
They view the triumph from afar,
And seize it with their eye.

6 When that illustrious day shall rise,
And all thine armies shine
In robes of vict'ry through the skies,
The glory shall be thine.

431 *The Heavenly Race.—Phil. 3: 14.*   C. M.

1 Awake, my soul! stretch every nerve,
And press with vigor on:
A heavenly race demands thy zeal,
A bright, immortal crown.

2 A cloud of witnesses around
Hold thee in full survey:
Forget the steps already trod,
And onward urge thy way.

3 'Tis God's all animating voice,
That calls thee from on high;
'Tis his own hand presents the prize
To thine aspiring eye,—

4 That prize with peerless glories bright,
Which shall new luster boast,
When victor's wreaths and monarch's gems
Shall blend in common dust.

5 Blest Saviour, introduced by thee,
Have I my race begun;
And, crowned with vict'ry, at thy feet
I'll lay my honors down.

432 *The Cross and the Crown.*   C. M.

1 Must Jesus bear the cross alone,
And all the world go free?
No; there's a cross for every one,
And there's a cross for me.

2 How happy are the saints above
Who once went sorrowing here;
But now they taste unmingled love,
And joy without a tear.

3 The consecrated cross I'll bear,
Till death shall set me free,
And then go home my crown to wear—
For there's a crown for me!

THE CHRISTIAN WARFARE.

DEVIZES. C. M.

433 *"It is I; be not afraid."*
Matt. 14: 27. **C. M.**

1 When waves of trouble round me swell,
My soul is not dismayed;
I hear a voice I know full well:
"'Tis I; be not afraid."

2 When black the threatening clouds appear,
And storms my path invade,
That voice shall calm each rising fear:
"'Tis I; be not afraid."

3 There is a gulf that must be crossed:
Saviour! be near to aid;
Whisper, when my frail bark is tossed,
"'Tis I; be not afraid."

4 There is a dark and fearful vale,—
Death hides within its shade;
Oh, say, when flesh and heart shall fail,
"'Tis I; be not afraid!"

434 *"The cross before the crown."* **C. M**

1 O, speed' thee, Christian! on thy way,
And to thine armor cling;
With girded loins the call obey
Which grace and mercy bring.

2 There is a battle to be fought,
An upward race to run,
A crown of glory to be sought,
A vict'ry to be won.

3 Oh, faint not, Christian! for thy sighs
Are heard before the throne;
The race must come before the prize,
The cross before the crown.

435 *"Through flood and flames."* **C. M.**

1 We seek a rest beyond the skies,
In everlasting day;
Through flood and flames the passage lies,
But Jesus guards the way.

2 The swelling flood, the raging flame,
Hear and obey His word;
Then let us triumph in His name,
Our Saviour is the Lord.

436 *"Haste Thee to help me."*
Psalm 22. **C. M.**

1 O, help us, Lord!—each hour of need
Thy heavenly succor give;
Help us in thought, and word, and deed,
Each hour on earth we live.

2 Oh, help us when our spirits bleed,
With contrite anguish sore;
And when our hearts are cold and dead,
Oh, help us, Lord, the more!

3 Oh, help us, through the power of faith,
More firmly to believe!
For still the more the servant hath
The more shall he receive.

4 O, help us, Jesus! from on high
We know no help but thee;
Oh, help us so to live and die,
As thine in heaven to be!

Doxology. **C. M.**

The Father's Name we loudly raise,
The Son we all adore,
The Holy Ghost, One God, we praise,
Both now and evermore.

THE CHRISTIAN WARFARE.

MISSIONARY CHANT. L. M.

437 *"Stand up, my soul, shake off thy fears."* **L. M.**

1 Stand up, my soul! shake off thy fears,
And gird the Gospel armor on;
March to the gates of endless joy,
Where Jesus, thy great Captain's gone.

2 Hell and thy sins resist thy course;
But hell and sin are vanquished foes:
Thy Jesus nailed them to the cross,
And sung the triumph when he rose.

3 Then let my soul march boldly on;
Press forward to the heavenly gate:
There peace and joy eternal reign,
And glitt'ring robes for conquerors wait.

4 There shall I wear a starry crown,
And triumph in almighty grace,
While all the armies of the skies
Join in my glorious Leader's praise.

438 *"They shall mount up with wings as eagles.—Isa. 40: 31."* **L. M.**

1 Awake, our souls! away our fears!
Let every trembling thought be gone;
Awake, and run the heavenly race,
And put a cheerful courage on.

2 True, 'tis a strait and thorny road,
And mortal spirits tire and faint;
But they forget the mighty God,
Who feeds the strength of every saint—

3 The mighty God, whose matchless power
Is ever new and ever young,
And firm endures, while endless years
Their everlasting circles run.

4 From thee, the overflowing spring,
Our souls shall drink a fresh supply;
While such as trust their native strength
Shall melt away, and droop, and die.

5 Swift as an eagle cuts the air
We'll mount aloft to thine abode;
On wings of love our souls shall fly,
Nor tire amid the heavenly road!

439 *"Lord; save us, we perish!"* **L. M.**

1 The billows swell, the winds are high;
Clouds overcast my wint'ry sky:
Out of the depths to thee I call;
My fears are great, my strength is small.

2 O Lord, the pilot's part perform,
And guide and guard me through the storm,
Defend me from each threatening ill:
Control the waves; say, "Peace! be still."

3 Amid the roaring of the sea,
My soul still hangs her hope on thee;
Thy constant love, thy faithful care,
Is all that saves me from despair.

4 Though tempest-tossed and half a wreck,
My Saviour through the floods I seek:
Let neither winds nor stormy main
Force back my shattered bark again.

440 *"Stand therefore—taking the shield of faith."—Eph. 6: 12.* **L. M.**

1 Awake, my soul! lift up thine eyes;
See where thy foes against thee rise,
In long array, a numerous host;
Awake, my soul, or thou art lost!

THE CHRISTIAN WARFARE.

LUTON. L. M.

2 Thou tread'st upon enchanted ground;
Perils and snares beset thee round;
Beware of all; guard every part;
But most, the traitor in thy heart.

3 Come then, my soul! now learn to wield
The weight of thine immortal shield;
Put on the armor, from above,
Of heavenly truth, and heavenly love.

4 The terror and the charm repel,
And powers of earth, and powers of hell;
The Man of Calvary triumphed here:
Why should his faithful followers fear?

441   *"Go, labor on."*   **L. M.**

1 Go, labor on; your hands are weak,
Your knees are faint, your soul cast down;
Yet falter not; the prize you seek
Is near,—a kingdom and a crown!

2 Go, labor on, while it is day;
The world's dark night is hastening on;
Speed, speed thy work,—cast sloth away!
It is not thus that souls are won.

3 Men die in darkness at your side,
Without a hope to cheer the tomb;
Take up the torch and wave it wide—
The torch that lights time's thickest gloom.

4 Toil on,—faint not,—keep watch and pray!
Be wise the erring soul to win;
Go forth into the world's highway;
Compel the wanderer to come in.

442   *The Christian Race.*   **L. M.**

1 Amidst a world of hopes and fears,
A world of cares, and toils, and tears,
Where foes alarm, and tempests beat,
And pleasures kill, and glories cheat:

2 Send down, O Lord! a heavenly ray,
To guide me in the doubtful way;
And o'er me hold Thy shield of power,
To guard me in the dang'rous hour.

3 Teach me the flatt'ring paths to shun,
In which the thoughtless many run,
Who for a shade the substance miss,
And grasp their ruin in their bliss.

4 May never pleasure, wealth, or pride,
Allure my wand'ring soul aside;
But through this maze of mortal ill,
Safe lead me to Thy heav'nly hill.

5 There glories shine, and pleasures roll,
That charm, delight, transport the soul,
And every longing wish shall be
Possess'd of boundless bliss in Thee.

Doxology.   **L. M.**

Eternal Father! throned above,
Thou fountain of redeeeming love!
Eternal Word! who left thy throne
For man's rebellion to atone;
Eternal Spirit, who dost give
That grace whereby our spirits live·
Thou God of our salvation, be
Eternal praises paid to thee!

THE CHRISTIAN WARFARE.

BARBER. S. M.

443 *Mark 13: 37.*

1 A charge to keep I have,
A God to glorify;
A never-dying soul to save,
And fit it for the sky.

2 To serve the present age,
My calling to fulfill;
O may it all my pow'rs engage
To do my Master's will.

3 Arm me with jealous care,
As in thy sight to live:
And O thy servant, Lord, prepare
A strict account to give.

4 Help me to watch and pray,
And on thyself rely:
Assur'd if I my trust betray,
I shall for ever die.

444 *"Watch and pray."*

1 My soul! be on thy guard;
Ten thousand foes arise;
The hosts of sin are pressing hard
To draw thee from the skies.

2 Oh, watch, and fight, and pray!
The battle ne'er give o'er;
Renew it boldly every day,
And help divine implore.

3 Ne'er think the victory won,
Nor once at ease sit down;
Thy arduous work will not be done
Till thou obtain thy crown.

S. M.

4 Fight on, my soul, till death
Shall bring thee to thy God!
He'll take thee at thy parting breath,
Up to his blest abode.

445 *"So fight I, not as one that beateth the air."* **S. M.**

1 My soul! weigh not thy life
Against thy heavenly crown,
Nor suffer Satan's deadliest strife
To beat thy courage down.

2 With prayer and crying strong,
Hold on the fearful fight;
And let the breaking day prolong
The wrestling of the night.

3 The battle soon will yield,
If thou thy part fulfill;
For, strong as is the hostile shield,
Thy sword is stronger still.

S. M.

4 Thine armor is divine,—
Thy feet with vict'ry shod:
And on thy head shall quickly shine
The diadem of God!

446 *"Rejoicing in hope."* **S. M.**

1 Come, we that love the Lord,
And let our joys be known;
Join in a song of sweet accord,
And thus surround the throne.

2 Let those refuse to sing
Who never knew our God;
But favorites of the heavenly King
May speak their joys abroad.

THE CHRISTIAN WARFARE.

LISBON. S. M.

3 The men of grace have found
Glory begun below;
Celestial fruits on earthly ground
From faith and hope may grow.

4 The hill of Zion yields
A thousand sacred sweets,
Before we reach the heavenly fields,
Or walk the golden streets.

5 Then let our songs abound,
And every tear be dry:
We're marching through Immanuel's ground
To fairer worlds on high.

447   *The Lord will guide.*   S. M.

1 The Lord Himself will keep
His people safe from harm;
Will hold the helm, and guide the ship,
With His Almighty arm.

2 Then let the tempests roar,
The billows heave and swell;
We trust to reach the peaceful shore
Where all the ransomed dwell:

3 And when we gain the land,
How happy shall we be!
How shall we bless the mighty hand
That led us through the sea!

448   *Heb. 1: 14*   S. M.

1 Heirs of unending life,
While yet we sojourn here,
Oh let us our salvation work
With trembling and with fear.

2 God will support our hearts
With might before unknown;
The work to be performed is ours,
The strength is all His own.

3 'Tis He that works to will,
'Tis He that works to do;
His is the power by which we act,
His be the glory too!

449   *Psalm 23.*   S. M.

1 While my Redeemer's near,
My Shepherd and my Guide,
I bid farewell to anxious fear;
My wants are all supplied.

2 To ever fragrant meads
Where rich abundance grows,
His gracious hand indulgent leads,
And guards my sweet repose.

3 Dear Shepherd, if I stray,
My wandering feet restore;
To Thy fair pastures guide my way,
And let me rove no more.

Doxology.   S. M.

Praise to the Father be;
Praise to His Only Son;
Praise to the blessed Paraclete,
While endless ages run.

LOVE TO GOD, AND

CHESTNUT STREET. C. M.

450 *"Thou knowest that I love Thee."* **C. M.**
John 21: 15—17.

1 Do not I love thee, O my Lord?
Behold my heart and see;
And turn the dearest idol out
That dares to rival thee.

2 Do not I love thee from my soul?
Then let me nothing love:
Dead be my heart to every joy
When Jesus cannot move.

3 Is not thy name melodious still
To mine attentive ear?
Doth not each pulse with pleasure bound
My Saviour's voice to hear?

4 Hast thou a lamb in all thy flock
I would disdain to feed?
Hast thou a foe before whose face
I fear thy cause to plead?

5 Would not my heart pour forth its blood
In honor of thy name?
And challenge the cold hand of death
To damp th' immortal flame?

6 Thou know'st I love thee, dearest Lord;
But, oh! I long to soar
Far from the sphere of mortal joys,
And learn to love thee more.

451 *The beloved Name.* **C. M.**

1 Blest Jesus! when my soaring thoughts
O'er all thy graces rove,
How is my soul in transport lost,—
In wonder, joy, and love!

2 Not softest strains can charm my ears,
Like thy beloved name;
Nor aught beneath the skies inspire
My heart with equal flame.

3 Where'er I look, my wondering eyes
Unnumbered blessings see;
But what is life, with all its bliss,
If once compared with thee?

4 Hast thou a rival in my breast?
Search, Lord, for thou canst tell
If aught can raise my passions thus,
Or please my soul so well.

5 No: thou art precious to my heart,
My portion and my joy:
For ever let thy boundless grace
My sweetest thoughts employ.

452 *The Chief Grace.* **C. M.**

1 Happy the heart where graces reign,
Where love inspires the breast;
Love is the brightest of the train,
And strengthens all the rest.

2 Knowledge—alas! 't is all in vain,
And all in vain our fear;
Our stubborn sins will fight and reign,
If love be absent there.

3 This is the grace that lives and sings,
When faith and hope shall cease;
'Tis this shall strike our joyful strings,
In realms of endless peace.

MAN.

BOARDMAN. C. M.

4 Before we quite forsake our clay,
Or leave this dark abode,
The wings of love bear us away,
To see our smiling God.

453 *"Love as brethren."* C. M.

1 How sweet, how heavenly is the sight,
When those who love the Lord
In one another's peace delight,
And so fulfill his word!

2 When each can feel his brother's sigh,
And with him bear a part!
When sorrow flows from eye to eye,
And joy from heart to heart!

3 When, free from envy, scorn, and pride,
Our wishes all above,
Each can his brother's failings hide
And show a brother's love!

4 Let love, in one delightful stream,
Through every bosom flow,
And union sweet, and dear esteem
In every action glow.

5 Love is the golden chain that binds
The happy souls above;
And he's an heir of heaven who finds
His bosom glow with love.

454 *The Spirit of Peace.—Ps. 133.* C. M.

1 Spirit of peace! celestial Dove!
How excellent thy praise!
No richer gift than Christian love
Thy gracious power displays.

2 Sweet as the dew on herb and flower
That silently distills,
At evening's soft and balmy hour,
On Zion's fruitful hills,—

3 So, with mild influence from above,
Shall promised grace descend,
Till universal peace and love
O'er all the earth extend!

455 *"Beloved, let us love one another."* C. M.

1 Our God is love: and all His saints
His image bear below;
The heart with love to God inspir'd,
With love to man will glow.

2 O may we love each other, Lord,
As we are loved of Thee:
For none are truly born of God,
Who live in enmity.

3 Heirs of the same immortal bliss,
Our hopes and fears the same,
The cords of love our hearts should bind,
The law of love inflame.

4 So shall the vain contentious world
Our peaceful lives approve,
And wondering say, as they of old,
"See how these Christians love."

Doxology. C. M.

To Father, Son, and Holy Ghost,
The God whom we adore,
Be glory as it was, is now,
And shall be evermore.

LONGING.

BETHANY. 6s & 4s.

456 *"Nearer to God."* 6s & 4s.

1 Nearer, my God! to thee,
Nearer to thee!
E'en though it be a cross
That raiseth me!
Still all my song shall be,
Nearer, my God! to thee,
Nearer to thee!

2 Though like the wanderer,
The sun gone down,
Darkness be over me,
My rest a stone,
Yet in my dreams I'd be
Nearer, my God! to thee,
Nearer to thee!

3 There let the way appear,
Steps unto heaven!
All that thou sendest me,
In mercy given;
Angels to beckon me
Nearer, my God! to thee,
Nearer to thee!

4 Then, with my waking thoughts
Bright with thy praise,
Out of my stony griefs
Bethel I'll raise;
So by my woes to be
Nearer, my God! to thee,
Nearer to thee!

5 Or if, on joyful wing
Cleaving the sky,
Sun, moon and stars forgot,
Upward I fly,
Still all my song shall be,
Nearer, my God! to thee,
Nearer to thee!

457 *"More love for Christ."* 6s & 4s.

1 More love to thee, O Christ!
More love to thee!
Hear thou the prayer I make
On bended knee;
This is my earnest plea:
More love, O Christ! to thee,
More love to thee!

2 Once earthly joy I craved,
Sought peace and rest;
Now thee alone I seek—
Give what is best;
This all my prayer shall be:
More love, O Christ! to thee,
More love to thee!

3 Let sorrow do its work,
Send grief and pain;
Sweet are thy messengers,
Sweet their refrain,
When they can sing with me,
More love, O Christ! to thee,
More love to thee!

4 Then shall my latest breath
Whisper thy praise;
This be the parting cry
My heart shall raise,
This still its prayer shall be:
More love, O Christ! to thee,
More love to thee!

LONGING.

FATHERLAND. 6s & 4.

458 *Cant. 2: 16* 6s & 4s.

1 Fade, fade, each earthly joy;
Jesus is mine!
Break, every tender tie;
Jesus is mine!
Dark is the wilderness,
Earth has no resting-place,
Jesus alone can bless;
Jesus is mine!

2 Tempt not my soul away;
Jesus is mine!
Here would I ever stay;
Jesus is mine!
Perishing things of clay,
Born but for one brief day,
Pass from my heart away;
Jesus is mine!

3 Farewell, ye dreams of night,
Jesus is mine!
Lost in this dawning bright;
Jesus is mine!
All that my soul has tried,
Left but a dismal void;
Jesus has satisfied;
Jesus is mine!

4 Farewell, mortality;
Jesus is mine!
Welcome, eternity;
Jesus is mine!
Welcome, O loved and blest,
Welcome, sweet scenes of rest,
Welcome, my Savior's breast;
Jesus is mine!

459 *"Trust in Christ."* 6s & 4s.

1 No, not despairngly
Come I to Thee;
No, not distrustingly
Bend I the knee;
Sin hath gone over me;
Yet is this still my plea,
Jesus hath died.

2 Lord, I confess to Thee
Sadly my sin;
All I am, tell I thee;
All I have been;
Purge Thou my sin away,
Wash Thou my soul this day;
Lord, make me clean.

3 Faithful and just art Thou,
Forgiving all;
Loving and kind art Thou
When poor ones call:
Lord, let the cleansing blood,
Blood of the Lamb of God,
Pass o'er my soul!

Doxology. 6s & 4s.

To God, the Father, Son,
All praise be given!
And Spirit, Three in One,
  All praise be given!
Crown him in every song;
To him your hearts belong
Let all his praise prolong
  On earth, in heaven!

LONGING.

CORONATION. C. M.

460   *Rev. 21: 10.*   C. M.

1 O mother dear, Jerusalem,
When shall I come to thee!
When shall my sorrows have an end,
Thy joys when shall I see!

2 O happy harbor of God's saints!
O sweet and pleasant soil!
In thee no sorrow can be found,
Nor grief, nor care, nor toil.

3 No dimming cloud o'ershadows thee,
Nor gloom, nor darksome night;
But every soul shines as the sun,
For God Himself gives light.

4 Thy walls are made of precious stone,
Thy bulwarks diamond-square,
Thy gates are all of orient pearl—
O God! if I were there!

5 Right through thy streets, with pleasing sound
The flood of life doth flow,
And on the banks, on either side,
The trees of life do grow.

6 Those trees each month yield ripened fruit,
For ever more they spring;
And all the nations of the earth
To thee their honors bring.

7 There the blest souls that hardly 'scaped
The snare of death and hell,
Triumph in joy eternally,
Whereof no tongue can tell.

8 O mother dear, Jerusalem!
When shall I come to thee?
When shall my sorrows have an end?
Thy joys when shall I see?

461   *Rev. 7: 15.*   C. M.

1 Jerusalem, my happy home,
Name ever dear to me!
When shall my labors have an end
In joy and peace, in thee?

2 When shall these eyes thy heaven-built walls
And pearly gates behold?
Thy bulwarks with salvation strong,
And streets of shining gold?

3 Oh when, thou city of my God,
Shall I thy courts ascend,
Where congregations ne'er break up,
And Sabbaths have no end?

4 There happier bowers than Eden's bloom,
Nor sin nor sorrow know:
Blest seats! through rude and stormy scenes,
I onward press to you.

5 Apostles, martyrs, prophets, there
Around my Saviour stand;
And soon my friends in Christ below,
Will join the glorious band.

6 Jerusalem, my happy home!
My soul still pants for thee;
Then shall my labors have an end,
When I thy joys shall see.

LONGING.

NEWBOLD. C. M.

462 *"Earnestly desiring to be clothed upon."* C. M.

1 Father! I long, I faint, to see
The place of thine abode;
I'd leave thine earthly courts, and flee
Up to thy seat, my God!

2 There all the heavenly hosts are seen;
In shining ranks they move;
And drink immortal vigor in,
With wonder and with love.

3 Then at thy feet, with awful fear,
Th' adoring armies fall;
With joy they shrink to nothing there,
Before th' eternal All.

4 The more thy glories strike my eyes,
The humbler I shall lie;
Thus while I sink, my joys shall rise
Immeasurably high.

463 *"When shall I see my Father's face?"* C. M.

1 On Jordan's stormy banks I stand,
And cast a wishful eye
To Canaan's fair and happy land,
Where my possessions lie.

2 Oh the transporting, rapturous scene,
That rises to my sight!
Sweet fields arrayed in living green,
And rivers of delight!

3 O'er all those wide extended plains
Shines one eternal day;
There God, the Sun, forever reigns,
And scatters night away.

4 No chilling winds, no poisonous breath
Can reach that healthful shore;
Sickness and sorrow, pain and death
Are felt and feared no more.

5 When shall I reach that happy place,
And be forever blest?
When shall I see my Father's face,
And in his bosom rest.

6 Filled with delight, my raptured soul
Can here no longer stay;
Though Jordan's waves around me roll,
Fearless I'd launch away.

464 *Holiness of Heaven.* 1 Cor. 2: 9, 10. C. M.

1 Nor eye hath seen, nor ear hath heard,
Nor sense nor reason known,
What joys the Father has prepared
For those that love his Son.

2 But the good Spirit of the Lord
Reveals a heaven to come;
The beams of glory in his word
Allure and guide us home.

3 Pure are the joys above the sky,
And all the region peace,
No wanton lips, nor envious eye
Can see or taste the bliss.

4 Those holy gates forever bar
Pollution, sin, and shame;
None shall obtain admittance there,
But followers of the Lamb.

LONGING.

LUTHER. S. M.

465 *The Pilgrim's Song.* S. M.

1 A few more years shall roll,
A few more seasons come;
And we shall be with those that rest,
Asleep within the tomb.

2 Then, O my Lord, prepare
My soul for that great day;
Oh, wash me in thy precious blood,
And take my sins away!

3 A few more storms shall beat
On this wild, rocky shore;
And we shall be where tempests cease,
And surges swell no more.

4 Then, O my Lord, prepare
My soul for that calm day;
Oh, wash me in thy precious blood,
And take my sins away!

5 A few more struggles here,
A few more partings o'er,
A few more toils, a few more tears,
And we shall weep no more.

6 Then, O my Lord, prepare
My soul for that blest day;
Oh, wash me in thy precious blood,
And take my sins away!

7 A few more Sabbaths here
Shall cheer us on our way;
And we shall reach the endless rest,
Th' eternal Sabbath-day.

8 Then, O my Lord, prepare
My soul for that sweet day;
Oh, wash me in thy precious blood,
And take my sins away!

9 'Tis but a little while,
And he shall come again,
Who died that we might live, who lives
That we with him may reign.

10 Then, O my Lord, prepare
My soul for that glad day;
Oh, wash me in thy precious blood,
And take my sins away!

466 *"How shall we sing—in a strange land?"—Psalm 137.* S. M.

1 Far from my heavenly home,
Far from my Father's breast,
Fainting, I cry, "Blest Spirit, come,
And speed me to my rest!"

2 Upon the willows long
My harp has silent hung;
How should I sing a cheerful song,
Till thou inspire my tongue?

3 My spirit homeward turns,
And fain would thither flee;
My heart, O Zion, droops and yearns,
When I remember thee.

4 To thee, to thee I press—
A dark and toilsome road;
When shall I pass the wilderness,
And reach the saints' abode?

LONGING.

OLNEY. S. M.

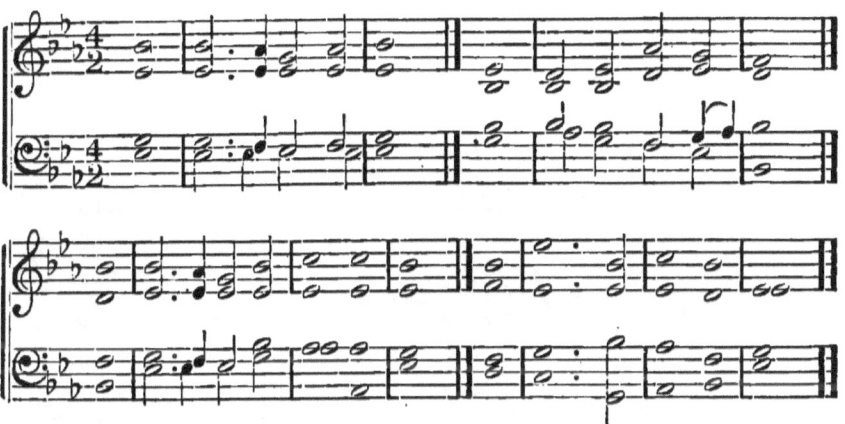

5 God of my life, be near;
On thee my hopes I cast:
Oh, guide me through the desert here,
And bring me home at last!

467 *"Forever with the Lord."* S. M.
1 Thess. 4: 17.

1 "Forever with the Lord!"
Amen! so let it be;
Life from the dead is in that word;
'Tis immortality!

2 My Father's house on high,
Home of my soul! how near,
At times, to faith's foreseeing eye,
Thy golden gates appear!

3 "Forever with the Lord!"
Father, if 'tis thy will,
The promise of thy gracious word
Ev'n here to me fulfill.

4 Be thou at my right hand;
So shall I never fail:
Uphold thou me and I shall stand;
Help, and I shall prevail.

5 So, when my latest breath
Shall rend the vail in twain,
By death I shall escape from death,
And life eternal gain.

6 Knowing "as I am known,"
How shall I love that word,

And oft repeat before the throne,
"Forever with the Lord!"

468 *"The former things are passed away."* S. M.

1 The people of the Lord
Are on their way to heaven;
There they obtain their great reward,
The prize will there be given.

2 'Tis conflict here below;
'Tis triumph there, and peace:
On earth we wrestle with the foe;
In heaven our conflicts cease.

3 'Tis gloom and darkness here;
'Tis light and joy above:
There all is pure, and all is clear;
There all is peace and love.

4 There rest shall follow toil,
And ease succeed to care;
The victors there divide the spoil;
They sing and triumph there.

5 Then, let us joyful sing!
The conflict is not long:
We hope in heaven to praise our King
In one eternal song.

Doxology. S. M.

To God, the Father, Son,
And Spirit, glory be,
As was, and is, and shall remain
Through all eternity!

LONGING, AND

DE FLEURY. 8s.

469 *"Having a desire to depart."* 8s.

1 To Jesus, the crown of my hope,
My soul is in haste to be gone;
Oh, bear me, ye cherubim, up,
And waft me away to his throne.

2 My Saviour, whom absent I love;
Whom, not having seen, I adore;
Whose name is exalted above
All glory, dominion and power.

3 Dissolve thou these bands that detain
My soul from her portion in thee,
Ah! strike off this adamant chain,
And make me eternally free.

4 When that happy era begins,
When arrayed in thy glories I shine,
Nor grieve any more, by my sins,
The bosom on which I recline,—

5 Oh, then shall the vail be removed!
And round me thy brightness be pour'd;
I shall meet him whom absent I loved,
I shall see whom unseen I adored.

6 And then, never more shall the fears,
The trials, temptations, and woes,
Which darken this valley of tears,
Intrude on my blissful repose.

470 *"The rock that is higher than I."* 8s.

1 Encompassed with clouds of distress,
Just ready all hope to resign,
I pant for the light of thy face,
And fear it will never be mine;
Disheartened with waiting so long,
I sink at thy feet with my load:
All plaintive I pour out my song,
And stretch forth my hands unto God.

2 If sometimes I strive as I mourn
My hold on thy promise to keep,
The billows more fiercely return,
And plunge me again in the deep;
O'erwhelmed and cast out from thy sight,
The tempter suggests in that hour
The Lord has forgotten me quite,
My God will be gracious no more.

3 Shine, Lord! and my terrors shall cease;
The blood of atonement apply;
And lead me to Jesus for peace,
The Rock that is higher than I.
Almighty to rescue thou art;
Thy grace is my shield and my tower;
Oh, gladden my desolate heart;
Let this be the day of thy power.

471 Rev. 1; 5, 6. 8s.

1 My gracious Redeemer I love,
His praises aloud I'll proclaim,
And join with the armies above,
To shout his adorable name.

PRAYER.

INSPIRER AND HEARER. 8s.

2 To gaze on his glories divine
Shall be my eternal employ,
And feel them incessantly shine
My boundless, ineffable joy.

3 He freely redeemed with his blood
My soul from the confines of hell,
To live on the smiles of my God,
And in his sweet presence to dwell;

4 To shine with the angels of light,
With saints and with seraphs to sing,
To view with eternal delight
My Jesus, my Saviour, my King.

5 Ye palaces, sceptres and crowns,
Your pride with disdain I survey;
Your pomps are but shadows and sounds,
And pass in a moment away.

6 The crown that my Saviour bestows
Yon permanent sun shall outshine;
My joy everlastingly flows,
My God, my Redeemer, is mine..

472 Heb. 1: 14. 8s.

1 Inspirer and Hearer of prayer,
Thou Shepherd and Guardian of mine!
My all to thy covenant care
I sleeping and waking resign;
If thou art my shield and my sun,
The night is no darkness to me;
And fast as my moments roll on,
They bring me but nearer to thee.

2 Thy ministering spirits descend
To watch while thy saints are asleep;
By day and by night they attend,
The heirs of salvation to keep;
Bright seraphs, despatched from the throne,
Repair to their stations assigned;
And angels elect are sent down
To guard the redeemed of mankind.

3 Thy worship no interval knows;
Their fervor is still on the wing;
And while they protect my repose,
They chant to the praise of my King.
I, too, at the season ordained,
Their chorus for ever shall join,
And love and adore without end
Their faithful Creator, and mine.

473 "The first and the last." 8s.

1 This Lord is the Lord we adore,
Our faithful, unchangeable friend,
Whose love is as large as his power,
And neither knows measure nor end.
'Tis Jesus, the First and the Last,
Whose Spirit shall guide us safe home;
We'll praise him for all that is past,
And trust him for all that's to come.

PRAYER.

OLIVE'S BROW. L. M.

474 *The Mercy-seat.* L. M.

1 From every stormy wind that blows,
From every swelling tide of woes,
There is a calm, a sure retreat;
'T is found beneath the mercy-seat.

2 There is a place where Jesus sheds
The oil of gladness on our heads,—
A place, than all besides, more sweet;
It is the blood-bought mercy-seat.

3 There is a scene where spirits blend,
Where friend holds fellowship with friend;
Though sundered far, by faith they meet
Around one common mercy-seat!

4 There, there, on eagle wings we soar,
And sense and sin molest no more,
And heaven comes down our souls to greet,
And glory crowns the mercy-seat!

5 Oh! let my hand forget her skill,
My tongue be silent, cold, and still,
This throbbing heart forget to beat,
If I forget the mercy-seat.

475 *"We have an advocate with the Father."—1 John 2: 1.* L. M.

1 Where is my God?—does he retire
Beyond the reach of humble sighs?
Are these weak breathings of desire
Too languid to ascend the skies?

2 Look up, my soul, with cheerful eye!
See where the great Redeemer stands,
The glorious Advocate on high,
With precious incense in his hands.

3 He sweetens every humble groan;
He recommends each broken prayer;
Recline thy hope on him alone
Whose power and love forbid despair.

4 Teach my weak heart, O gracious Lord,
With stronger faith to call thee mine;
Bid me pronounce the blissful word,
My Father—God, with joy divine.

476 *The blessed Hour.* L. M.

1 Blest hour! when mortal man retires
To hold communion with his God,
To send to heaven his warm desires,
And listen to the sacred word.

2 Blest hour! when God himself draws nigh
Well pleased his people's voice to hear,
To hush the penitential sigh,
And wipe away the mourner's tear.

3 Blest hour! for, where the Lord resorts,
Foretastes of future bliss are given,
And mortals find his earthly courts
The house of God—the gate of heaven.

4 Hail, peaceful hour! supremely blest,
Amid the hours of worldly care;
The hour that yields the spirit rest,
That sacred hour—the hour of prayer.

5 And when my hours of prayer are past,
And this frail tenement decays,
Then may I spend in heaven at last
A never-ending hour of praise.

PRAYER.

WOODWORTH. L. M.

477 *Matt. 18: 20.* **L. M.**

1 Where two or three, with sweet accord,
Obedient to their sovereign Lord,
Meet to recount his acts of grace,
And offer solemn prayer and praise;—

2 There will the gracious Saviour be,
To bless the little company;
There, to unvail his smiling face,
And bid his glories fill the place.

3 We meet at thy command, O Lord!
Relying on thy faithful word;
Now send the Spirit from above,
And fill our hearts with heavenly love.

478 *"The love of Christ, which passeth knowledge."* **L. M.**

1 Come, dearest Lord! descend and dwell
By faith and love in every breast;
Then shall we know, and taste, and feel
The joys that can not be expressed.

2 Come, fill our hearts with inward strength,
Make our enlarged souls possess,
And learn the height, and breadth, and length,
Of thine immeasurable grace.

3 Now to the God whose power can do
More than our thoughts and wishes know,
Be everlasting honors done
By all the church, through Christ his Son!

479 *The Worth of Prayer.* **L. M.**

1 What various hindrances we meet
In coming to a mercy-seat!
Yet who that knows the worth of prayer,
But wishes to be often there!

2 Prayer makes the darkened clouds withdraw;
Prayer climbs the ladder Jacob saw,
Gives exercise to faith and love,
Brings every blessing from above.

3 Restraining prayer, we cease to fight;
Prayer makes the Christian's armor bright;
And Satan trembles when he sees
The weakest saint upon his knees.

4 Have you no words? ah! think again;
Words flow apace when you complain,
And fill a fellow-creature's ear
With the sad tale of all your care.

5 Were half the breath thus vainly spent
To heaven in supplication sent,
Our cheerful song would oftener be,
"Hear what the Lord hath done for me!"

480 *Christ present in the Sanctuary.* **L. M.**

1 How sweet to leave the world awhile,
And seek the presence of our Lord!
Dear Saviour, on thy people smile,
And come, according to thy word.

2 From busy scenes we now retreat,
That we may here converse with thee:
Ah, Lord, behold us at thy feet!
Let this the "gate of heaven" be.

3 "Chief of ten thousand!" now appear,
That we by faith may see thy face;
Oh, speak, that we thy voice may hear,
And let thy presence fill this place!

HORTON. 7s.

481 *"My times are in Thy hand."*
Psalm 31. 7s.

1 Sovereign Ruler of the skies,
Ever gracious, ever wise!
All my times are in thy hand;
All events at thy command.

2 Times of sickness, times of health,
Times of penury and wealth,—
All must come, and last, and end,
As shall please my heavenly Friend.

3 O Thou gracious, wise, and just!
In thy hands my life I trust;
Have I somewhat dearer still?—
I resign it to thy will.

4 Thee at all times will I bless;
Having Thee, I all possess:
Ne'er can I bereaved be,
While I do not part with thee.

482 *"Cast thy burden upon the Lord."*
Psalm 55. 7s.

1 Cast thy burden on the Lord;
Lean thou only on his word:
Ever will he be thy stay,
Though the heavens shall melt away.

2 Ever in the raging storm,
Thou shalt see his cheering form,
Hear his pledge of coming aid:
"It is I, be not afraid."

3 Cast thy burden at his feet;
Linger near his mercy-seat:
He will lead thee by the hand
Gently to the better land.

4 He will gird thee by his power,
In thy weary, fainting hour;
Lean, then, loving, on his word;
Cast thy burden on the Lord.

483 *Support in Christ.* 7s.

1 Everlasting arms of love
Are beneath, around, above:
He who left his throne of light,
And unnumbered angels bright;

2 He who on th' accursed tree
Gave his precious life for me—
He it is that bears me on,
His the arm I lean upon.

3 He who now, enthroned above,
Still retains his heart of love,
Marking still each falling tear
Of his burdened pilgrims here;

4 He who wields creation's rod,
He my Brother, yet my God;
Faithful he, whate'er betide,
Is my everlasting Guide!

5 All things hasten to decay,
Earth and seas will pass away:
Soon will yonder circling sun
Cease his blazing course to run.

6 Scenes will vary, friends grow strange,
But the Changeless can not change:
Gladly will I journey on,
With his arm to lean upon.

ETERNAL LIFE.

VON WEBER. 7s.

484 *"The God of my life."* 7s.

1 Source and Giver of repose,
From thee all my comfort flows:
Peace and happiness are thine;
Mine they are, if thou art mine.

2 Thee to praise and thee to know,
Constitute my bliss below;
Thee to see and thee to love
Constitute my bliss above.

3 Lord! it is not life to live,
If thy presence thou deny:
Lord! if thou thy presence give,
'T is no longer death to die.

485 *"God shall wipe away all tears from their eyes."*

1 High in yonder realms of light,
Dwell the raptured saints above;
Far beyond our feeble sight,
Happy in Immanuel's love:

2 Pilgrims in this vale of tears,
Once they knew, like us below,
Gloomy doubts, distressing fears,
Torturing pain and heavy woe.

3 But these days of weeping o'er,
Passed this scene of toil and pain,
They shall feel distress no more—
Never, never weep again:

4 'Mid the chorus of the skies,
'Mid th' angelic lyres above,
Hark! their songs melodious rise,
Songs of praise to Jesus' love!

5 All is tranquil and serene,
Calm and undisturbed repose:
There no cloud can intervene,
There no angry tempest blows:

6 Every tear is wiped away,
Sighs no more shall heave the breast,
Night is lost in endless day,
Sorrow—in eternal rest.

486 *"Come up hither."*—Rev. 4: 1. 7s.

1 "Come up hither; come away:"
Thus the ransomed spirits sing;
Here is cloudless, endless day;
Here is everlasting spring.

2 Come up hither; come and dwell
With the living hosts above;
Come, and let your bosoms swell
With their burning songs of love.

3 Come up hither; come and share
All the sacred joys that rise,
Like an ocean, everywhere
Through the myriads of the skies.

4 Come up hither; come and shine
In the robes of spotless white;
Palms, and harps, and crowns are thine;
Hither, hither wing your flight.

5 Come up hither; hither speed:
Rest is found in heaven alone;
Here is all the wealth you need;
Come, and make this wealth your own.

COMFORT IN AFFLICTIONS, AND

HAMBURG. L. M.

487 *"He is my defense; I shall not be moved."* Psalm 62. L. M.

1 My spirit looks to God alone;
My rock and refuge is his throne:
In all my fears, in all my straits,
My soul on his salvation waits.

2 Trust him, ye saints, in all your ways;
Pour out your hearts before his face;
When helpers fail, and foes invade,
God is our all-sufficient Aid.

488 *God our Refuge.* Psalm 46. L. M.

1 God is the refuge of his saints,
When storms of sharp distress invade;
Ere we can offer our complaints,
Behold him present with his aid.

2 Let mountains from their seats be hurled
Down to the deep, and buried there,
Convulsions shake the solid world;
Our faith shall never yield to fear.

3 There is a stream, whose gentle flow
Supplies the city of our God,
Life, love, and joy, still gliding through,
And watering our divine abode.

4 That sacred stream, thine holy word,
Our grief allays, our fear controls;
Sweet peace thy promises afford,
And give new strength to fainting souls.

5 Zion enjoys her Monarch's love,
Secure against a threatening hour;
Nor can her firm foundations move,
Built on his truth and armed with power.

489 *"The Rock of my strength."* L. M.

1 Rejoice, ye saints, rejoice and praise
The blessings of redeeming grace!
Jesus, your everlasting tower,
Stands firm against the tempest's power.

2 He is a refuge ever nigh;
His love endures as mountains high;
His name's a rock, which winds above,
And waves below, can never move.

3 While all things change, he changes not;
He ne'er forgets, though oft forgot;
His love will ever be the same;
His word, enduring as his name.

4 Rejoice, ye saints, rejoice and praise
The blessings of his wondrous grace!
Jesus, your everlasting tower,
Can bear, unmoved, the tempest's power.

490 Psalm 46. L. M.

1 God will our strength and refuge prove,
In all distress a present aid;
And though the trembling earth remove,
We will not fear or be dismayed;

2 Though hills be cast amid the sea,
And angry billows round them break,
Though waters roar and troubled be,
And mountains, with their swelling, shake.

3 A river flows whose living streams
Make glad the city of our God,
The tents where heavenly glory beams,
Where God most high hath his abode.

DEATH.

GRATITUDE. L. M.

4 God has in her his dwelling made,
And she shall nevermore be moved;
Her God shall early give her aid,
As he her help hath ever proved.

491 *"Welcome to me the darkest night."* **L. M.**

1 Welcome to me the darkest night,
If there the Saviour's presence bright
Beam forth upon the soul dismayed,
And say, "'Tis I: be not afraid!"

2 Welcome the fiercest waves that roll
Their deepening floods to whelm my soul,
If he rebuke the storm of ill,
And bid the tempest, "Peace, be still!"

3 Welcome the thorniest path, if there
The print-marks of his feet appear:
If in his footsteps we may tread,
And follow where our Lord hath led.

4 I will not ask what else is mine,
If thou, O Lord, account me thine;
For what but joy can be my lot,
If God, my God, reject me not?

492 *"He shall sit as a refiner of silver."* **L. M.**

1 Why should I murmur or repine,
O Lamb of God, who bled for me?
What are my griefs compared with thine,—
Thy tears, thy groans, thine agony!

2 If thou the furnace dost employ,
Thou sittest as refiner near,
To purge away the base alloy,
Till thine own image bright appear.

3 Though oft thy way is in the sea,
Thy footsteps in the winged storm;
Though crested billows threaten me,—
Love slumbers in their frowning form!

4 Submissive would I kiss the rod,
Needful each stroke, I humbly own:
Help me to trust thee, O my God!
If now thy wisdom be unknown.

493 *"Lord, make me to know the measure of my days."—Ps. 39.* **L. M.**

1 Almighty Maker of my frame,
Teach me the measure of my days;
Teach me to know how frail I am,
And spend the remnant to thy praise.

2 My days are shorter than a span,
A little point my life appears;
How frail at best is dying man!
How vain are all his hopes and fears!

3 Oh, spare me, and my strength restore,
Ere my few hasty minutes flee!
And when my days on earth are o'er,
Let me forever dwell with thee.

4 Oh, be that noble portion mine!
My God, I bow before thy throne;
Earth's fleeting treasures I resign,
And fix my hopes on thee alone.

Doxology. **L. M.**

Praise God, from whom all blessings flow!
Praise him, all creatures here below!
Praise him above, ye heavenly host!
Praise Father, Son, and Holy Ghost!

COMFORT IN AFFLICTIONS, AND

DUNDEE. C. M.

494 *"Be still, for it is he."* C. M.

1 The Christian would not have his lot,
Be other than it is;
For while his Father rules the world,
He knows that world is his.

2 He knows that he who gave the best,
Will give him all beside;
Assured each seeming good he asks
Is evil, if denied.

3 When clouds of sorrow gather round,
His bosom owns no fear;
He knows, where'er his portion be,
His God will still be there.

4 And when the threaten'd storm has burst,
Whate'er the trial be;
Something yet whispers him within,
"Be still, for it is he!"

495 *"The Lord gave, and the Lord hath taken away."—Job 1: 21.* C. M.

1 It is the Lord,—enthroned in light,
Whose claims are all divine,
Who hath an undisputed right
To govern me and mine.

2 It is the Lord—who gives me all,
My wealth, my friends, my ease;
And of his bounties may recall
Whatever part he please.

3 It is the Lord, my cov'nant God,—
Thrice blessed be his name,—
Whose gracious promise, sealed with blood,
Must ever be the same.

4 Can I, with hopes so firmly built,
Be sullen, or repine?
No; gracious God! take what thou wilt:
To thee I all resign.

496 *"My meditation of Him shall be sweet."* C. M.

1 When languor and disease invade
This trembling house of clay,
'Tis sweet to look beyond my pain,
And long to fly away;

2 Sweet to look inward, and attend
The whispers of his love;
Sweet to look upward to the place
Where Jesus pleads above;

3 Sweet to reflect how grace divine
My sins on Jesus laid:
Sweet to remember that His blood
My debt of sufferings paid.

4 Sweet, in the confidence of faith,
To trust his firm decrees;
Sweet to lie passive in his hands,
And know no will but his.

5 If such the sweetness of the streams,
What must the fountain be
Where saints and angels draw their bliss
Direct, O Lord, from thee?

497 *"All things are yours." 1 Cor. 3: 22.* C. M.

1 If God is mine, then present things
And things to come are mine;
Yea, Christ, his word, and Spirit too,
And glory all divine.

DEATH.

ARLINGTON. C. M.

2 If he is mine, then from his love
He every trouble sends;
All things are working for my good,
And bliss his rod attends.

3 If he is mine, I need not fear
The rage of earth and hell;
He will support my feeble power,
Their utmost force repel.

4 If he is mine, let friends forsake,
Let wealth and honors flee:
Sure, he who giveth me himself,
Is more than these to me.

5 If he is mine, I'll boldly pass
Through death's dark, lonely vale;
He is my comfort and my stay,
When heart and flesh shall fail.

6 Oh, tell me, Lord, that thou art mine;
What can I wish beside?
My soul shall at the fountain live,
When all the streams are dried.

498 *"It is appointed unto men once to die."* **C. M.**

1 If I must die, oh! let me die
With hope in Jesus' blood—
The blood that saves from sin and guilt,
And reconciles to God.

2 If I must die, then let me die
In peace with all mankind,
And change these fleeting joys below
For pleasures all refined.

3 If I must die—and die I shall—
Let some kind seraph come,
And bear me on his friendly wing
To my celestial home.

4 Of Canaan's land, from Pisgah's top,
May I but have a view,
Though Jordan should o'erflow its banks,
I'll boldly venture through.

499 *"Be not dismayed, for I am thy God."* **C. M.**

1 Thou must go forth alone, my soul!
Thou must go forth alone,
To other scenes, to other worlds,
That mortal hath not known.

2 Thou must go forth alone, my soul,
To tread the narrow vale;
But he, whose word is sure, hath said
His mercy shall not fail.

3 Thou must go forth alone, my soul,
To meet thy God above:
But shrink not—he has said, my soul,
He is a God of love!

4 His rod and staff shall comfort thee
Across the dreary road,
Till thou shalt join the blessed ones
In heaven's serene abode.

Doxology. **C. M.**

To God the Father, God the Son,
And God the Holy Ghost,
All glory be from Saints on earth,
And from the Angel-host.

DEATH, RESURRECTION AND JUDGMENT HYMN. L. M.

500 *"I have fought a good fight."*
2 Tim. 4: 6—8.   L. M.

1 The hour of my departure 's come;
I hear the voice that calls me home;
Now, O my God! let trouble cease,
And let thy servant die in peace.

2 The race appointed I have run;
The combat 's o'er, the prize is won;
And now my witness is on high,
And now my record 's in the sky.

3 Not in mine innocence I trust;
I bow before thee in the dust;
And through my Saviour's blood alone
I look for mercy at thy throne.

4 I come, I come, at thy command;
I give my spirit to thy hand;
Stretch forth thine everlasting arms,
And shield me in the last alarms.

501 *"That they may rest from their labors."*   L. M.

1 Sweet is the scene when Christians die,
When holy souls retire to rest;
How mildly beams the closing eye!
How gently heaves th' expiring breast!

2 So fades a summer cloud away;
So sinks the gale when storms are o'er;
So gently shuts the eye of day;
So dies a wave along the shore.

3 Triumphant smiles the victor's brow,
Fanned by some guardian angel's wing;
O Grave! where is thy victory now?
And where, O death! where is thy sting?

502 *"Why is His chariot so long in coming?"*   L. M.

1 Gently, my Saviour, let me down,
To slumber in the arms of death;
I rest my soul on thee alone,
Ev'n till my last, expiring breath.

2 Soon will the storm of life be o'er,
And I shall enter endless rest;
There I shall live to sin no more,
And bless thy name, forever blest.

3 Bid me possess sweet peace within;
Let childlike patience keep my heart;
Then shall I feel my heaven begin,
Before my spirit hence depart.

4 Oh, speed thy chariot, God of love,
And take me from this world of woe;
I long to reach those joys above,
And bid farewell to all below.

5 There shall my raptured spirit raise
Still louder notes than angels sing,—
High glories to Immanuel's grace,
My God, my Saviour and my King!

503 *"Why should we weep for those who die?"*   L. M.

1 Why should we weep for those who die?
Those blessed ones who weep no more?
Jesus hath called them to the sky,
And gladly have they gone before.

2 A few short days they lingered here,
Th' appointed span of trial knew;
Dropped—early dropped the parting tear,
And early now have parted, too.

JUDGMENT.

REST. L. M.

3 Up, up, in swift ascent, they rise,
Star after star of living light!
Why should we mourn that midnight skies
Become with added glories bright?

504 *"The Lord will come."* L. M.
           2 Thess. 1: 7.

1 The Lord will come! the earth shall quake;
The mountains to their center shake;
And, withering from the vault of night,
The stars withdraw their feeble light.

2 The Lord will come! but not the same
As once in lowly form he came, —
A silent Lamb before his foes,
A weary man, and full of woes.

3 The Lord will come! a dreadful form,
With wreath of flame, and robe of storm,
On cherub-wings, and wings of wind,
Anointed Judge of human kind!

4 Can this be he, who wont to stray
A pilgrim on the world's highway,
By power oppressed, and mocked by pride,—
The Nazarene, the Crucified?

5 While sinners in despair shall call,
"Rocks, hide us! mountains, on us fall!"
The saints, ascending from the tomb,
Shall sing for joy, "The Lord is come!"

505 *The Day of Wrath.* L. M.
       (A Hymn of the Thirteenth Century.)

1 That day of wrath! that dreadful day,
When heaven and earth shall pass away!
What power shall be the sinner's stay?
How shall he meet that dreadful day?

2 When, shriveling like a parched scroll,
The flaming heavens together roll;
When louder yet, and yet more dread,
Swells the high trump that wakes the dead!—

3 Oh! on that day — that wrathful day,
When man to judgment wakes from clay,
Be thou the trembling sinner's stay,
Tho' heaven and earth shall pass away!

506 Luke 21: 31. L. M.

1 He reigns, the Lord, the Saviour, reigns,
Praise him in evangelic strains;
Let the whole earth in songs rejoice,
And distant islands join their voice.

2 Deep are his counsels and unknown,
But grace and truth support his throne;
Though gloomy clouds his way surround,
Justice is their eternal ground.

3 In robes of judgment, lo! he comes,
Shakes the wide earth and cleaves the tombs;
Before him burns devouring fire,
The mountains melt, the seas retire.

4 His enemies, with sore dismay,
Fly from the sight and shun the day;
Then lift your heads, ye saints, on high,
And sing, for your redemption's nigh.

Doxology. L. M.

Now to the Father, and the Son
Who rose from death, be glory given,
With Thee, O Holy Comforter,
Henceforth, by all in earth and heaven.

RESURRECTION, JUDGMENT AND

CAMBRIDGE. C. M.

507 *"Them also which sleep in Jesus."*
1 Thess. 4: 14—17.   C. M.

1 As Jesus died and rose again,
Victorious, from the dead;
So his disciples rise, and reign
With their triumphant Head.

2 The time draws nigh, when, from the clouds,
Christ shall with shouts descend;
And the last trumpet's awful voice
The heavens and earth shall rend.

3 Then they who live shall changed be,
And they who sleep shall wake;
The graves shall yield their ancient charge
And earth's foundation shake.

4 The saints of God, from death set free,
With joy shall mount on high;
The heavenly host with praises loud
Shall meet them in the sky.

5 Together to their Father's house
With joyful hearts they go:
And dwell forever with the Lord,
Beyond the reach of woe.

508 *"In my flesh shall I see God."*
Job. 19: 25, 26.   C. M.

1 My faith shall triumph o'er the grave,
And trample on the tomb;
I know that my Redeemer lives,
And on the clouds shall come.

2 I know that he shall soon appear
In power and glory meet:
And death, the last of all his foes,
Lie vanquished at his feet.

3 Then, though the grave my flesh devour,
And hold me for its prey,
I know my sleeping dust shall rise
On the last judgment-day.

4 I, in my flesh, shall see my God,
When he on earth shall stand;
I shall with all his saints ascend
To dwell at his right hand.

5 Then shall he wipe all tears away,
And hush the rising groan;
And pains and sighs and griefs and fears
Shall ever be unknown.

509   1 Thess. 4: 14.   C. M.

1 Hark to the trump! behold it breaks
The sleep of ages now;
And lo, the light of glory shines
On many an aching brow.

2 Changed in a moment, full of life,
The quick, the dead, arise,
Responsive to the angel's voice
That calls us to the skies.

3 Ascending through the crowded air,
On eagle wings we soar,
To dwell in the full joy of love,
And sorrow there no more.

4 O Lord, the bright and blessed hope
That cheered us through the past,
Of full, eternal rest in thee,
Is all fulfilled at last.

5 Past conflict now, O Lord, 't is ours,
Through everlasting days,
To sing our songs of victory,
To thine eternal praise.

ETERNAL LIFE.

ARMENIA. C. M.

5 Past conflict now, O Lord, 'tis ours,
Through everlasting days,
To sing our songs of victory,
To thine eternal praise.

510 *The Judgment-seat of Christ.* **C. M.**
Matt. 25: 41.

1 That awful day will surely come,
Th' appointed hour makes haste,
When I must stand before my Judge,
And pass the solemn test.

2 Thou lovely Chief of all my joys,
Thou Sovereign of my heart!
How could I bear to hear thy voice
Pronounce the sound "Depart!"

3 Oh, wretched state of deep despair!
To see my God remove,—
And fix my doleful station where
I must not taste his love!

4 Jesus, I throw my arms around,
And hang upon thy breast:
Without a gracious smile from thee,
My spirit cannot rest.

5 Oh, tell me that my worthless name
Is graven on thy hands!
Show me some promise in thy book,
Where my salvation stands.

6 Give me one kind, assuring word,
To sink my fears again;

And cheerfully my soul shall wait
Her threescore years and ten.

511 *No Sin in Heaven.* **C. M.**

1 Far from these narrow scenes of night,
Unbounded glories rise,
And realms of infinite delight,
Unknown to mortal eyes.

2 Fair, distant land! could mortal eyes
But half its charms explore,
How would our spirits long to rise,
And dwell on earth no more!

3 No cloud those blissful regions know—
Realms ever bright and fair!
For sin, the source of mortal woe,
Can never enter there.

4 Oh, may the heavenly prospect fire
Our hearts with ardent love!
Till wings of faith, and strong desire
Bear every thought above.

5 Prepare us, Lord, by grace divine,
For thy bright courts on high;
Then bid our spirits rise and join
The chorus of the sky.

Doxology. **C. M.**

The Father's name we loudly raise,
The Son we all adore,
The Holy Ghost, One God, we praise,
Both now and evermore.

RESURRECTION, JUDGMENT, AND

OLMUTZ. S. M.

512 *"My flesh also shall rest in hope."* S. M.

1 Rest for the toiling hand,
Rest for the anxious brow,
Rest for the weary, way-worn feet,
Rest from all labor now;—

2 Rest for the fevered brain,
Rest for the throbbing eye;
Through these parched lips of thine no more
Shall pass the moan or sigh.

3 Soon shall the trump of God
Give out the welcome sound,
That shakes thy silent chamber walls,
And breaks the turf-sealed ground.

4 Ye dwellers in the dust,
Awake! come forth and sing;
Sharp has your frost of winter been,
But bright shall be your spring.

5 'Twas sown in weakness here;
'Twill then be raised in power:
That which was sown an earthly seed,
Shall rise a heavenly flower!

513 1 Thess. 4: 16. S. M.

1 Waked by the trumpet's sound,
I from the grave must rise,
And see the Judge with glory crowned,
And see the flaming skies.

2 O Thou that wouldst not have
One wretched sinner die,
Who diedst Thyself my soul to save
From endless misery!

3 Show me the way to shun
Thy dreadful wrath severe;
That when Thou comest on Thy throne,
I may with joy appear!

514 1 Thess. 4: 16. S. M.

1 And will the Judge descend,
And must the dead arise,
And not a single soul escape
His all-discerning eyes?

2 How will my heart endure
The terrors of that day,
When earth and heaven before His face
Astonished shrink away?

3 But ere the trumpet shakes
The mansions of the dead,
Hark, from the Gospel's cheering sound
What joyful tidings spread!

4 Ye sinners, seek His grace
Whose wrath ye cannot bear;
Fly to the shelter of His cross,
And find salvation there.

5 So shall that curse remove,
By which the Saviour bled;
And the last awful day shall pour
His blessings on your head.

515 *"Every one of us shall give account of himself to God."* S. M.

1 Thou Judge of quick and dead,
Before whose bar severe,
With holy joy, or guilty dread,
We all shall soon appear!—

ETERNAL LIFE.

DENNIS. S. M.

2 Our anxious souls prepare
For that tremendous day;
Come, fill us now with watchful care,
And stir us up to pray;

3 To pray, and wait the hour,
That awful hour unknown,
When, robed in majesty and power,
Thou shalt from heaven come down!

4 Oh, may we all be found
Obedient to thy word,—
Attentive to the trumpet's sound,
And looking for our Lord.

5 Oh, may we all ensure
A home among the blest;
And watch a moment to secure
An everlasting rest!

516 *"And to wait for his Son."* S. M.

1 He comes! the Conqueror comes!
Death falls beneath his sword;
The joyful prisoners burst their tombs,
And rise to meet their Lord.

2 The trumpet sounds—Awake!
Ye dead, to judgment come!
The pillars of creation shake,
While hell receives her doom.

3 Thrice happy morn for those
Who love the ways of peace;
No night of sorrow e'er shall close
Upon its perfect bliss.

517 *"There remaineth therefore a rest."* S. M.

1 And is there, Lord, a rest
For weary souls designed,
Where not a care shall stir the breast,
Or sorrow entrance find?

2 Is there a blissful home,
Where kindred minds shall meet,
And live, and love, nor ever roam
From that serene retreat?

3 Are there bright, happy fields,
Where naught that blooms shall die;
Where each new scene fresh pleasure yields,
And healthful breezes sigh?

4 Are there celestial streams,
Where living waters glide,
With murmurs sweet as angel dreams,
And flowery banks beside?

5 Forever blessed they,
Whose joyful feet shall stand —
While endless ages waste away—
Amid that glorious land!

6 My soul would thither tend,
While toilsome years are given;
Then let me, gracious God, ascend
To sweet repose in heaven!

Doxology. S. M.

Praise to the Father be;
Praise to His Only Son;
Praise to the blessed Paraclete,
While endless ages run.

ETERNAL LIFE AND

SESSIONS. L. M.

518 *"The Lamb is the light thereof."* L. M.

1 O for a sweet, inspiring ray,
To animate our feeble strains,
From the bright realms of endless day—
The blissful realms where Jesus reigns!

2 There, low before his glorious throne,
Adoring saints and angels fall;
And, with delightful worship, own
His smile their bliss, their heaven, their all.

3 Immortal glories crown his head,
While tuneful hallelujahs rise,
And love and joy, and triumph spread
Through all the assemblies of the skies.

4 He smiles,—and seraphs tune their songs,
To boundless rapture, while they gaze;
Ten thousand thousand joyful tongues
Resound his everlasting praise.

5 There all the followers of the lamb
Shall join at last the heavenly choir:
Oh, may the joy-inspiring theme
Awake our faith and warm desire!

519 *"Who dwell in light."* L. M.

1 O happy saints, who dwell in light
And walk with Jesus clothed in white,
Safe landed on that peaceful shore
Where pilgrims meet to part no more.

2 Released from sin and toil and grief,
Death was their gate to endless life;
An opened gate to let them fly
And find their happy home on high.

3 And now they range the heavenly plains,
And sing their hymns in melting strains;
And now their souls begin to prove
The height and depths of Jesus' love.

4 He cheers them with eternal smile;
They sing hosannas all the while;
Or, overwhelmed with rapture sweet,
Sink down adoring at his feet.

5 Ah, Lord! with tardy steps I creep,
And sometimes sing and sometimes weep;
Yet strip me of this house of clay,
And I will sing as loud as they.

520 *Rev. 5: 9.* L. M.

1 Hark! how the choral song of heaven
Swells full of peace and joy above!
Hark! how they strike their golden harps,
And raise the tuneful notes of love!

2 No anxious care nor thrilling grief,
No deep despair nor gloomy woe,
They feel while high their lofty strains
In noblest, sweetest concord flow.

3 When shall we join the heavenly host
Who sing Immanuel's praise on high,
And leave behind our fears and doubts,
To swell the chorus of the sky?

4 Oh, come, thou rapture-bringing morn,
And usher in this joyful day;
We long to see thy rising sun
Drive all these clouds of grief away.

HEAVEN.

OLIVE'S BROW. L. M.

521 *"And dying is but going home."*
1 Cor. 2: 9.   L. M.

1 Now let our souls, on wings sublime,
Rise from the vanities of time,
Draw back the parting vail, and see
The glories of eternity.

2 Born by a new, celestial birth,
Why should we grovel here on earth?
Why grasp at vain and fleeting toys,
So near to heaven's eternal joys?

3 Shall aught beguile us on the road,
While we are walking back to God?
For strangers into life we come,
And dying is but going home.

4 Welcome, sweet hour of full discharge,
That sets our longing souls at large,
Unbinds our chains, breaks up our cell,
And gives us with our God to dwell.

5 To dwell with God, to feel his love,
Is the full heaven enjoyed above;
And the sweet expectation now
Is the young dawn of heaven below.

522 *"One in our hope of rest above."*   L. M.

1 Still one in life and one in death,
One in our hope of rest above;
One in our joy, our trust, our faith,
One in each other's faithful love.

2 Yet must we part, and, parting, weep;
What else has earth for us in store?
Our farewell pangs, how sharp and deep!
Our farewell words, how sad and sore!

3 Yet shall we meet again in peace,
To sing the song of festal joy,
Where none shall bid our gladness cease,
And none our fellowship destroy.

4 Where none shall beckon us away,
Nor bid our festival be done;
Our meeting-time th' eternal day,
Our meeting-place th' eternal throne.

5 There, hand in hand, firm-linked at last,
And, heart to heart, enfolded all,
We'll smile upon the troubled past,
And wonder why we wept at all.

523 *"Willing rather to be absent from the body."*   L. M.

1 Descend from heaven, immortal Dove!
Stoop down and take us on thy wings;
And mount, and bear us far above
The reach of these inferior things,—

2 Beyond, beyond this lower sky,
Up where eternal ages roll,
Where solid pleasures never die,
And fruits immortal feast the soul.

3 Oh for a sight, a pleasing sight,
Of our almighty Father's throne!
There sits our Saviour, crowned with light,
Clothed in a body like our own.

Doxology.   L. M.

Eternal Father of the Word,
Eternal Son, co-equal King,
Eternal Spirit, God and Lord,
To thee unceasing praise we bring.

ETERNAL LIFE, AND

HAVEN. C. M.

524 *"Sweet fields, beyond the swelling flood."* **C. M.**

1 There is a land of pure delight,
Where saints immortal reign;
Infinite day excludes the night,
And pleasures banish pain.

2 There everlasting spring abides,
And never-withering flowers:
Death, like a narrow sea, divides
This heavenly land from ours.

3 Sweet fields, beyond the swelling flood,
Stand dressed in living green;
So to the Jews old Canaan stood,
While Jordan rolled between.

4 But timorous mortals start and shrink,
To cross this narrow sea;
And linger, shivering, on the brink,
And fear to launch away.

5 Oh, could we make our doubts remove,
Those gloomy doubts that rise,
And see the Canaan that we love,
With unbeclouded eyes!—

6 Could we but climb where Moses stood,
And view the landscape o'er,
Not Jordan's stream, nor death's cold flood
Should fright us from the shore.

525 *"I saw a new heaven and a new earth."—Rev. 21: 1–5.* **C. M.**

1 Lo! what a glorious sight appears
To our believing eyes!
The earth and seas are passed away,
And the old rolling skies.

2 From the third heaven, where God resides,
That holy, happy place,
The new Jerusalem comes down,
Adorned with shining grace.

3 Attending angels shout for joy,
And the bright armies sing:
"Mortals! behold the sacred seat
Of your descending King.

4 "The God of glory down to men
Removes his blest abode,—
Men, the dear objects of his grace,
And he, the loving God.

5 "His own soft hands shall wipe the tears,
From every weeping eye;
And pains, and groans, and griefs, and fears,
And death itself shall die."

6 How long, dear Saviour! oh, how long
Shall this bright hour delay?
Fly swifter round, ye wheels of time,
And bring the welcome day!

526 *"Caught up together with them in the clouds."* **C. M.**

1 Hope of our hearts! O Lord, appear,
Thou glorious Star of day!
Shine forth, and chase the dreary night,
And all our fears away.

2 Strangers on earth we wait for thee:
Oh, leave the Father's throne!
Come with a shout of victory, Lord,
And claim us as thine own!

HEAVEN.

HEBER. C. M.

3 Oh, bid the bright archangel then
The trump of God prepare,
To call thy saints, the quick, the dead,
To meet thee in the air!

4 No resting-place we seek on earth,
No loveliness we see;
Our eye is on the royal crown
Prepared for us and thee.

5 But, oh! the thought of sharing, Lord,
Thy glorious throne above,
What is it to the brighter hope
Of dwelling in thy love?

527 *"Now they desire a better country."* **C. M.**

1 Oh! could our thoughts and wishes fly
Above these gloomy shades,
To those bright worlds beyond the sky
Which sorrow ne'er invades!

2 There joys unseen by mortal eyes,
Or reason's feeble ray,
In ever-blooming prospect rise,
Unconscious of decay.

3 Lord! send a beam of light divine
To guide our upward aim;
With one reviving touch of thine
Our languid hearts inflame.

4 Then shall, on faith's sublimest wing,
Our ardent wishes rise
To those bright scenes, where pleasures spring
Immortal in the skies.

528 *"Lord, I believe a rest remains."* **C. M.**

1 Lord, I believe a rest remains,
To all thy people known;
A rest where pure enjoyment reigns,
And thou art loved alone;—

2 A rest where all our souls' desire
Is fixed on things above;
Where fear and sin and grief expire,
Cast out by perfect love.

3 Oh that I now the rest might know,
Believe and enter in!
Now, Saviour! now the power bestow,
And let me cease from sin.

4 Remove the hardness of my heart,
The unbelief remove;
To me the rest of faith impart—
The Sabbath of thy love.

529 *"The sons of God."* **C. M.**
     Rom. 8: 19-23.

1 The whole creation groans and waits
Till we, who love thee, Lord,
Shall stand within thy temple gates,
And shine—the sons of God.

2 One with the Lord and all his saints!
Thy nature in our own!
Thy crown our rich inheritance!
Heirs to thy royal throne!

Doxology. **C. M.**

Let God the Father, and the Son,
And Spirit, be adored,
Where there are works to make him known,
Or saints to love the Lord!

MORNING AND EVENING HYMNS.

For Family Devotions and Church use.

MORNING.

DENFIELD. C. M.

530 *Morning Hymn.* **C. M.**

1 God of my life, my morning song
To thee I cheerful raise;
Thy acts of love 'tis good to sing,
And pleasant 'tis to praise,

2 Preserv'd by thy Almighty arm,
I pass'd the shades of night,
Serene, and safe from ev'ry harm,
To see the morning light.

3 While numbers spent the night in sighs,
And restless pains and woes,
In gentle sleep I clos'd my eyes,
And rose from sweet repose.

4 Oh let the same Almighty care
Through all this day attend:
From ev'ry danger, ev'ry snare,
My heedless steps defend.

5 Smile on my minutes as they roll,
And guide my future days;
And let thy goodness fill my soul
With gratitude and praise.

531 *Morning Hymn.* **C. M.**

1 Giver and Guardian of our sleep,
To praise Thy name we wake;
Still, Lord, Thy helpless servants keep,
For Thine own mercy's sake!

2 The blessing of another day
We thankfully receive;
Oh may we only Thee obey,
And to Thy glory live.

3 Upon us lay Thy mighty hand;
Our words and thoughts restrain;
And bow our souls to Thy command,
Nor let our faith be vain.

532 *Morning Hymn.* **C. M.**

1 O God, that madest earth and sky,
The darkness and the day,
Give ear to this Thy family,
And help us when we pray!

2 The cross our Master bore for us,
For Him we fain would bear;
But mortal strength to weakness turns,
And courage to despair.

3 Then mercy on our failings, Lord!
Our sinking faith renew!
And when Thy sorrows visit us,
Oh send Thy patience too!

EVENING.

COWPER. C. M.

533 *"Thou, Lord, only makest me dwell in safety."* **C. M.**

1 Lord, thou wilt hear me when I pray;
I am forever thine,
I fear before thee all the day,
Nor would I dare to sin.

2 And while I rest my weary head,
From cares and business free,
'Tis sweet conversing on my bed
With my own heart and thee.

3 I pay this evening sacrifice;
And when my work is done,
Great God! my faith and hope relies
Upon thy grace alone.

4 Thus, with my thoughts composed to peace,
I give mine eyes to sleep;
Thy hand in safety keeps my days,
And will my slumbers keep.

534 *Evening Hymn.* **C. M.**

1 I love to steal awhile away
From every cumbering care,
And spend the hours of setting day
In humble, grateful prayer.

2 I love, in solitude, to shed
The penitential tear;
And all His promises to plead
Where none but God is near.

3 I love to think on mercies past,
And future good implore;
And all my cares and sorrows cast
On Him whom I adore.

4 I love, by faith, to take a view
Of brighter scenes in heaven;
The prospect doth my strength renew,
While here by tempests driven.

5 Thus, when life's toilsome day is o'er,
May its departing ray
Be calm as this impressive hour,
And lead to endless day.

535 *Evening Hymn.* **C. M.**

1 Now from the altar of our hearts
Let flames of love arise;
Assist us, Lord! to offer up
Our evening sacrifice.

2 Minutes and mercies multiplied
Have made up all this day;
Minutes came quick, but mercies were
More fleet, more free, than they.

3 New time, new favors and new joys
Do a new song require;
Till we shall praise thee as we would,
Accept our hearts' desire.

4 Lord of our time! whose hand hath set
New time upon our score,
Thee may we praise for all our time,
When time shall be no more.

Doxology. **C. M.**

To Father, Son, and Holy Ghost,
The God whom we adore,
Be glory as it was, is now,
And shall be evermore.

MORNING.

WOODWORTH. L. M.

536 *An ancient Psalm of the Morning.* **L. M.**

1 O Christ! with each returning morn
Thine image to our heart be borne;
And may we ever clearly see
Our God and Saviour, Lord, in thee!

2 All hallowed be our walk this day;
May meekness form our early ray,
And faithful love our noontide light,
And hope our sunset, calm and bright.

3 May grace each idle thought control,
And sanctify our wayward soul;
May guile depart, and malice cease,
And all within be joy and peace.

4 Our daily course, O Jesus, bless;
Make plain the way of holiness:
From sudden falls our feet defend,
And cheer at last our journey's end.

537 *The Morning Sacrifice.* **L. M.**

1 Awake, my soul, and with the sun
Thy daily stage of duty run;
Shake off dull sloth, and joyful rise
To pay thy morning sacrifice.

2 Awake, lift up thyself, my heart,
And with the angels bear thy part,
Who all night long unwearied sing
High praises to th' eternal King.

3 Glory to thee, who safe hast kept,
And hast refreshed me while I slept;
Grant, Lord, when I from death shall wake,
I may of endless life partake.

4 Lord, I my vows to thee renew:
Scatter my sins as morning dew;
Guard my first springs of thought and will,
And with thyself my spirit fill.

5 Direct, control, suggest this day,
All I design, or do, or say;
That all my powers, with all their might,
In thy sole glory may unite.

538 *Morning Hymn.* **L. M.**

1 New every morning is the love
Our wakening and uprising prove;
Thro' sleep and darkness safely brought,
Restored to life and power and thought.

2 New mercies each returning day
Hover around us while we pray,
New perils past, new sins forgiven,
New thoughts of God, new hopes of heaven.

3 If, on our daily course, our mind
Be set to hallow all we find,
New treasures still, of countless price,
God will provide for sacrifice.

4 The trivial round, the common task,
Will furnish all we need to ask,
Room to deny ourselves, a road
To bring us daily nearer God.

5 Only, O Lord! in thy dear love,
Fit us for perfect rest above,
And help us this and every day
To live more nearly as we pray.

EVENING.

HURSLEY. L. M.

539   *"Abide with us."*   L. M.

1 Sun of my soul! thou Saviour dear,
It is not night if thou be near:
Oh, may no earth-born cloud arise
To hide thee from thy servant's eyes!

2 When soft the dews of kindly sleep
My wearied eyelids gently steep,
Be my last thought,—how sweet to rest
Forever on my Saviour's breast!

3 Abide with me from morn till eve,
For without thee I cannot live;
Abide with me when night is nigh,
For without thee I dare not die.

4 Be near to bless me when I wake,
Ere through the world my way I take;
Abide with me till in thy love
I lose myself in heaven above.

540   *"Hide me under the shadow of Thy wings."*   L. M.

1 Glory to thee, my God, this night,
For all the blessings of the light:
Keep me, oh, keep me, King of kings!
Beneath the shadow of thy wings.

2 Forgive me, Lord! through thy dear Son,
The ill which I this day have done;
That with the world, myself, and thee,
I, ere I sleep, at peace may be.

3 Teach me to live, that I may dread
The grave as little as my bed;
Teach me to die, that so I may
Rise glorious at thy judgment day.

4 Be thou my guardian while I sleep,
Thy watchful station near me keep;
My heart with love celestial fill,
And guard me from th' approach of ill.

5 Lord, let my soul forever share
The bliss of thy paternal care!
'T is heaven on earth, 't is heaven above,
To see thy face, and sing thy love.

541   *"I will both lay me down in peace and sleep."*   L. M.

1 Thus far the Lord has led me on;
Thus far his power prolongs my days;
And every evening shall make known
Some fresh memorial of his grace.

2 Much of my time has run to waste,
And I, perhaps, am near my home;
But he forgives my follies past:
He gives me strength for days to come.

3 Faith in thy name forbids my fear;
Oh, may thy presence ne'er depart!
And in the morning make me hear
The love and kindness of thy heart.

4 Thus, when the night of death shall come,
My flesh shall rest beneath the ground,
And wait thy voice to rouse my tomb,
With sweet salvation in the sound.

Doxology.   L. M.

Glory to thee, O God, most high!
Father, we praise thy majesty!
The Son, the Spirit, we adore,
One Godhead, blest for evermore!

MORNING.

LUTHER. S. M.

542 *Christ the Day-star.* S. M.

1 We lift our hearts to thee,
Thou Day-star from on high:
The sun itself is but thy shade,
Yet cheers both earth and sky.

2 Oh, let thy rising beams
Dispel the shades of night;
And let the glories of thy love,
Come like the morning light!

3 How beauteous nature now!
How dark and sad before!—
With joy we view the pleasing change,
And nature's God adore.

4 May we this life improve,
To mourn for errors past;
And live this short revolving day
As if it were our last.

543 *Morning Hymn.* S. M.

1 Serene I laid me down
Beneath God's guardian care;
I slept, and I awoke and found
My kind Preserver near.

2 Oh, how shall I repay
The bounties of my God?
This feeble spirit pants beneath
The pleasing, painful load.

3 Dear Saviour! to thy cross
I bring my sacrifice;
Tinged with thy blood, it shall ascend
With fragrance to the skies.

5 My life I would anew
Devote, O Lord! to thee,
And in thy service I would spend
A long eternity.

544 *Morning Hymn.* S. M.

1 My God! permit my tongue
This joy, to call Thee mine;
And let my early cries prevail,
To taste Thy love divine.

2 My thirsty fainting soul
Thy mercy doth implore;
Not travelers in desert lands,
Can pant for water more.

3 For life, without Thy love,
No relish can afford:
No joy can be compared to this,
To serve and please the Lord.

4 In wakeful hours at night,
I call my God to mind;
I think how wise Thy counsels are,
And all Thy dealings kind.

5 Since Thou hast been my help,
To Thee my spirit flies;
And on Thy watchful providence
My cheerful hope relies.

545 *Morning Hymn.* S. M.

1 Blest be Thy love, dear Lord,
That taught us this sweet way,
Only to love Thee for Thyself,
And for that love obey.

EVENING.

LISBON. S. M.

2 O Thou, our souls' chief Hope!
We to Thy mercy fly;
Where'er we are, Thou canst protect,
Whate'er we need, supply.

3 Whether we sleep or wake,
To Thee we both resign;
By night we see, as well as day,
If Thy light on us shine.

4 Whether we live or die,
Both we submit to Thee;
In death we live, as well as life,
If Thine in death we be.

546 *Evening Hymn.* S. M.

1 The day, O Lord! is spent;
Abide with us, and rest;
Our hearts' desires are fully bent
On making thee our guest.

2 We have not reached that land,
That happy land, as yet,
Where holy angels round thee stand
Whose sun can never set.

3 Our sun is sinking now;
Our day is almost o'er;
O Sun of Righteousness! do thou
Shine on us evermore.

547 *Evening Hymn.* S. M.

1 The day is past and gone,
The evening shades appear;
Oh, may I ever keep in mind
The night of death draws near.

2 I lay my garments by,
Upon my bed to rest;
So death will soon remove me hence,
And leave my soul undressed.

3 Lord! keep me safe this night,
Secure from all my fears;
May angels guard me while I sleep
Till morning light appears.

4 And when my days are past,
And I from time remove,
Lord! may I in thy bosom rest,
The bosom of thy love.

548 *Evening Hymn.* S. M.

1 To-morrow, Lord! is thine,
Lodged in thy sov'reign hand;
And if its sun arise and shine,
It shines by thy command.

2 The present moment flies,
And bears our life away:
Oh, make thy servants truly wise,
That they may live to-day.

3 One thing demands our care;
Oh, be it still pursued,
Lest, slighted once, the season fair
Should never be renewed.

4 To Jesus may we fly
Swift as the morning light,
Lest life's young golden beam should die
In sudden, endless night.

MORNING.

WARE. L. M.

549   *Morning Song.*   L. M.

1 God of the morning, at whose voice
The cheerful sun makes haste to rise,
And like a giant doth rejoice
To run his journey through the skies:

2 From the fair chambers of the east
The circuit of his race begins;
And, without weariness or rest,
Round the whole earth he flies and shines.

3 O like the sun, may I fulfil
The appointed duties of the day;
With ready mind and active will
March on and keep my heavenly way!

4 But I shall rove, and lose the race,
If God, my Sun, should disappear,
And leave me in this world's wide maze,
To follow every wandering star.

5 Give me thy counsel for my guide,
And then receive me to thy bliss:
All my desires and hopes beside
Are faint and cold compared with this.

550   *Morning Hymn.*   L. M.

1 Forth in thy name, O Lord, I go,
My daily labor to pursue,
Thee, only thee, resolved to know,
In all I think, or speak, or do.

2 The task thy wisdom hath assigned,
O let me cheerfully fulfil;
In all my works thy presence find,
And prove thy good and perfect will.

3 Thee may I set at my right hand,
Whose eyes my inmost substance see,
And labor on at thy command,
And offer all my works to thee.

4 Give me to bear thy easy yoke,
And every moment watch and pray;
And still to things eternal look,
And hasten to thy glorious day;

5 For thee delightfully employ
Whate'er thy bounteous grace hath given,
And run my course with even joy,
And closely walk with thee to heaven.

551   *Morning Hymn.*   L. M.

1 Lord! let my heart still turn to Thee,
In all my hours of waking thought;
Nor let this heart e'er wish to flee,
Or think, or feel, where Thou art not.

2 In every hour of pain and woe,
When nought on earth this heart can cheer,
When sighs will burst and tears will flow,
Lord, hush the sigh and chase the tear.

3 In every dream of earthly bliss,
Do Thou, dear Jesus, present be;
Nor let a thought of happiness
On earth intrude apart from Thee!

4 To my last ling'ring thought at night,
Do Thou, Lord Jesus, still be near;
And ere the dawn of opening light,
In still, small accents wake mine ear.

EVENING.

HAMBURG. L. M.

552 *Evening Hymn.* L. M.

1 My God! how endless is thy love!
Thy gifts are ev'ry evening new,
And morning mercies from above
Gently distill like early dew.

2 Thou spread'st the curtain of the night,
Great Guardian of my sleeping hours!
Thy sov'reign word restores the light,
And quickens all my drowsy powers.

3 I yield my powers to thy command,
To thee I consecrate my days;
Perpetual blessings from thy hand
Demand perpetual songs of praise.

553 *Evening Hymn.* L. M.

1 All praise to thee, my God! this night,
For all the blessings of the light;
Keep me, oh keep me, King of kings!
Beneath thine own almighty wings.

2 Forgive me, Lord! for thy dear Son,
The ill that I this day have done,
That with the world, myself and thee
I, ere I sleep, at peace may be.

3 Teach me to live that I may dread
The grave as little as my bed,
To die that this vile body may
Rise glorious at the awful day.

4 Oh may my soul on thee repose,
And may sweet sleep mine eyelids close—
Sleep that shall me more vigorous make
To serve my God when I awake.

5 When in the night I sleepless lie,
My soul with heavenly thoughts supply;
Let no ill dreams disturb my rest,
No power of darkness me molest.

6 Oh, when shall I in endless day
For ever chase dark sleep away,
And praise with the angelic choir
Incessant sing, and never tire?

554 *Evening Hymn.* L. M.

1 Great God! to thee my evening song
With humble gratitude I raise:
Oh, let thy mercy tune my tongue,
And fill my heart with lively praise.

2 My days, unclouded as they pass,
And every gentle, rolling hour,
Are monuments of wondrous grace,
And witness to thy love and power.

3 And yet this thoughtless, wretched heart,
Too oft regardless of thy love
Ungrateful can from thee depart,
And, fond of trifles, vainly rove.

4 Seal my forgiveness in the blood
Of Jesus; his dear name alone
I plead for pardon, gracious God!
And kind acceptance at thy throne.

5 Let this blest hope mine eyelids close,
With sleep refresh my feeble frame;
Safe in thy care may I repose,
And wake with praises to thy name.

555 *Matt. 11: 28,29.* 11s & 10s.

1 Come, ye disconsolate! where'er ye languish,
Come to the mercy-seat, fervently kneel;
Here bring your wounded hearts; here tell your anguish;
Earth has no sorrow, that heaven cannot heal.

2 Joy of the desolate! Light of the straying!
Hope, when all others die, fadeless and pure!
Here speaks the Comforter, in God's name saying,
Earth has no sorrow, that heaven cannot cure.

3 Here see the Bread of life; see waters flowing
Forth from the throne of God, boundless in love:
Come to the feast prepared; come, ever knowing,
Earth has no sorrow, but heaven can remove.

556 *The Star in the East.* 11s & 10s.

1 Brightest and best of the sons of the morning!
Dawn on our darkness, and lend us thine aid;
Star of the East, the horizon adorning,
Guide where our infant Redeemer is laid.

2 Cold on his cradle the dew-drops are shining;
Low lies his head with the beasts of the stall:
Angels adore him, in slumbers reclining,
Maker, and Monarch, and Saviour of all!

3 Say, shall we yield him, in costly devotion
Odors of Edom, and offerings divine?
Gems of the mountain, and pearls of the ocean,
Myrrh from the forest, or gold from the mine?

4 Vainly we offer each ample oblation,
Vainly with gold would his favors secure:
Richer, by far, is the heart's adoration;
Dearer to God are the prayers of the poor.

5 Brightest and best of the sons of the morning!
Dawn on our darkness, and lend us thine aid;
Star of the East, the horizon adorning,
Guide where our infant Redeemer is laid.

MISCELLANEOUS.

MESSIAH; or, Harvest Home. 7s. Double.

557 *Harvest Home.* 7s.

1 Come, ye thankful people, come,
Raise the song of Harvest Home!
All is safely gathered in,
Ere the winter storms begin:
God our Maker doth provide
For our wants to be supplied:
Come to God's own temple, come,
Raise the song of Harvest Home!

2 We ourselves are God's own field,
Fruit unto his praise to yield:
Wheat and tares together sown,
Unto joy or sorrow grown:
First the blade, and then the ear,
Then the full corn shall appear:
Grant, O Harvest-Lord, that we
Wholesome grain and pure may be!

3 For the Lord our God shall come,
And shall take his harvest home:
From his field shall in that day
All offences purge away:
Give his angels charge at last
In the fire the tares to cast:
But the fruitful ears to store
In his garner evermore.

4 Then, thou Church Triumphant, come,
Raise the song of Harvest Home!
All are safely gathered in,
Free from sorrow, free from sin:
There, forever purified,
In God's garner to abide:
Come, ten thousand angels, come,
Raise the glorious Harvest Home!

558 *Ps. 84.* 7s.

1 Pleasant are thy courts above,
In the land of light and love;
Pleasant are thy courts below,
In this land of sin and woe.
Oh, my spirit longs and faints
For the converse of thy saints,
For the brightness of thy face,
For thy fullness, God of grace!

2 Lord, be mine this prize to win,
Guide me through this world of sin;
Keep me by thy saving grace,
Give me at thy side a place;
Sun and Shield alike thou art,
Guide and guard my erring heart;
Grace and glory flow from thee,
Shed, oh, shed them, Lord, on me,

MISCELLANEOUS.

WALNUT STREET CHANT; or, The Golden Gates. C. M.

559 *John 14: 3.*

1 The golden gates are lifted up,
The doors are opened wide,
The King of glory is gone in
Unto his Father's side.

2 Thou art gone up before us, Lord,
To make for us a place,
That we may be where now thou art,
And look upon God's face.

3 And ever on thine earthly path
A gleam of glory lies;
A light still breaks behind the cloud
That vailed thee from our eyes.

4 Lift up our hearts, lift up our minds,
Let thy dear grace be given,
That while we tarry here below,
Our treasure be in heaven!

5 That where thou art, at God's right hand,
Our hope, our love may be;
Dwell thou in us, that we may dwell
Forevermore in thee!

560 *Ps. 68: 19.* **C. M.**

1 Salvation!—oh, the joyful sound!
'T is pleasure to our ears;
A sovereign balm for every wound,
A cordial for our fears.

2 Buried in sorrow and in sin,
At hell's dark door we lay;—

C. M. But we arise by grace divine,
To see a heavenly day.

3 Salvation!—let the echo fly
The spacious earth around;
While all the armies of the sky
Conspire to raise the sound.

561 *Job. 1: 21.* **C. M.**

1 One prayer I have—all prayers in one—
When I am wholly thine;
Thy will, my God, thy will be done,
And let that will be mine.

2 All-wise, almighty, and all-good,
In thee I firmly trust;
Thy ways, unknown or understood,
Are merciful and just.

3 May I remember that to thee
Whate'er I have I owe;
And back, in gratitude, from me
May all thy bounties flow.

4 And though thy wisdom takes away,
Shall I arraign thy will?
No, let me bless thy name, and say,
"The Lord is gracious still."

5 A pilgrim through the earth I roam,
Of nothing long possessed;
And all must fail when I go home,
For this is not my rest.

MISCELLANEOUS.

BEETHOVEN; or, While O'er the Deep. L. M.

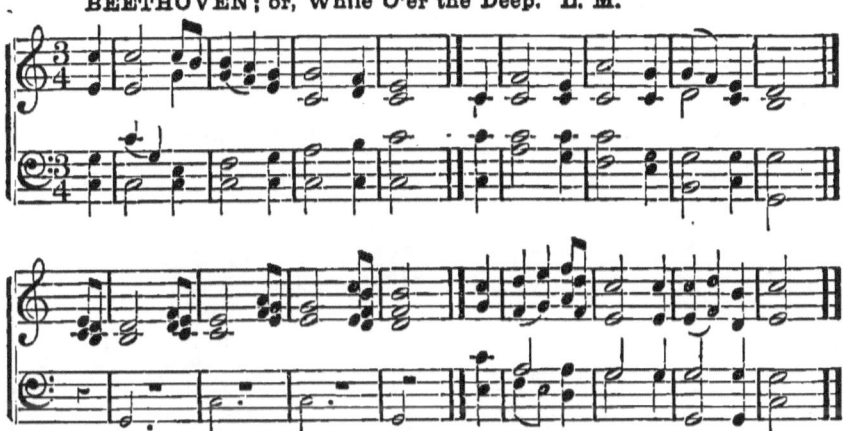

562   *Isa 63: 13.*   **L. M.**

1. While o'er the deep thy servants sail,
Send thou, O Lord, the prosperous gale;
And on their hearts where'er they go,
Oh, let thy heavenly breezes blow!

2 If on the morning's wings they fly,
They will not pass beyond thine eye;
The wanderer's prayer thou bend'st to hear,
And faith exults to know thee near.

3 When tempests rock the groaning bark,
Oh, hide them safe in Jesus' ark!
When in the tempting port they ride,
Oh, keep them safe at Jesus' side!

4 If life's wide ocean smile or roar,
Still guide them to the heavenly shore;
And grant their dust in Christ may sleep,
Abroad, at home, or in the deep.

563   *"So He bringeth them unto their desired haven."*   **L. M.**

1 Almighty Father, hear our cry,
As o'er the trackless deep we roam;
Be Thou our haven always nigh,
On homeless waters Thou our home!

2 O Jesus, Saviour, at whose voice
The tempest sank to perfect rest,
Bid Thou the mourner's heart rejoice,
And cleanse and calm the troubled breast.

3 O Holy Ghost, beneath whose power
The ocean woke to life and light,
Command Thy blessing in this hour,
Thy fostering warmth, Thy quickening might.

564   *Rev. 21 : 23.*   **L. M.**

1 A light streams downward from the sky,
An open door the radiance shows,
Through which the ransomed spirits fly,
To enter bliss no mortal knows.

2 Girded with gladness in that home,
No soul its sackcloth ever wears;
No sickness, griefs, or fears can come,
Nor burdened heart with heavy cares.

3 A tree of life, with pleasant shade,
Grows in that upper Paradise;
Renewed from Eden's early glade,
Its various fruit each want supplies.

4 There flowers of grace in beauty stand,
With fragrance of immortal bloom;
No blighting breath, nor icy hand,
Demands their sweetness for the tomb.

5 Sweet sinless home! my spirit longs
To mount the skies, and breathe thine air;
With grateful heart to join the songs,
Whose rolling tide flows ceaseless there!

Doxology.   **L. M.**

To God the Father, God the Son,
And God the Spirit, Three in One,
Be honor, praise, and glory given,
By all on earth, and all in heaven!

MISCELLANEOUS.

NORTHAMPTON, or When Adverse Winds.

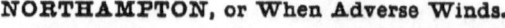

565   *Deut. 33: 25.*   **L. M.**

1 When adverse winds and waves arise,
And in my heart despondence sighs;
When life her throng of cares reveals,
And weakness o'er my spirit steals,
Grateful I hear the kind decree,
That "as my day, my strength shall be."

2 One trial more must yet be past,
One pang—the keenest and the last;
And when, with brow convulsed and pale,
My feeble, quivering heart-strings fail,
Redeemer! grant my soul to see
That "as her day, her strength shall be."

566   *Ps. 84: 3.*   **L. M.**

1 Forth from the dark and stormy sky,
Lord, to thine altar's shade we fly;
Forth from the world its hope and fear,
Father, we seek thy shelter here;
Weary and weak, thy grace we pray;
Turn not, O Lord, thy guests away.

2 Long have we roamed in want and pain,
Long have we sought thy rest in vain;
Wildered in doubt, in darkness lost,
Long have our souls been tempest-tossed;
Low at thy feet our sins we lay;
Turn not, O Lord, thy guests away.

567   *Phil. 4: 19.*   **L. M.**

1 None loves me, Saviour, with thy love;
None else can meet such needs as mine;
Oh! grant me, as thou shalt approve,
All that befits a child of thine!
From every fear and doubt release,
And give me confidence and peace.

2 Give me a faith shall never fail,
One that shall always work by love;
And then, whatever foes assail,
They shall but higher courage move
More boldly for the truth to strive,
And more by faith in thee to live.

568   *Jer. 8: 22.*   **L. M.**

1 Peace, troubled soul, whose plaintive moan
Hath taught each scene the notes of woe;
Cease thy complaint, suppress thy groan,
And let thy tears forget to flow;
Behold, the precious balm is found,
To lull thy pain, to heal thy wound.

MISCELLANEOUS.

MARRIAGE. S. M.

569 *John 2: 2.*

1 How welcome was the call,
And sweet the festal lay,
When Jesus' deigned in Cana's hall
To bless the marriage day.

2 O Lord of life and love,
Come Thou again to-day;
And bring a blessing from above
That ne'er shall pass away.

3 O bless, as erst of old,
The Bridegroom and the Bride;
Bless with the holier stream that flowed
Forth from Thy pierced side.

4 Before Thine altar-throne
This mercy we implore;
As Thou dost knit them, Lord, in one,
So bless them evermore.

570 *Love of God.* S. M.

1 In every trying hour
My soul to Jesus flies;
I trust in his almighty power,
When swelling billows rise.

2 His comforts bear me up;
I trust a faithful God;
The sure foundation of my hope
Is in my Saviour's blood.

3 Loud hallelujahs sing
To our Redeemer's name;
In joy or sorrow—life or death—
His love is still the same.

571 *2 Cor. 5: 7.* S. M.

1 If, through unruffled seas,
Toward heaven we calmly sail,
With grateful hearts, O God, to thee,
We'll own the favoring gale.

2 But should the surges rise,
And rest delay to come,
Blest be the sorrow—kind the storm,
Which drives us nearer home.

3 Soon shall our doubts and fears
All yield to thy control:
Thy tender mercies shall illume
The midnight of the soul.

4 Teach us, in every state,
To make thy will our own;
And when the joys of sense depart,
To live by faith alone.

572 *Ps. 126: 5.* S. M.

1 The harvest dawn is near,
The year delays not long;
And he who sows with many a tear,
Shall reap with many a song.

2 Sad to his toil he goes,
His seed with weeping leaves;
But he shall come, at twilight's close,
And bring his golden sheaves.

MISCELLANEOUS.

SING OF JESUS. 8s & 5s.

573   *Rev. 5: 9—13.*   8s & 5s.

1 Sing of Jesus, sing forever
Of the love that changes never!
Who, or what, from Him can sever
Those He makes His own?

2 With His blood the Lord hath bought them,
When they knew Him not He sought them,
And from all their wanderings brought them;
His the praise alone.

3 Through the desert Jesus leads them,
With the bread of heaven he feeds them,
And through all their way He speeds them
To their home above.

4 There they see the Lord who bought them,
Him who came from Heaven and sought them,
Him who by His Spirit taught them,
Him they serve and love.

574   *Rev. 5: 9—13.*   8s & 5s.

1 Saints in glory! we together
Know the song that ceases never;
Song of songs Thou art, O Saviour,
All that endless day.

2 Theme of Adam when forgiven,
Theme of Abraham, David, Stephen;
Souls, ye chant it entering Heaven,
Now, henceforth, alway.

3 O the God-man! O Immanuel!
Cloud by day! Jehovah-Angel!
Fire by night! He led His Israel,
So He leads us home.

4 Come, ye angels, round us gather,
While to Jesus we draw nearer;
In His throne He'll seat forever,
Those for whom he died.

5 Underneath His throne, a river
Clear as crystal flows forever,
Like His fulness, failing never:
Hail enthroned Lamb!

6 Oh the unsearchable Redeemer!
Shoreless Ocean, sounded never!
Yesterday, to-day, forever,
Jesus Christ, the same.

MISCELLANEOUS.

THE VOICE OF FREE GRACE. 12s.

Sing the small notes for the 576th hymn.

2 Ye souls that are wounded! oh, flee to the Saviour!
He calls you in mercy, 'tis infinite favor;
Your sins are increasing, escape to the mountain—
His blood can remove them, it flows from the fountain.
  Hallelujah to the Lamb, etc.

3 O Jesus! ride onward, triumphantly glorious!
O'er sin, death, and hell, thou art more than victorious;
Thy name is the theme of the great congregation,
While angels and men raise the shout of salvation.
  Hallelujah to the Lamb, etc.

4 With joy shall we stand, when escaped to the shore;
With harps in our hands, we'll praise him the more;

We'll range the sweet plains on the banks of the river,
And sing of salvation forever and ever!
  Hallelujah to the Lamb, etc.

576   *John 11: 25.*   **12s.**

1 Thou art gone to the grave! but we will not deplore thee,
Though sorrows and darkness encompass the tomb;
The Saviour hath passed through its portals before thee;
And the Lamp of his love is thy guide through the gloom.

2 Thou art gone to the grave! but we will not deplore thee,
Since God was thy ransom, thy guardian, thy guide;
He gave thee, he took thee, and he will restore thee;
And death hath no sting, since the Saviour hath died.

MISCELLANEOUS.

WE PRAISE THEE, O GOD. 11s & 12s.

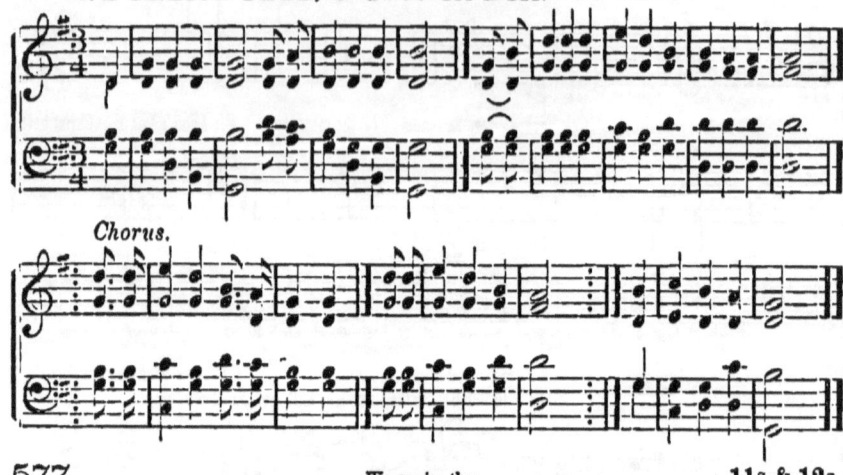

577 *We praise thee.* 11s & 12s.

1 We praise thee, O God! for the Son of thy love,
For Jesus, who died, and is now gone above.
  CHORUS.—Hallelujah! thine the glory, Hallelujah! Amen.
  Hallelujah! thine the glory, We praise thee again.

2 We praise thee, O God! for thy Spirit of light!
Who has shown us the Saviour, and scattered our night.—*Cho.*

3 All glory and praise to the Lamb that was slain,
Who hath borne all our sins, and has cleansed every stain.—*Cho.*

4 Revive us again: fill each heart with thy love!
May our souls be rekindled with fire from above.—*Cho.*

578 *Rejoice and be glad.* 11s & 12s.

1 Rejoice and be glad! the Redeemer has come!
Go look on his cradle, his cross, and his tomb.
  CHORUS.—Sound his praises, tell the story, of him who was slain.
  Sound his praises, tell with gladness he liveth again.

2 Rejoice and be glad! it is sunshine at last!
The clouds have departed, the shadows are past.

3 Rejoice and be glad! for the blood hath been shed!
Redemption is finished, the price hath been paid.

4 Rejoice and be glad! now the pardon is free!
The Just for the unjust, has died on the tree.

5 Rejoice and be glad! for the Lamb that was slain
O'er death is triumphant, and liveth again.

6 Rejoice and be glad! for our King is on high,
He pleadeth for us, on his throne in the sky.

7 Rejoice and be glad! for he cometh again;
He cometh in glory, the Lamb that was slain.

MISCELLANEOUS.

EVENTIDE. 10s.

579   *Abide with me.*   10s.

1 Abide with me! Fast falls the eventide;
  The darkness deepens; Lord, with me abide!
  When other helpers fail, and comforts flee,
  Help of the helpless, oh, abide with me!

2 Swift to its close ebbs out life's little day;
  Earth's joys grow dim, its glories pass away;
  Change and decay in all around I see;
  O thou who changest not, abide with me!

3 Come not in terrors, as the King of kings,
  But kind and good, with healing in thy wings;
  Tears for all woes, a heart for every plea:
  Come, Friend of sinners, thus abide with me!

4 I need thy presence every passing hour;
  What but thy grace can foil the tempter's power?
  Who like thyself my guide and stay can be?
  Through cloud and sunshine, oh, abide with me!

5 I fear no foe, with thee at hand to bless;
  Ills have no weight, and tears no bitterness:
  Where is death's sting? where, grave, thy victory?
  I triumph still, if thou abide with me.

6 Hold thou thy cross before my closing eyes;
  Shine through the gloom, and point me to the skies;
  Heaven's morning breaks, and earth's vain shadows flee!
  In life, in death, O Lord, abide with me!

MISCELLANEOUS.

O HOLY SAVIOUR. 8s & 6s.

580 *John 15: 5.*   **8s & 6s.**

1 O holy Saviour, Friend unseen!
Since on thine arm thou bid'st me lean,
Help me, throughout life's varying scene,
By faith to cling to thee,—to thee.

2 Blest with this fellowship divine,
Take what thou wilt, I'll ne'er repine;
E'en as the branches to the vine,
My soul would cling to thee,—to thee.

3 Far from my home, fatigued, oppressed,
Here have I found a place of rest;
An exile still, yet not unblest,
While I can cling to thee,—to thee.

4 What though the world deceitful prove,
And earthly friends and hopes remove?
With patient, uncomplaining love
Still would I cling to thee,—to thee.

5 Oft, when I seem to tread alone
Some barren waste, with thorns o'ergrown,
Thy voice of love in gentlest tone,
Whispers, "Still cling to me,—to me."

6 Though faith and hope may long be tried,
I ask not, need not, aught beside;
How safe, how calm, how satisfied,
The souls that cling to thee,—to thee!

581 *John 13: 1.*   **8s & 6s.**

1 O Thou the contrite sinner's Friend,
Who loving, lov'st them to the end,
On this alone my hopes depend,
That thou wilt plead for me,—for me.

2 When, weary in the Christian race,
Far off appears my resting place,
And fainting I mistrust thy grace,
Then, Saviour! plead for me,—for me.

3 When I have erred, and gone astray,
Afar from thine and wisdom's way,
And see no glimmering guiding ray,
Still, Saviour! plead for me,—for me.

4 When Satan, by my sins made bold,
Strives from thy cross to loose my hold,
Then, with thy pitying arms, enfold,
And plead, oh plead for me,—for me.

5 And, when my dying hour draws near,
Darkened with anguish, guilt, and fear,
Then to my fainting sight appear,
Pleading in heaven for me,—for me.

6 When the full light of heavenly day
Reveals my sins in dread array,
Say thou hast washed them all away;
Oh, say thou plead'st for me,—for me.

MISCELLANEOUS.

ALL GLORY, PRAISE, AND HONOR. 7s & 6s.

582 *All Glory, Praise, and Honor.* **7s & 6s.**

1 All glory, praise, and honor
To thee, Redeemer King!
To whom the lips of children
Made sweet hosannas ring.

   Cho.—All glory, praise and honor
      To thee, Redeemer King!
      To whom the lips of children
      Made sweet hosannas ring.

2 Thou art the King of Israel,
Thou David's royal Son,
Who in the Lord's name comest,
The King and blessed one. *Cho.*

3 The company of angels
Are praising thee on high;
And mortal men, and all things
Created make reply. *Cho.*

4 The people of the Hebrews
With palms before thee went;
Our praise and prayer and anthems
Before thee we present. *Cho.*

5 To thee before thy passion
They sang their hymns of praise;
To thee amidst thy glory
Our melody we raise. *Cho.*

6 Thou didst accept their praises;
Accept the prayers we bring,
Who in all good delightest,
Thou good and gracious king! *Cho.*

583 *Come, let us sing.* **7s & 6s.**

1 Come, let us sing of Jesus,
While hearts and accents blend;
Come, let us sing of Jesus,
The sinner's only Friend. *Cho.*

2 His holy soul rejoices,
Amid the choirs above,
To hear our youthful voices
Exulting in his love. *Cho.*

3 We love to sing of Jesus,
Who died our souls to save;
We love to sing of Jesus,
Triumphant o'er the grave. *Cho.*

4 And in our hour of danger
We'll trust his love alone
Who once slept in a manger,
And now sits on the throne. *Cho.*

MISCELLANEOUS.

GOING HOME. L. M.

1. My heavenly home is bright and fair; Nor pain, nor death can enter there;
Its glittering towers the sun out-shine; That heavenly man-sion shall be mine;

Chorus.
I'm go-ing home, I'm go-ing home, I'm go-ing home to die no more,
To die no more, to die no more, I'm go-ing home to die no more.

584   **L. M.**

2 My Father's house is built on high,
Far, far above the starry sky;
When from this earthly prison free,
That heavenly mansion mine shall be.
    Cho.

3 While here, a stranger far from home.
Afliction's waves may round me foam;
And, tho' like Lazarus, sick and poor,
My heavenly mansion is secure. *Cho.*

4 Let others seek a home below,
Which flames devour, or waves o'erflow,
Be mine a happier lot, to own
A heavenly mansion near the throne.
    Cho.

5 Then fail the earth, let stars decline,
And sun and moon refuse to shine,
All nature sink and cease to be,
That heavenly mansion stands for me.
    Cho.

585   Ps. 119: 151.   **L. M.**

1 O Love Divine! that stooped to share
Our sharpest pang, our bitterest tear,
On thee we cast each earth-born care,
We smile at pain while thou art near.
    Cho.

2 Though long the weary way we tread,
And sorrow crown each ling'ring year,
No path we shun, no darkness dread,
Our heart still whisp'ring, thou art near.
    Cho.

3 On thee we fling our burd'ning woe,
O Love Divine, for ever dear;
Content to suffer while we know,
Living or dying, thou art near.

MISCELLANEOUS.

REST FOR THE WEARY. 8s & 7s.

586   *Rest for the Weary.*   8s & 7s.

1 In the Christian's home in glory,
There remains a land of rest;
There my Saviour's gone before me,
To fulfil my soul's request.

CHO.—There is rest for the weary,
    There is rest for the weary,
    There is rest for the weary,
    There is rest for you.
    On the other side of Jordan,
    In the sweet fields of Eden,
    Where the tree of life is blooming,
    There is rest for you.

2 He is fitting up my mansion,
Which eternally shall stand,
For my stay shall not be transient,
In that holy, happy land.   *Cho.*

3 Pain or sickness ne'er shall enter,
Grief nor woe my lot shall share;
But in that celestial center,
I a crown of life shall wear.   *Cho.*

4 Death itself shall then be vanquished,
And his sting shall be withdrawn;
Shout for gladness, oh, ye ransomed,
Hail with joy the rising morn!   *Cho.*

5 Sing, oh, sing, ye heirs of glory,
Shout your triumph as you go;
Zion's gate will open for you,
You shall find an entrance through.
                                     Cho.

587   *Deut.* 12: 9.   8s & 7s.

1 This is not my place of resting,—
Mine's a city yet to come;
Onward to it I am hasting,
On to my eternal home.   *Cho.*

2 In it all is light and glory;
O'er it shines a nightless day;
Every trace of sin's sad story,
All the curse, hath passed away.   *Cho.*

3 There the Lamb, our Shepherd, leads us
By the streams of life along,
On the freshest pastures feeds us,
Turns our sighing into song.   *Cho.*

4 Soon we pass this desert dreary,
Soon we bid farewell to pain;
Never more are sad or weary,
Never, never sin again.   *Cho.*

THY WAY, NOT MINE.

6s. Double.

588 *Job 23: 11.*

1 Thy way, not mine, O Lord,
However dark it be!
Lead me by thine own hand;
Choose out the path for me.
I dare not choose my lot:
I would not, if I might;
Choose thou for me, my God,
So shall I walk aright.

2 The kingdom that I seek
Is thine: so let the way
That leads to it be thine,
Else I must surely stray.
Take thou my cup, and it
With joy or sorrow fill,
As best to thee may seem;
Choose thou my good and ill.

3 Choose thou for me my friends,
My sickness or my health;
Choose thou my cares for me,
My poverty or wealth.
Not mine, not mine the choice,
In things or great or small;
Be thou my Guide, my Strength,
My Wisdom, and my All.

589 *Heb. 12: 7.* **6s.**

1 Be tranquil, O my soul,
Be quiet every fear!
Thy Father hath control,
And he is ever near.
Ne'er of thy lot complain,
Whatever may befall;
Sickness, or care, or pain,
'Tis well-appointed all.

2 A Father's chastening hand
Is leading thee along;
Nor distant is the land,
Where swells the immortal song.
Oh, then, my soul, be still!
Await heaven's high decree;
Seek but thy Father's will,
It shall be well with thee.

590 *John 16: 33.*

1 Cheer up, desponding soul!
Thy longing pleased I see;
'Tis part of that great whole
Wherewith I longed for thee:
Wherewith I longed for thee,
And left my Father's throne
From death to set thee free,
And claim thee for my own.

2 To claim thee for my own
I suffered on the cross;
Oh, were my love but known,
All else would be as dross!
All else would be as dross,
And souls, through grace divine,
Would count their gains but loss,
To live forever mine.

591 *Isa. 33: 17.*

1 There is a blessed home
Beyond this land of woe,
Where trials never come,
Nor tears of sorrow flow;
Where faith is lost in sight,
And patient hope is crowned,
And everlasting light
Its glory throws around.

2 There is a land of peace;
Good angels know it well;
Glad songs that never cease
Within its portals swell;
Around its glorious throne
Ten thousand saints adore
Christ, with the Father one,
And Spirit, evermore.

3 Oh, joy all joys beyond!
To see the Lamb who died,
And count each sacred wound,
In hands, and feet, and side;
To give to him the praise
Of every triumph won,
And sing through endless days
The great things he hath done.

4 Look up, ye saints of God!
Nor fear to tread below
The path your Saviour trod
Of daily toil and woe;
6s. Wait but a little while
In uncomplaining love;
His own most gracious smile
Shall welcome you above.

592 *Mark 14: 36.* 6s.

1 My Jesus, as thou wilt!
Oh! may thy will be mine;
Into thy hand of love
I would my all resign;
Through sorrow, or through joy,
Conduct me as thine own,
And help me still to say,
My Lord, thy will be done!

2 My Jesus, as thou wilt!
Though seen through many a tear,
Let not my star of hope
Grow dim or disappear:
6s. Since thou on earth hast wept,
And sorrowed oft alone,
If I must weep with thee,
My Lord, thy will be done!

3 My Jesus, as thou wilt!
All shall be well for me;
Each changing future scene
I gladly trust with thee:
Straight to my home above
I travel calmly on,
And sing, in life or death,
My Lord, thy will be done!

593 *Ps. 116: 7.* 6s.

1 My spirit longs for thee
To dwell within my breast;
Although unworthy I
Of so divine a Guest!
Of so divine a Guest
Unworthy though I be,
Yet hath my heart no rest
Until it come to thee!

2 Until it come to thee,
In vain I look around:
In all that I can see
No rest is to be found!
No rest is to be found,
But in thy bleeding love,
Oh, let my wish be crowned,
And send it from above!

MISCELLANEOUS.

UPLIFT YOUR BANNER. L. M.

594   *Uplift the Banner!*   L. M.

1 Uplift the banner! Let it float
Sky-ward and sea-ward, high and wide;
The sun shall light its shining folds,
The Cross, on which the Saviour died.

2 Uplift the banner! Angels bend
In anxious silence o'er the sign,
And vainly seek to comprehend
The wonder of the love divine.

3 Uplift the banner! Heathen lands
Shall see from far the glorious sight,
And nations, gathering at the call,
Their spirits kindle in its light.

4 Uplift the banner! Let it float
Sky-ward and sea-ward, high and wide;
Our glory only in the Cross,
Our only hope the Crucified.

5 Uplift the banner! Wide and high
Sea-ward and sky-ward let it shine:
Nor skill, nor might, nor merit ours;
We conquer only in that sign.

595   John 17: 21.   L. M.

1 Let me be with thee where thou art,
My Saviour, my eternal Rest;
Then only will this longing heart
Be fully and forever blest.

2 Let me be with thee where thou art,
Thine unvailed glory to behold;
Then only will this wandering heart
Cease to be false to thee and cold.

3 Let me be with thee where thou art,
Where spotless saints thy name adore;
Then only will this sinful heart
Be evil and defiled no more.

4 Let me be with thee where thou art,
Where none can die, where none remove;
There neither death nor life will part
Me from thy presence and thy love.

596   John 12: 21.   L. M.

1 Far from my thoughts, vain world, begone!
Let my religious hours alone:
Fain would mine eyes my Saviour see—
I wait a visit, Lord! from thee.

2 My heart grows warm with holy fire,
And kindles with a pure desire:
Come, my dear Jesus! from above,
And feed my soul with heavenly love.

3 Blest Saviour! what delicious fare—
How sweet thine entertainments are!
Never did angels taste above
Redeeming grace and dying love.

MISCELLANEOUS.

JESUS LEAD THE WAY. 5s &.8s.

597   *Luke 5: 11.*   5s & 8s.

1 Jesus! lead the way
To eternal day:
And although the way be cheerless,
We will follow, calm and fearless:
Guide us by thy hand
To our Fatherland.

2 If the way be drear,
If the foe be near,
If our days be very dreary,
And our burdens very weary,
Lead us by thy hand,
To our Fatherland.

3 When we seek relief
From a long-felt grief,
Then in all our woe and weakness,
Grant us patience, grant us meekness,
Guide us by thy hand
To our Fatherland.

4 Jesus! still lead on,
Till our rest be won;
Heavenly Leader! still direct us,
Still support, console, protect us,
Till we safely stand,
In our Fatherland.

598 .   *Jesus, slain for me.*   5s & 8s.

1 Jesus, who can be
Once compared with Thee!
Source of rest and consolation,
Life, and light, and full salvation;
Son of God, with Thee
None compared can be!

2 Jesus, slain for me
On the accursed tree!
From all sin me to deliver
And from death to save forever!
I am by thy blood
Reconciled to God.

3 Grant me steadiness,
Lord, to run my race,
Following Thee with love most tender,
So that Satan may not hinder
Me by craft or force;
Further Thou my course.

4 When I hence depart,
Strengthen Thou my heart,
Where Thou art, O Lord, convey me;
In Thy righteousness array me;
That at Thy right hand
Joyful I may stand.

MISCELLANEOUS.

THY WILL BE DONE. 8s & 4s.

599   *Acts* 21 : 14.   8s & 4s.

1 "Thy will be done!" In devious way
The hurrying stream of life may run;
Yet still our grateful hearts shall say,
  "Thy will be done!"

2 "Thy will be done!" If o'er us shine
A gladdening and a prosperous sun;
This prayer will make it more divine,—
  "Thy will be done!"

3 "Thy will be done!" Though shrouded o'er
Our path with gloom; one comfort, one
Is ours,—to breathe, while we adore,
  "Thy will be done!"

600   *Acts* 21: 14.   8s & 4s.

1 My God, my Father! while I stray
Far from my home on life's rough way,
Oh, teach me from my heart to say,
  Thy will be done!

2 What though in lonely grief I sigh
For friends beloved, no longer nigh?
Submissive still would I reply,
  Thy will be done!

3 Though thou hast called me to resign
What most I prized, it ne'er was mine;
I have but yielded what was thine;
  Thy will be done!

4 Should grief or sickness waste away
My life in premature decay,
My Father! still I strive to say,
  Thy will be done!

5 Let but my fainting heart be blest
With thy sweet Spirit for its guest;
My God! to thee I leave the rest:
  Thy will be done!

6 Renew my will from day to day;
Blend it with thine, and take away
All that now makes it hard to say,
  Thy will be done!

7 Then when on earth I breathe no more
The prayer oft mixed with tears before,
I'll sing upon a happier shore,
  Thy will be done!

601   *Hallelujah!*   8s & 4s.

1 The strife is o'er, the battle done;
The triumph of the Lord is won;
Oh let the song of praise be sung!
  Hallelujah!

2 The powers of death have done their worst,
And Jesus hath His foes dispersed;
Let shouts of praise and joy outburst!
  Hallelujah!

3 On that third morn He rose again
In glorious majesty to reign;
Oh let us swell the joyful strain!
  Hallelujah!

4 Lord, by the stripes which wounded Thee,
From death's dread sting Thy servants free,
That we may live, and sing to Thee!
  Hallelujah!

MISCELLANEOUS.

LORD, WITH GLOWING HEART. 8s & 7s.

602 *Grace.* 8s & 7s.

1 Lord, with glowing heart I'd praise thee
For the bliss thy love bestows;
For the pardoning grace that saves me,
And the peace that from it flows:
Help, O God, my weak endeavor;
This dull soul to rapture raise;
Thou must light the flame, or never
Can my love be warmed to praise.

2 Praise, my soul, the God that sought thee,
Wretched wanderer, far astray;
Found thee lost, and kindly brought thee
From the paths of death away;
Praise, with love's devoutest feeling,
Him who saw thy guilt-born fear,
And, the light of hope revealing,
Bade the blood-stained cross appear.

3 Lord, this bosom's ardent feeling
Vainly would my lips express:
Low before thy footstool kneeling,
Deign thy suppliant's prayer to bless;
Let thy grace, my soul's chief treasure,
Love's pure flame within me raise;
And, since words can never measure,
Let my life show forth thy praise.

603 1 Cor. 3: 6. 8s & 7s.

1 Vain were all our toil and labor,
Did not God that labor bless;
Vain, without his grace and favor,
Every talent we possess.

2 Vainer still the hope of heaven,
That on human strength relies;
But to him shall help be given,
Who in humble faith applies.

3 Seek we, then, the Lord's Anointed;
He shall grant us peace and rest:
Ne'er was suppliant disappointed,
Who through Christ his prayer addressed.

604 John 19: 30. 8s, 7s & 4s.

1 Hark! the voice of love and mercy
Sounds aloud from Calvary;
See!—it rends the rocks asunder—
Shakes the earth—and vails the sky:
"It is finished!"—
Hear the dying Saviour cry.

2 "It is finished!"—oh, what pleasure
Do these charming words afford!
Heavenly blessings, without measure,
Flow to us through Christ, the Lord:
"It is finished!"—
Saints! the dying words record.

3 Tune your harps anew, ye seraphs!
Join to sing the pleasing theme:
All in earth and heaven, uniting,
Join to praise Immanuel's name:
Hallelujah!—
Glory to the bleeding Lamb!

MISCELLANEOUS.

GOOD; or, How Sweetly Flowed. — Geo. Kingsley.

605   L. M.

1 How sweetly flowed the gospel's sound
From lips of gentleness and grace,
When list'ning thousands gathered round,
And joy and reverence filled the place!

2 From heaven he came, of heaven he spoke,
To heaven he led his foll'wers' way;
Dark clouds of gloomy night he broke,
Unveiling an immortal day.

3 "Come, wanderers! to my Father's home,
Come, all ye weary ones! and rest:"
Yes, sacred Teacher; we will come,
Obey thee, love thee, and be blest.

606   *Matt. 11: 28.*   L. M.

1 With tearful eyes I look around;
Life seems a dark and stormy sea;
Yet, 'mid the gloom, I hear a sound,
A heavenly whisper, "Come to me."

2 It tells me of a place of rest;
It tells me where my soul may flee:
Oh, to the weary, faint, oppressed,
How sweet the bidding, "Come to me!"

3 "Come, for all else must fail and die!
Earth is no resting-place for thee;
To heaven direct thy weeping eye,
I am thy portion; Come to me!"

4 O voice of mercy! voice of love!
In conflict, grief, and agony,
Support me, cheer me from above!
And gently whisper, "Come to me!"

607   L. M.

1 My hope is built on nothing less
Than Jesus' blood and righteousness;
I dare not trust the sweetest frame,
But wholly lean on Jesus' name.

2 When darkness veils his lovely face,
I rest on his unchanging grace;
In every high and stormy gale,
My anchor holds within the veil.

3 His oath, his covenant, his blood,
Support me in the whelming flood;
When all around my soul gives way,
He then is all my hope and stay.

4 When he shall come with trumpet sound,
O, may I then in him be found;
Drest in his righteousness alone,
Faultless to stand before the throne!

608   L. M.

1 O Spirit of the living God,
In all thy plenitude of grace,
Where'er the foot of man hath trod,
Descend on our apostate race.

2 Give tongues of fire, and hearts of love,
To preach the reconciling word;
Give power and unction from above,
Where'er the joyful sound is heard.

3 Baptize the nations, far and nigh;
The triumphs of the cross record;
The name of Jesus glorify,
Till every kindred call him Lord.

MISCELLANEOUS.

MATTOON; or, My Father's House.

609 S. M.

1 My Father's house on high!
Home of my soul! how near
At times, to faith's foreseeing eye,
Thy golden gates appear!

2 I hear at morn and even
At noon and midnight hour,
The choral harmonies of heaven
Angelic music pour.

3 Oh, then my spirit faints
To reach the land I love—
The bright inheritance of saints,
My glorious home above.

610 S. M.

1 One sweetly solemn thought
Comes to me o'er and o'er,—
Nearer my home, to-day, am I
Than e'er I've been before.

2 Nearer my Father's house,
Where many mansions be;
Nearer to-day the great white throne;
Nearer the crystal sea.

3 Nearer the bound of life,
Where burdens are laid down;
Nearer to leave the heavy cross;
Nearer to gain the crown.

4 Father, perfect my trust!
Strengthen my power of faith!
Nor let me stand, at last, alone
Upon the shore of death.

611 S. M.

1 Servant of God, well done!
Rest from thy loved employ:
The battle fought, the victory won,
Enter thy Master's joy.

2 The pains of death are past;
Labor and sorrow cease;
And life's long warfare closed at last,
His soul is found in peace.

3 Soldier of Christ, well done!
Praise be thy new employ;
And, while eternal ages run,
Rest in thy Saviour's joy.

612 S. M.

1 Soldiers of Christ, arise,
And gird your armor on,
Strong in the strength which God supplies,
Through his eternal Son:

2 Strong in the Lord of hosts,
And in his mighty power,
Who in the strength of Jesus trusts,
Is more than conqueror.

3 From strength to strength go on;
Wrestle, and fight, and pray;
Tread all the powers of darkness down,
And win the well-fought day.

4 Still let the Spirit cry,
In all his soldiers, "Come,"
Till Christ the Lord descends from high,
And takes the conquerors home.

MISCELLANEOUS.

MEASE; or, God of the Morning Ray. 6s & 4s.   GEO. KING

613   *Acts* 17:28.   **6s & 4s.**
1 God of the morning ray,
  God of the rising day,
    Glorious in power!
In thee we live and move,
And thus we daily prove
  Thy condescending love
    Each passing hour.

2 God of our feeble race,
  God of redeeming grace,
    Spirit all-blest!
Our own eternal Friend,
Thy guardian influence lend,
From every snare defend—
    In thee we rest.

614   *Rev.* 14:3.   **6s & 4s.**
1 Sing, sing his lofty praise,
  Whom angels cannot raise,
    But whom they sing;
Jesus, who reigns above,
Object of angels' love,
Jesus, whose grace we prove,
    Jesus, our King.

2 Rich is the grace we sing,
  Poor is the praise we bring,
    Not as we ought;
But when we see his face,
In yonder glorious place,
Then shall we sing his grace,
    Sing without fault.

615   *Dan.* 12:3.   **6s & 4s.**
1 Sound, sound the truth abroad!
  Bear ye the word of God
    Through the wide world;
Tell what our Lord has done,
Tell how the day is won,
And from his lofty throne
    Satan is hurled.

2 Ye, who forsaking all,
  At your loved Master's call,
    Comforts resign:
Soon will your work be done;
Soon will the prize be won;
Brighter than yonder sun
    Then shall ye shine.

616   *Ps.* 150.   **6s**
1 Praise ye Jehovah's name;
Praise through his courts proclaim
    Rise and adore;
High o'er the heavens above,
Sound his great acts of love,
While his rich grace we prove,
    Vast as his power.

2 Now let the trumpet raise
Sounds of triumphant praise,
    Wide as his fame;
There let the harp be found;
Organs, with solemn sound,
Roll your deep notes around,
    Filled with his name.

3 While his high praise you sing,
Shake every sounding string;
    Sweet the accord!
He vital breath bestows;
Let every breath that flows,
His noblest fame disclose:
    Praise ye the Lord.

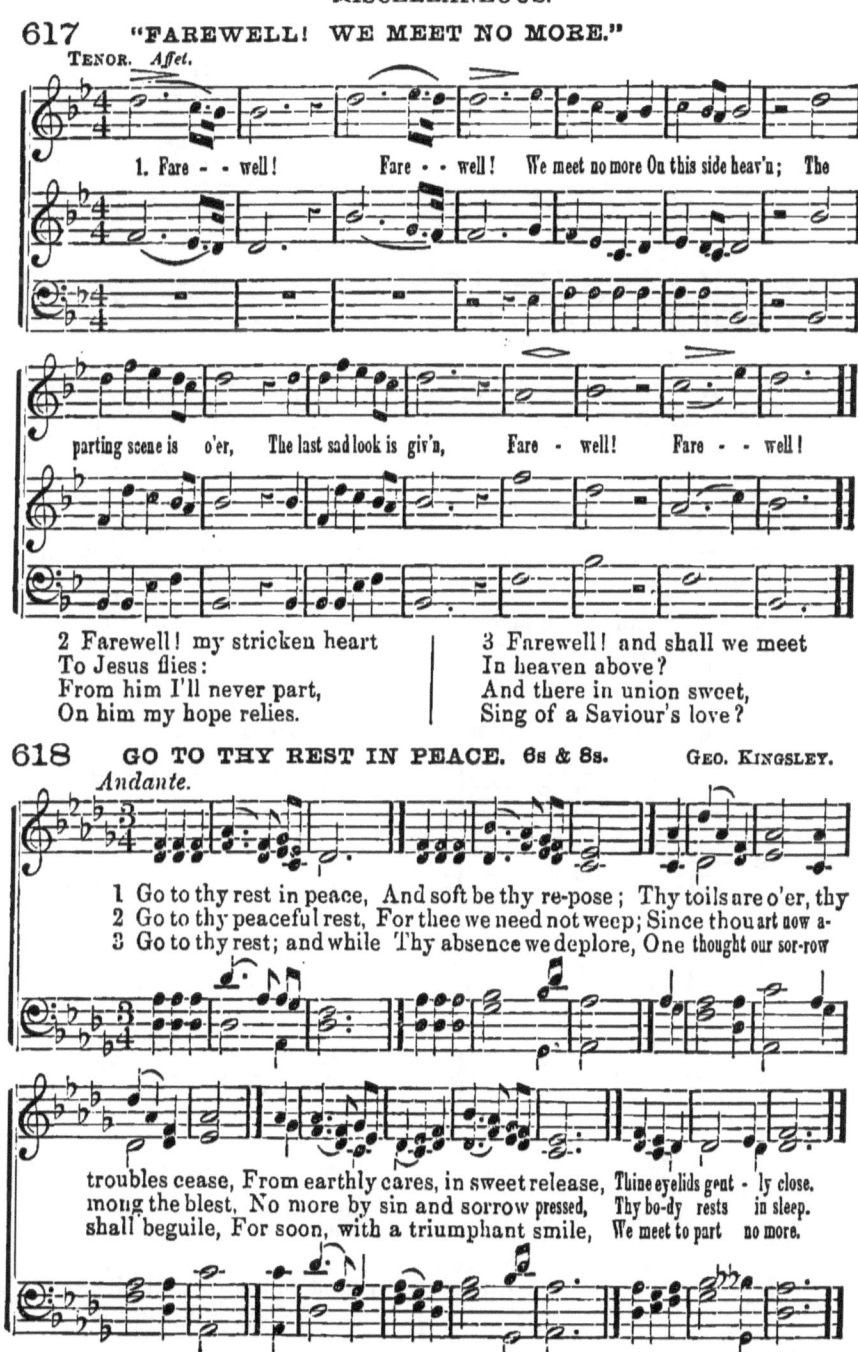

2 Farewell! my stricken heart
To Jesus flies:
From him I'll never part,
On him my hope relies.

3 Farewell! and shall we meet
In heaven above?
And there in union sweet,
Sing of a Saviour's love?

618 GO TO THY REST IN PEACE. 6s & 8s. GEO. KINGSLEY.

1 Go to thy rest in peace, And soft be thy repose; Thy toils are o'er, thy troubles cease, From earthly cares, in sweet release, Thine eyelids gently close.
2 Go to thy peaceful rest, For thee we need not weep; Since thou art now among the blest, No more by sin and sorrow pressed, Thy body rests in sleep.
3 Go to thy rest; and while Thy absence we deplore, One thought our sorrow shall beguile, For soon, with a triumphant smile, We meet to part no more.

MISCELLANEOUS.

A SOLDIER'S DIRGE. Chant.   Geo. Kingsley.

619

1 The flag hangs low, in mournful waves;
The gathering | crowds are | dumb; |
Dim paths that wind among the graves,
Wait | for the | muffled | drum! |
In martial files, with brows all bare,
Mute comrades | guard the | ground; |
The bell's sad tolling swells the air,
In | waves of | sorrowing | sound. ‖

2 Breathe dirges o'er your hero's rest,
Ye for whose | cause he | bled; |
Yours the dear land whose yearning breast,
Takes | home the | honored | dead. |
O God of our forefathers' trust!
God of the | brave and | free; |
Our hands have crowned his martyr'd dust,
We | leave the | dead with | thee. ‖

IT CAME UPON THE MIDNIGHT CLEAR. Chant.

620   C. M.

1 It came upon the midnight clear,
That glorious | song of | old,
From angels bending near the earth
To | touch their | harps of | gold;
"Peace to the earth, good-will to man,
From heaven's all- | gracious | King;"
The earth in solemn stillness lay,
To | hear the | angels | sing.

2 Still through the cloven skies they come,
With peaceful | wings un- | furled;
And still celestial music floats
O'er | all the | weary | world;
Above its sad and lowly plains
They bend on | heavenly | wing,
And ever, o'er its Babel sounds,
The | blessed | angels | sing.

MISCELLANEOUS.

FROM THE RECESSES. Chant.

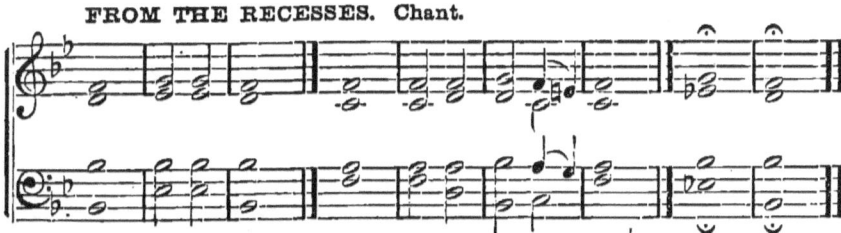

621

1 From the recesses of a lowly spirit,
  Our humble prayer ascends; O | Father! | hear it, ‖
  Upsoaring on the wings of awe and meekness!
      | For-·· | give its | weakness!

2 We see thy hand; it leads us, it supports us:
  We hear thy voice; it | counsels and it | courts us: ‖
  And then we turn away; and still thy kindness
      | For-·· | gives our | blindness.

3 Oh, how long-suffering, Lord! but thou delightest
  To win with | love the | wandering; ‖ thou invitest,
  By smiles of mercy, not by frowns or terrors,
      | Man ·· | from his | errors.

4 Father and Saviour! plant within each bosom
  The | seeds of | holiness, ‖ and bid them blossom
  In fragrance and in beauty bright and vernal,
      | And ·· | spring e- | ternal.

AGNUS DEI. Chant.

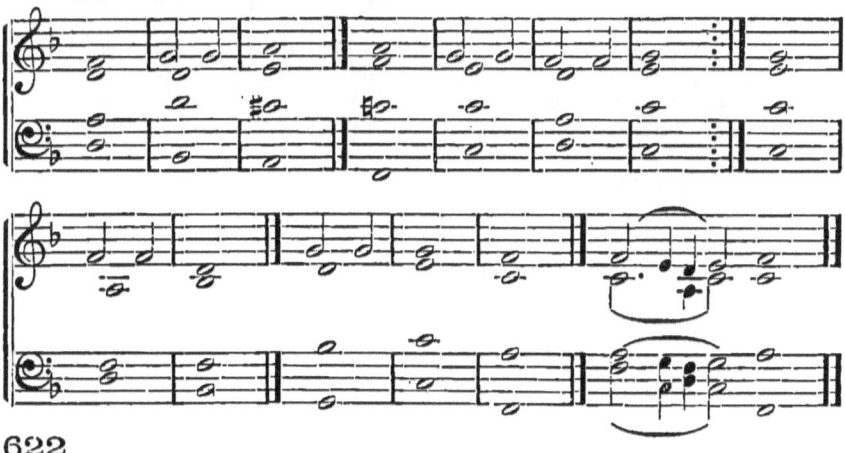

622

1 O Christ, thou Lamb of God, that takest away the | sins · of the | world, ‖
    have | mercy | upon | us. ‖
2 O Christ, thou Lamb of God, that takest away the | sins · of the | world, ‖ have
    | mercy | upon | us. ‖
3 O Christ, thou Lamb of God, that takest away the | sins · of the | world, ‖
    grant us | thy | peace. ‖ A-men. ‖

MISCELLANEOUS.

BEAUTIFUL ZION. Chant.

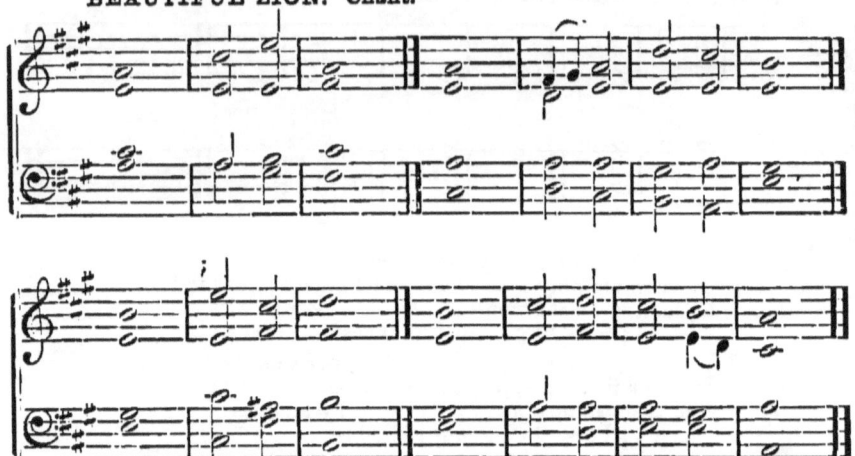

623

1 Beautiful Zion, built above,
Beautiful city, | that I | love,
Beautiful gates of pearly white,
Beautiful | temple, | God its | light!
He who was slain on | Calva- | ry
Opens those | pearly | gates to | me.

2 Beautiful heaven, where all is light,
Beautiful angels, | clothed in | white,
Beautiful strains that never tire,
Beautiful | harps through | all the | choir!
There shall I join the | chorus | sweet,
Worshiping | at the | Saviour's | feet.

3 Beautiful crowns on every brow,
Beautiful palms the | conquerors | show,
Beautiful robes the ransomed wear,
Beautiful | all who | enter | there!
Thither I press with | eager | feet;
There shall my | rest be | long and | sweet.

4 Beautiful throne for Christ our King,
Beautiful songs the | angels | sing,
Beautiful rest, all wanderings cease,
Beautiful | home of | perfect | peace!
There shall my eyes the | Saviour | see;
Haste to this | heavenly | home with | me!

BEYOND THE SMILING. Chant.

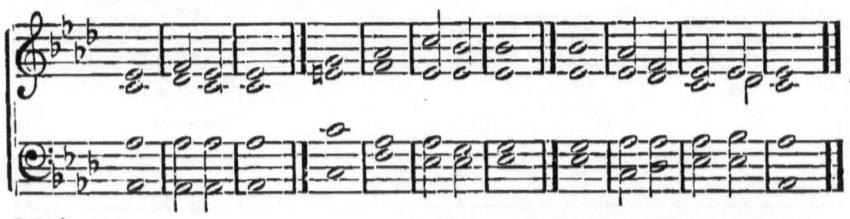

624

1 Beyond the smiling and the weeping
   I | shall be | soon; ||
Beyond the waking and the sleeping, |
Beyond the sowing and the reaping
   I | shall be | soon! ||
Love, rest and home—
Sweet hope! Lord, | tarry | not, but | come!

2 Beyond the blooming and the fading
   I | shall be | soon; ||
Beyond the shining and the shading, |
Beyond the hoping and the dreading,
   I | shall be | soon! ||
Love, rest and home—
Sweet hope! Lord, | tarry | not, but | come!

MISCELLANEOUS.

GLORIA IN EXCELSIS. Chant.

625 PART I.

Glory be to | God on | high, ‖ and on earth | peace, good- | will ·· towards | men. ‖
We praise thee, we bless thee, we | worship | thee, ‖ we glorify thee, we give thanks to thee | for thy | great — | glory. ‖

PART II.

O Lord God, | heavenly | King, ‖ God the | Father | Al- — | mighty! ‖
O Lord, the only-begotten Son | Jesus | Christ, ‖
O Lord God, Lamb of God, | Son ·· of the | Fa- — | ther, ‖

PART III.

That takest away the | sins ·· of the | world, ‖ have mercy up- | on — | us. ‖
Thou that takest away the | sins ·· of the | world, ‖ have mercy up- | on — | us. ‖
Thou that takest away the | sins ·· of the | world, ‖ receive | our — | prayer.
Thou that sittest at the right hand of | God the | Father, ‖ have mercy up- | on — | us. ‖

PART I.

For thou only | art — | holy, ‖ thou | only | art the | Lord. ‖
Thou only, O Christ, with the | Holy | Ghost, ‖ art most high in the | glory ·· of | God the | Father. | A- | men. ‖

MISCELLANEOUS.

626   *John 13: 5.*   6s & 4s.

1 I need Thee every hour,
Most gracious Lord:
No tender voice like Thine
Can peace afford.

Refr.—I need Thee, oh! I need Thee:
    Every hour I need Thee;
    O bless me now, my Saviour!
    I come to Thee.

2 I need Thee every hour;
Stay Thou near by;
Temptations lose their power
When Thou art nigh.

3 I need Thee every hour,
In joy or pain:
Come quickly and abide,
Or life is vain.

4 I need Thee every hour;
Teach me Thy will;
And Thy rich promises
In me fulfil.

5 I need Thee every hour,
Most Holy One;
Oh, make me Thine indeed,
Thou blessed Son.

627   *2 Cor. 6: 2.*   7s.

1 Heavenly Father, bless me now;
At the cross of Christ I bow;
Take my guilt and grief away;
Hear and heal me now, I pray.

Refr.—Bless me now, bless me now;
    Heavenly Father, bless me now.

2 Now, O Lord, this very hour,
Send thy grace and show thy power;
While I rest upon thy word,
Come and bless me now, O Lord.

3 Now, oh, now, for Jesus' sake,
Lift the clouds, the fetters break;
While I look, and as I cry,
Touch and cleanse me ere I die.

628   *Ps. 40: 17.*   L. M.

1 Sweet hour of prayer, sweet hour of prayer,
That calls me from a world of care,
And bids me at my Father's throne
Make all my wants and wishes known;
In seasons of distress and grief
My soul has often found relief,
And oft escaped the tempter's snare,
By thy return, sweet hour of prayer.

2 Sweet hour of prayer, sweet hour of prayer,
Thy wings shall my petition bear,
To him whose truth and faithfulness
Engage the waiting soul to bless;
And since he bids me seek his face,
Believe his word and trust his grace,
I'll cast on him my every care,
And wait for thee, sweet hour of prayer.

3 Sweet hour of prayer, sweet hour of prayer,
May I thy consolation share,
Till from Mount Pisgah's lofty height
I view my home and take my flight;
This robe of flesh I'll drop, and rise,
To seize the everlasting prize;
And shout, while passing through the air
Farewell farewell, sweet hour of prayer.

629   *Gal. 6: 7.*   9s & 7s.

1 Sowing the seed by the daylight fair,
Sowing the seed by the noon-day glare,
Sowing the seed by the fading light,
Sowing the seed in the solemn night;
Oh, what shall the harvest be?
Oh, what shall the harvest be?

Refr.—Sown in the darkness or sown in the light,
    Sown in our weakness or sown in our might,
    Gathered in time or eternity.
    Sure, ah, sure will the harvest be.

2 Sowing the seed by the wayside high,
Sowing the seed on the rocks to die,
Sowing the seed where the thorns will spoil,
Sowing the seed in the fertile soil;
Oh, what shall the harvest be?
Oh, what shall the harvest be?

3 Sowing the seed of a lingering pain,
Sowing the seed of a maddened brain,
Sowing the seed of a tarnished name,
Sowing the seed of eternal shame;
Oh, what shall the harvest be?
Oh, what shall the harvest be?

MISCELLANEOUS.

4 Sowing the seed with an aching heart,
Sowing the seed while the tear-drops start,
Sowing in hope till the reapers come,
Gladly to gather the harvest home;
Oh, what shall the harvest be?
Oh, what shall the harvest be?

630   Ps. 32: 8.   7s.

1 Holy Spirit, faithful guide,
Ever near the Christian's side;
Gently lead us by the hand,
Pilgrims in a desert land;
Weary souls for e'er rejoice,
While they hear that sweetest voice,
Whispering softly, wanderer come!
Follow me, I'll guide thee home.

2 Ever present, truest Friend,
Ever near thine aid to lend,
Leave us not to doubt and fear,
Groping on in darkness drear,
When the storms are raging sore,
Hearts grow faint, and hopes give o'er,
Whispering softly, wanderer come!
Follow me, I'll guide thee home.

3 When our days of toil shall cease,
Waiting still for sweet release,
Nothing left but heaven and prayer,
Wond'ring if our names were there,
Wading deep the dismal flood,
Pleading nought but Jesus' blood,
Whispering softly, wanderer come!
Follow me, I'll guide thee home :

631   Prov. 18: 24.   8s & 7s.

1 What a friend we have in Jesus,
All our sins and griefs to bear;
What a privilege to carry,
Everything to God in prayer.
Oh! what peace we often forfeit,
Oh! what needless pain we bear,
All because we do not carry,
Everything to God in prayer.

2 Have we trials and temptations?
Is there trouble anywhere?
We should never be discouraged,
Take it to the Lord in prayer.
Can we find a Friend so faithful,
Who will all our sorrows share?
Jesus knows our every weakness,
Take it to the Lord in prayer.

3 Are we weak and heavy laden,
Cumbered with a load of care?
Precious Saviour, still our refuge,—
Take it to the Lord in prayer.
Do thy friends despise, forsake thee?
Take it to the Lord in prayer;
In His arms He'll take and shield thee,
Thou wilt find a solace there.

632   Acts 26: 28.   9s, 6s & 4s.

1 "Almost persuaded" now to believe;
"Almost persuaded" Christ to receive;
Seems now some soul to say:
"Go, Spirit, go thy way,
Some more convenient day,
On thee I'll call."

2 "Almost persuaded," come, come to-day;
"Almost persuaded," turn not away.
Jesus invites you here,
Angels are lingering near,
Prayers rise from hearts so dear;
O wanderer, come!

3 "Almost persuaded," harvest is past!
"Almost persuaded," doom comes at last!
"Almost" cannot avail;
"Almost" is but to fail!
Sad, sad that bitter wail,—
"Almost," but lost!

MISCELLANEOUS.

MT. BLANC. P. M.

1. We are on our journey home, Where Christ, our Lord, is gone; We shall meet around his throne When he makes his people one, In the new, In the new Jerusalem. In the new Jerusalem.

633   Rev. 21: 2.   **P. M.**

2 We can see that distant home,
Though clouds rise dark between;
Faith views the radiant dome,
And a lustre flashes keen
  From the new Jerusalem.

3 Our hearts are breaking now
Those mansions fair to see;
O Lord! thy heavens bow,
And raise us up with thee,
  To the new Jerusalem.

I'M A PILGRIM.

634   **P. M.**

1 I'm a pilgrim and I'm a stranger;
I can tarry, I can tarry but a night;
Do not detain me, for I am going
To where the fountains are ever flowing.
  I'm a pilgrim, etc.

2 There the glory is ever shining;
Oh, my longing heart, my longing heart is there;
Here in this country so dark and dreary
I long have wandered forlorn and weary.
  I'm a pilgrim, etc.

3 There's the city to which I journey;
My Redeemer, my Redeemer is its light;
There is no sorrow, nor any sighing,
Nor any tears there, nor any dying.
  I'm a pilgrim, etc.

CLOSING HYMNS.

OLD HUNDRED. L. M.

635   **L. M.**
1 Dismiss us with thy blessing, Lord!
Help us to feed upon thy word;
All that has been amiss forgive,
And let thy truth within us live.

2 Though we are guilty, thou art good;
Wash all our works in Jesus' blood;
Give every fettered soul release,
And bid us all depart in peace.

636   **L. M.**
1 Lord, now we part in thy blest name,
In which we here together came;
Grant us, our few remaining days,
To work thy will and spread thy praise.

2 Teach us in life and death to bless,
Thee, Lord, our strength and righteousness;
Grant that we all may meet above
Where we shall better sing thy love.

637   *Phil. 4: 7.*   **L. M.**
1 The peace which God alone reveals,
And by his word of grace imparts,
Which only the believer feels,
Direct, and keep, and cheer our hearts!

2 And may the holy, Three in One,
The Father, Word, and Comforter,
Pour an abundant blessing down
On every soul assembled here!

638   **L. M.**
1 Praises to him whose love has given,
In Christ his Son, the life of heaven;
Who for our darkness gives us light,
And turns to day our deepest night.

2 Praises to him, in grace, who came,
To bear our woe and sin and shame;
Who lived to die, who died to rise,
The God-accepted sacrifice.

3 Praises to him the chain who broke,
Opened the prison, burst the yoke,
Sent forth the captives glad and free,
Heirs of an endless liberty.

4 Praises to him who sheds abroad
Within our hearts the love of God;
The spirit of all truth and peace,
Fountain of joy and holiness.

5 To Father, Son, and Spirit, now
The hands we lift, the knees we bow;
To thee, Jehovah, thus we raise
The sinners' endless song of praise!

639   *Brief Call to Praise. Psalm* 117. **L. M.**
1 From all that dwell below the skies,
Let the creator's praise arise;
Let the Redeemer's name be sung,
Through every land, by every tongue.

2 Eternal are thy mercies, Lord;
Eternal truth attends thy word;
Thy praise shall sound from shore to shore,
Till suns shall rise and set no more!

DOXOLOGIES.

640 GLORIA PATRI.

Glo-ry be to the Father, and to the Son, and to the Ho-ly Ghost; As it was in the be-gin-ning, is now, and ev-er shall be, world without end. A-men. A-men.

1   L. M.
Praise God from whom all blessings flow;
Praise Him, all creatures here below;
Praise Him above, ye heavenly host;
Praise Father, Son, and Holy Ghost.

2   L. M.
To God the Father, God the Son,
And God the Spirit, Three in One,
Be honor, praise, and glory given,
By all on earth, and all in heaven!

3   C. M.
To Father, Son, and Holy Ghost,
The God whom we adore,
Be glory as it was, is now,
And shall be evermore.

4   S. M.
The Father and the Son
And Spirit we adore;
We praise, we bless, we worship thee,
Both now and evermore!

5   7s.
Sing we to our God above
Praise eternal as his love;
Praise him, all ye heavenly host—
Father, Son, and Holy Ghost!

6   8s & 7s.
Honor, glory, might, dominion,
To the Father and the Son,
With the everlasting Spirit,
While eternal ages run.

7   C. M., Double.
The God of mercy be adored,
Who calls our souls from death,
Who saves by His redeeming Word
And new-creating Breath:
To praise the Father and the Son
And Spirit All-Divine,
The One in Three, and Three in One,
Let saints and angels join.

8   7s & 6s.
To thee be praise forever,
Thou glorious King of kings!
Thy wondrous love and favor
Each ransomed spirit sings:
We'll celebrate thy glory
With all thy saints above,
And shout the joyful story
Of thy redeeming love.

**   7s & 6s.**
Father, Son, and Holy Ghost,
One God whom we adore,
Join we with the heavenly host
To praise thee evermore;

DOXOLOGIES.

Live, by heaven and earth adored,
Three in One, and One in Three,
Holy, holy, holy Lord,
All glory be to thee!

9   6s & 4s.

To God, the Father, Son,
And Spirit, Three in One,
   All praise be given!
Crown him in every song;
To him your hearts belong
Let all his praise prolong
   On earth, in heaven!

10   H. M.

To God the Father's throne
Your highest honors raise;
Glory to God the Son,
To God the Spirit praise:
   With all our powers,
   Eternal King!
Thy name we sing,
While faith adores.

11   10s.

To Father, Son and Spirit, ever blest,
Eternal praise and worship be addressed;
From age to age, ye saints, his name adore,
And spread his fame till time shall be no more.

12   11s.

O Father Almighty, to thee be addressed,
With Christ and the Spirit, one God ever blest,
All glory and worship, from earth and from heaven,
As was, and is now, and shall ever be given!

13   8s, 7s & 4s.

Great Jehovah, we adore thee,
God the Father, God the Son,
God the Spirit, joined in glory
On the same eternal throne;
   Endless praises
To Jehovah, Three in One!

14   L. P. M.

Now to the great and sacred three,
The Father, Son, and Spirit, be
Eternal praise and glory given
Through all the worlds where God is known,
By all the angels near the throne,
And all the saints in earth and heaven.

15   8s & 7s.

Praise the God of our salvation,
Praise the Father's boundless love;
Praise the Lamb, our expiation;
Praise the Spirit from above;
Praise the Fountain of salvation,
Him by whom our spirits live;
   Undivided adoration
To the one Jehovah give!

16   7s.

Praise the name of God most high;
Praise him, all below the sky;
Praise him, all ye heavenly host—
Father, Son, and Holy Ghost!
As through countless ages past,
Evermore his praise shall last.

17   C. P. M.

To Father, Son, and Holy Ghost,
The God, whom Heaven's triumphant host,
And saints on earth adore;
Be glory as in ages past,
And now it is, and so shall last,
When time shall be no more.

INDEX OF FIRST LINES.

HYMN.	AUTHOR.
579 Abide with me! Fast falls the eventide.......	*H. F. Lyte.*
368 A broken heart, my God, my King.....	*I. Watts.*
290 According to thy gracious word..............	*J. Montgomery.*
443 A charge to keep I have...............	*C. Wesley.*
465 A few more years shall roll.........	*H. Bonar.*
118 Again our earthly cares we.........	*J. Newton.*
170 Alas! and did my Saviour bleed........	*Watts.*
174 Alas! what hourly dangers rise..	*Anne Steele.*
564 A light streams downward from...........	*Mrs. Hinsdale.*
48 All hail the power of Jesus'.......	*E. Perronet.*
582 All glory, praise and honor........	*Theodulph.*
553 All praise to thee, my God, this......	*T. Ken.*
150 All praise to thee, Eternal Lord........	*Luther.*
563 Almighty Father, hear our cry............	*Anon.*
493 Almighty maker of my frame.............	*Steele.*
632 "Almost persuaded," now to believe...	*Bliss.*
430 Am I a soldier of the cross..............	*Watts.*
442 Amidst a world of hopes and...........	*Anon.*
517 And is there, Lord, a rest ?........	*R. Palmer.*
427 And must I part with all............	*B. Beddome.*
302 And must this body die?..................	*Watts.*
514 And will the Judge descend.........	*Doddridge.*
206 Angels, roll the rock away............	*T. Scott.*
121 Another six days' work is done....	*J. Stennet.*
373 Approach, my soul, the mercy seat..	*Newton.*
240 Arise, O King of grace, arise..............	*Watts.*
231 Arm of the Lord, awake, awake.................	*W. Shrubsole.*
58 Around the Saviour's lofty throne..	*T. Kelly.*
10 Ascend thy throne, Almighty King.............	*Beddome.*
507 As Jesus died and rose again.......	*M. Bruce.*
313 Asleep in Jesus! blessed sleep...............	*Mrs. M. Mackay.*
388 As when the weary traveler...........	*Newton.*
281 At the Lamb's high feast........	*(tr) Campbell.*
42 Awake, and sing the song......	*W. Hammond.*
537 Awake, my soul, and with...............	*Ken.*
56 Awake, my soul, in joyful............	*S. Medley.*
440 Awake, my soul, lift up..............	*Barbauld.*

HYMN.	AUTHOR.
431 Awake, my soul, stretch every..	*P. Doddridge.*
5 Awake, my tongue, thy tribute..	*J. Needham.*
438 Awake, our souls, away our fears......	*Watts.*
623 Beautiful Zion, built above.............	*Anon.*
3 Before Jehovah's awful throne...........	*Watts.*
94 Begin, my soul, the exalted lay.......	*J. Ogilvie.*
339 Behold a stranger at the door.........	*J. Grigg.*
273 Behold the sure foundation stone.....	*Watts.*
300 Behold the western evening light...	*Peabody.*
393 Behold what wondrous grace..............	*Watts.*
20 Beneath a numerous train.............	
589 Be tranquil, O my soul..............	*Hastings.*
624 Beyond the smiling and the weeping..	*Bonar.*
378 Blessed Saviour! thee I love.......	*G Duffield.*
7 Bless, O my soul, the living God.........	*Watts.*
246 Blest are the sons of peace..............	*Watts.*
221 Blest be the tie that binds..........	*J. Fawcett.*
545 Blest be thy love, dear Lord.........	*J. Austin.*
39 Blest be thou, O God of Israel........	*Anon.*
476 Blest hour, when mortal man...........	*Raffles.*
451 Blest Jesus, when my soaring..	*Heginbotham.*
154 Blow ye the trumpet..................	*C. Wesley.*
283 Bread of heaven! on thee we.....	*J. Conder.*
145 Brightness of the Father's glory..	*R. Robinson.*
556 Brightest and best of the sons......	*R. Heber.*
387 By faith in Christ I walk...............	*Newton.*
131 Calm on the listening ear................	*Sears.*
482 Cast thy burden on the Lord...........	*R. Hill.*
307 Cease, ye mourners, cease to...........	*Collyer.*
590 Cheer up, desponding soul................	*Byrom.*
80 Children of the heavenly King...	*J. Cennick.*
157 Christ is our corner-stone.........	*(tr) Chandler.*
205 Christ the Lord, is risen............	*C. Wesley.*
90 Come, all ye saints of God.............	*J. Boden.*
109 Come, dearest Lord, and bless...	*J. Dobell.*
116 Come, dearest Lord, and feed.............	*Mason.*
210 Come, divine and peaceful guest...........	*Anon.*
478 Come, dearest Lord, descend and.........	*Watts.*
196 Come, gracious Spirit, heavenly......	*Browne.*
343 Come hither, all ye weary................	*Watts.*
217 Come, Holy Spirit, come...............	*J. Hart.*

230

INDEX OF FIRST LINES.

HYMN.	AUTHOR.	HYMN.	AUTHOR.
211	Come, Holy Spirit, heavenly..............Watts.	256	Father of mercies! condescend.........Morell.
353	Come, humble sinner, in whose......E. Jones.	227	Father of heaven! whose love.........Cooper.
103	Come, Jesus, Redeemer, abide......R. Palmer.	462	Father! I long, I faint to see...............Watts.
249	Come, Kingdom of our God................Johns.	336	Father! oh, hear me now.....................Hall.
285	Come, let us join our cheerful.............Watts.	297	Few are thy days and full of............Logan.
243	Come, let us join our friends.........C. Wesley.	467	Forever with the Lord!...........Montgomery.
583	Come, let us sing of Jesus.................Bethune.	566	Forth from the dark and stormy sky..Heber.
163	Come, let us sing the song of songs.......	550	Forth in thy name, O Lord, I......C. Wesley.
	....Montgomery.	141	For thy mercy and thy grace.........Downton.
135	Come, Lord, and tarry not..................Bonar.	117	Frequent the day of God returns.....Browne.
403	Come, my soul, thy suit prepare......Newton.	639	From all that dwell below the............Watts.
126	Come, O Creator, Spirit blest........(tr) Caswell.	474	From every stormy wind that......H. Stowell.
347	Come, says Jesus' sacred voice......Barbauld.	258	From Greenland's icy mountains.......Heber.
44	Come, sound his praise abroad.............Watts.	621	From the recesses of a lowly spirit..Bowring.
223	Come, thou Almighty King........C. Wesley.		
407	Come, thou Fount of every............Robinson.	310	Gently, Lord, oh, gently lead us....Hastings.
143	Come, thon long-expected...........C. Wesley.	502	Gently, my Saviour, let me down......R. Hill.
436	Come up hither! come away..............Nevin.	531	Giver and Guardian of.................C. Wesley.
340	Come, weary souls with sins..............Steele.	23	Give thanks to God; he resigns.......... Watts.
446	Come, we that love the Lord..............Watts.	305	Give to the wind thy fears........P. Gerhardt.
555	Come, ye disconsolate...................T. Moore.	408	Glorious things of thee are spoken...Newton.
557	Come, ye thankful people, come........Alford.	625	Glory be to God on high, and on ....
25	Come, ye that know and fear..........Burder.	234	Glory be to God the Father..............Bonar.
144	Crown his head with endless..........W. Goode.	30	Glory be to God on high...............C. Wesley.
		640	Glory be to the Father, and to... ....
252	Daughter of Zion! from the dust................	244	Glory to God, whose witness train..............
	....Montgomery.		....(tr) Moravian.
236	Day of judgment! day of wonders...Newton.	540	Glory to thee, my God, this...................Ken.
62	Dearest of all the names above.........Watts.	88	Glory to God on high.........................J. Allen.
173	Dear Father! to thy mercy-seat........Steele.	335	God bless our native land.................Dwight.
423	Dear Refuge of my weary soul.........Steele.	342	God calling yet; shall I not...(tr) Borthwick.
397	Dear Saviour! we are thine........Doddridge.	35	God eternal, mighty King.......(tr) De Deam.
350	Depth of mercy, can there be?......C. Wesley.	107	God in the gospel of his Son..........Beddome.
523	Descend from heaven, immortal.........Watts.	488	God is the refuge of his saints............Watts.
183	Did Christ o'er sinners weep?.........Beddome.	187	God of mercy, God of love..................Lyte.
635	Dismiss us with thy blessing................Hart.	530	God of my life, my morning song...............
450	Do not I love Thee, O my Lord....Doddridge.	414	God of my life, to thee I call............Cowper.
		410	God of my life, through all my...Doddridge.
470	Encompassed with clouds of distress....Anon.	549	God of the morning! at whose............Watts.
330	Eternal Source of every joy..........Doddridge.	613	God of the morning ray.................Hastings.
13	Eternal Spirit! we confess................... Watts.	490	God will our strength and refuge.......Anon.
483	Everlasting arms of love.................Macduff.	441	Go, labor on; your hands are..........Bonar.
311	Everything we love and cherish...............	277	Go, preach my gospel, saith the Lord.. Watts.
		379	Go to dark Gethsemane............Montgomery.
458	Fade, fade, each earthly joy......Mrs. Bonar.	618	Go to thy rest in peace.........................Anon.
383	Faith adds new charms to..................Watts.	394	Grace! 'tis a charming sound......Doddridge.
382	Faith is the brightest evidence............Watts.	209	Gracious Spirit, Love divine.........Stocker.
617	Farewell! Farewell! we meet no more.........	425	Grant me within thy courts a...Montgomery.
	....Anon.	123	Great God! attend while Zion............Watts.
466	Far from my heavenly home..............Lyte.	266	Great God! now condescend.........Fellows.
596	Far from my thoughts, vain world, begone..	554	Great God! to thee my evening........Steele.
	....Watts.	152	Great God! we sing that mighty..Doddridge.
511	Far from these narrow scenes...........Steele.	245	Great is the Lord our God.................Watts.
428	Father of love! our guide and............Irons.	4	Great One in Three............................Anon.

INDEX OF FIRST LINES.

HYMN.	AUTHOR.	HYMN.	AUTHOR.
124 Great Sun of Righteousness	Watts.	498 If I must die, oh let me die	Anon.
237 Guide me, O thou great Jehovah	Williams.	571 If through unruffled seas	Toplady.
		370 I heard the voice of Jesus say	Bonar.
165 Hail to the Lord's Anointed	Montgomery.	168 I lay my sins on Jesus	Bonar.
78 Hallelujah! raise, O raise	Conder.	125 I love the sacred book of God	Kelly.
452 Happy the heart where graces	Watts.	218 I love thy kingdom, Lord	Dwight.
242 Happy the souls to Jesus joined	C. Wesley.	534 I love to steal awhile away	Mrs. Brown.
147 Hark! an awful voice is	(tr) Caswell.	634 I'm a pilgrim, and I'm	Mrs. Dana.
153 Hark! hark! the notes of joy	A. Reed.	626 I need thee every hour	Mrs. Hawkes.
520 Hark how the choral song of	McAll.	570 In every trying hour	Anon.
309 Hark the sound of holy voices	Wordsworth.	472 Inspirer and Hearer of prayer	Toplady.
127 Hark the glad sound, the	Doddridge.	586 In the Christian's home in glory	Harmer.
604 Hark! the voice of love and mercy	Evans.	177 In the cross of Christ I glory	Bowring.
138 Hark! the herald angels sing	C. Wesley.	620 It came upon the midnight clear	E. H. Sears.
509 Hark to the trump, behold	Denny.	190 "It is finished!" shall we raise	Anon.
142 Hark! what mean those holy	Cawood.	303 It is not death to die	Bethune.
348 Haste, O sinner, now be wise	Scott.	495 It is the Lord, enthroned	Green.
345 Have mercy on me, O my God!	Anon.	322 I would not live alway, I ask	Muhlenberg.
299 Hear what the voice from heaven	Watts.		
627 Heavenly Father, bless me now	A. Clark.	21 Jehovah reigns; he dwells in light	Watts.
516 He comes, the conqueror comes		22 Jehovah reigns; his throne is	Watts.
192 He dies, the friend of sinners	Watts.	461 Jerusalem! my happy home	Dickson.
448 Heirs of unending life	Anon.	284 Jesus! all-atoning Lamb	C. Wesley.
506 He reigns, the Lord, the Saviour	Watts.	55 Jesus! and shall it ever be	Grigg.
485 High in yonder realms of light	Raffles.	291 Jesus, at whose supreme command	C. Wesley.
24 Holy and reverend is the name	Needham.	204 Jesus Christ is risen to-day	(tr).
40 Holy Ghost! dispel our	(tr) Toplady.	344 Jesus demands this heart of	Steele.
208 Holy Ghost! with light divine	Reed.	72 Jesus! engrave it on my heart	Medley.
33 Holy, Holy, Holy Lord	Montgomery.	178 Jesus! full of all compassion	Turner.
630 Holy Spirit, faithful guide	Wells.	363 Jesus! I come to thee	Bemen.
31 Holy Spirit! Love Divine	Anon.	396 Jesus! I live to thee	H Harbaugh.
52 Hosanna; raise the pealing hymn	Havergal.	85 Jesus, I love thy charming name	Doddridge.
74 Hosanna to the living Lord	Heber.	255 Jesus, immortal King! arise	Seymour.
526 Hope of our hearts, O Lord	Denny.	61 Jesus! in thy transporting name	Steele.
248 How beauteous are their feet	Watts.	413 Jesus! in whom but thee	Conder.
314 How blest the righteous, when he	Barbauld.	597 Jesus, lead the way	(tr) Zinzendorf.
220 How charming is the place	Stennet.	75 Jesus! lover of my soul	C. Wesley.
360 How heavy is the night	Watts.	82 Jesus, my Saviour! bind me fast	Beddome.
172 How oft, alas! this wretched	Steele.	349 Jesus! save my dying soul	C. Wesley.
113 How precious is the book divine	Fawcett.	158 Jesus shall reign where'er the sun	Watts.
453 How sweet, how heavenly is	Swain.	285 Jesus! Shepherd of the sheep	Anon.
605 How sweetly flowed the gospel's sound	Bowring.	86 Jesus! these eyes have never	Palmer.
		70 Jesus! the spring of joys divine	Steele.
64 How sweet the name of Jesus sounds	Newton.	66 Jesus! the very thought of thee	(tr) Bernard.
		65 Jesus! thou art the sinners'	Burnham.
480 How sweet to leave the world	Kelly.	54 Jesus! thou joy of loving hearts	(tr) Bernard.
318 How vain is all beneath the	Anon.	392 Jesus! thy blood and righteousness	
569 How welcome was the call	Baker.		(tr) Zinzendorf.
179 Humbly now, with deep contrition	Anon.	71 Jesus! thy boundless love to	(tr) J. Wesley.
		87 Jesus! thy name I love	Deck.
320 I am weary of straying! O fain	York.	267 Jesus! we thus obey	Anon.
2 I believe in God, the Father		112 Jesus, where'er thy people meet	Cowper.
96 I bless the Christ of God	Bonar.	293 Jesus! with all thy saints above	Watts.
497 If God is mine, then present things	Anon.	598 Jesus! who can be	(tr) Frelinghysen.

INDEX OF FIRST LINES.

HYMN.		AUTHOR.
128	Joy to the world, the Lord is come	Watts.
399	Joyful be the hours to-day	Kelly.
364	Just as I am, without one plea	Elliott.
9	Kingdoms and thrones to God	Watts.
352	Let every mortal ear attend	Watts.
595	Let me be with thee where thou art	
		C. Elliot.
214	Let songs of praises fill the sky	Cotterill.
222	Let us awake our joys	Kingsbury.
324	Let us with a gladsome mind	John Milton.
328	Let Sion praise the mighty God	Anon.
27	Lift up to God the voice of praise	Wardlaw.
195	Lift up your heads, ye gates...(tr)	Winkworth.
201	Lift up your heads, eternal gates	Tate.
79	Light of life! seraphic fire	C. Wesley.
254	Light of the lonely pilgrim's	Denny.
146	Light of those whose dreary	C. Wesley.
219	Like Noah's weary dove	Muhlenberg.
184	Like sheep we went astray	Watts.
12	Lo! God is here, let us adore	C. Wesley.
235	Lo! he comes with clouds	C. Wesley.
238	Lord, dismiss us with thy	Shirley.
276	Lord! I am thine, entirely thine	Davies.
424	Lord! I believe, thy power I own	Wreford.
528	Lord! I believe a rest remains	C. Wesley.
119	Lord! in the morning thou shalt	Watts.
16	Lord, in the temples of thy grace	Steele.
167	Lord Jesus! by thy passion	Anon.
386	Lord Jesus! we are one with thee	Deck.
357	Lord, like the publican I stand	Raffles.
18	Lord of all being! throned afar	Holmes.
636	Lord, now we part in thy blest	Heber.
551	Lord, let my heart still turn	Anon.
233	Lord of the harvest! bend thine	Hastings.
533	Lord! thou wilt hear me when I	Watts.
404	Lord! we come before thee now	Hammond.
263	Lord! what our ears have heard	Anon.
602	Lord, with glowing heart I'd praise thee	Key.
405	Love Divine! all love excelling	C. Wesley.
525	Lo! what a glorious sight appears	Watts.
51	Majestic sweetness sits enthroned	Stennet.
180	May the grace of Christ the Saviour	Newton.
321	Mid scenes of confusion and creature	Anon.
457	More love to thee, O Christ	Mrs. Prentiss.
207	Morning breaks upon the tomb	Collyer.
129	Mortals, awake, with angels join	Medley.
432	Must Jesus bear the cross alone	Allen.
334	My country! tis of thee	Smith.
53	My dear Redeemer and my Lord	Watts.
225	My faith looks up to thee	Palmer.
508	My faith shall triumph o'er the	Anon.
609	My Father's house on high	Montgomery.
186	My few revolving years	Beddome.

HYMN.		AUTHOR.
552	My God! how endless is thy love	Watts.
385	My God! my Father! blissful name	Steele.
600	My God! my Father! while I stray	C. Elliot.
544	My God! permit my tongue	Watts.
81	My God! the spring of all my joys	Watts.
471	My gracious Redeemer I love	Francis.
607	My hope is built on nothing less	Mote.
584	My heavenly home is bright and	Hunter.
592	My Jesus as thou wilt	(tr) Schmolke.
122	My opening eyes with rapture see	Hutton.
68	My Saviour! my Almighty friend	Watts.
445	My soul! weigh not thy life	Anon.
444	My soul! be on thy guard	Heath.
487	My spirit looks to God alone	Watts.
593	My spirit longs for thee	Byrom.
456	Nearer, my God, to thee	Mrs. Adams.
538	New, every morning, is the love	Keble.
389	No more, my God, I boast no	Watts.
567	None loves me Saviour, with thy love	
		(tr) German.
459	No, not despairingly	Anon.
464	Nor eye hath seen, nor	Watts.
181	Not all the blood of beasts	Watts.
139	Now begin the heavenly theme	Maden.
259	Now be the gospel banner	Hastings.
535	Now from the altar of our hearts	Mason.
337	Now I have found a friend	Hope.
73	Now in a song of grateful praise	Anon.
14	Now let my soul, eternal King	Heginbotham.
521	Now let our souls, on wings	Gibbons.
251	Now living waters flow	Anon.
286	Now may he, who from the dead	Newton.
100	O, bless the Lord, my soul	Montgomery.
261	O Bread, to pilgrims given	(tr) Palmer.
361	O cease, my wandering soul	Muhlenberg.
536	O Christ! with each returning morn	
		(tr) Latin.
69	O Christ! our true and	(tr) Winkworth.
622	O Christ, thou Lamb of God	
110	O come, loud anthems let us	Tate.
84	O! could I find from day to day	Cleveland.
91	O, could I speak the matchless worth	Medley.
527	O, could our thoughts and wishes	Steele.
409	O'er the gloomy hills of darkness	Williams.
182	O'erwhelmed in depths of woe	(tr) Caswell.
97	O everlasting Light	Bonar.
417	O, for a closer walk with God	Cowper.
381	O, for a faith that will not shrink	Bathurst.
374	O, for a heart to praise my God	C. Wesley.
426	O, for an overcoming faith	Watts.
202	O, for a shout of sacred joy	Watts.
518	O, for a sweet inspiring ray	Steele.

INDEX OF FIRST LINES.

HYMN.		AUTHOR.	HYMN.		AUTHOR.
60	O, for a thousand tongues to sing	C. Wesley.	151	Our Helper, God, we bless thy	Doddridge.
301	O, for the death of those	Montgomery.	194	Our Lord is risen from the dead	C. Wesley.
402	Oft in danger, oft in woe	White.	375	Out of the deeps of long distress	Watts.
105	O Garden of Olives, thou dear	De Fleury.	239	O, where are kings and empires	Coxe.
250	O God of sovereign grace	Melrose.	358	O, where shall rest be found	Montgomery.
264	O God of Abraham! hear	Hastings.	269	O wondrous is thy mercy	Anon.
295	O God! our help in ages past	Watts.			
532	O God! that madest earth and sky	Anon.	568	Peace, troubled soul, whose plaintive	Shirely.
29	O God! we praise thee and confess	Patrick.	271	Planted in Christ, the living	Smith.
275	O happy day! that seals my choice		558	Pleasant are thy courts above	Lyte.
		Doddridge.	326	Praise, O praise, our God and	Baker.
519	O happy saints! who dwell in light		36	Praise the Lord, ye heavens adore	
		Berridge			Kempthorne.
419	O happy soul! that lives	Watts.	38	Praise to thee, thou great Creator	Fawcett.
436	O help us, Lord, each hour of	Milman.	638	Praises to him, whose love has	Bonar.
226	O holy, holy, holy Lord	Eastburne.	325	Praise to God, immortal praise	Barbauld.
580	O holy Saviour, Friend unseen	C. Elliot.	616	Praise ye Jehovah's name	Goode.
98	O Holy Spirit! come and	Allen.	6	Praise ye the Lord; all nature join	Watts.
215	O Holy Spirit! Fount of Love	(tr)	257	Prayer is the soul's sincere	Montgomery.
46	O Jesus, God and man	Baker.	289	Prepare us, Lord, to view thy	Anon.
63	O Jesus! King most wonderful	(tr) Bernard.	356	Prostrate, dear Jesus, at thy feet	Stennet.
279	O Lord of hosts! whose glory fills	Neale.			
247	O Lord our God! arise	Wardlaw.	415	Redeemed from guilt; Redeemed	Lyte.
92	O Love Divine! how sweet thou	C. Wesley.	578	Rejoice and be glad	Bonar.
585	O Love Divine, that stooped to share	Holmes.	489	Rejoice, ye saints, rejoice and	Anon.
199	O Love, which lightens all	Monsell.	317	Remember, Lord, our mortal	Watts.
460	O mother dear! Jerusalem	Dickson.	512	Rest for the toiling band	Bonar.
561	One prayer I have—all prayers in one		111	Return, my soul, enjoy thy rest	Watts.
		Montgomery.	354	Return, O wanderer, now return	Collyer.
155	One sole baptismal sign	Robinson.	159	Rise, crowned with light, great	Pope.
610	One sweetly solemn thought	Carey.	376	Rock of Ages, cleft for me	Toplady.
463	On Jordan's stormy banks I stand	Stennet.	41	Round the Lord, in glory seated	Mant.
332	On thee, O Lord our God, we call	Anon.			
166	O sacred Head! now wounded	(tr) Bernard.	574	Saints in glory! we together	Mahmied.
132	O Saviour of our race	(tr) Winckworth.	380	Safely through another week	Newton.
193	O Saviour, who for man hast	Coffin.	329	Salvation doth to God belong	Doddridge.
608	O Spirit of the Living God	Montgomery.	560	Salvation! O the joyful sound	Watts.
434	O speed thee, Christian, on thy way	Anon.	377	Saviour of our ruined race	Hastings.
246	O that the Lord would guide my	Watts.	188	Saviour! when in dust to thee	Grant.
351	O these eyes, how dark and blind	Bonar.	268	See Israel's gentle Shepherd	Doddridge.
338	O thou best gift of heaven	Anon.	543	Serene I laid me down	Scott.
372	O thou, from whom all goodness	Haweis.	611	Servant of God, well done	Montgomery.
366	O thou that hearest, when sinners	Watts.	270	Shepherd of Israel! from above	Bathurst.
93	O thou, that hearest the prayer of	Toplady.	76	Shepherd of the ransomed flock	Anon.
581	O thou, the contrite sinners Friend	C. Elliot.	89	Shepherd of tender youth	(tr) Clement.
421	O thou, the Lord and Life of	Hall.	406	Shepherd of thine Israel, lead	
416	O thou, to whose all-searching	(tr) J. Wesley.	253	Shine, mighty God, on Zion	Watts.
171	O thou whose tender mercy hears	Steele.	367	Show pity, Lord, O Lord forgive	Watts.
274	O thou whose own vast temple stands		573	Sing of Jesus, sing forever	Kelly.
		Bryant.	614	Sing, sing his lofty praise	Kelly.
369	O turn, great Ruler of the skies	Merrick.	130	Sing to the Lord, ye distant	Watts.
455	Our God is Love, and all his	Cotterill.	355	Sinners, the voice of God regard	Fawcett.
1	Our Father, who art in heaven		346	Sinners, turn, why will ye die	C. Wesley.
398	Our heavenly Father calls	Doddridge.	312	Sister, thou wast mild and lovely	Smith.

INDEX OF FIRST LINES.

HYMN.	AUTHOR.	HYMN.	AUTHOR.
401	Sleep not, soldier of the cross.............Gaskell.	198	The morning purples all the sky............(tr).
612	Soldiers of Christ, arise.....................Wesley.	637	The peace which God alone reveals..Newton.
412	So let our lips and lives express..........Watts.	468	The people of the Lord.......................Anon.
230	Soon may the last glad song arise........Voke.	304	The pity of the Lord...........................Watts.
32	Songs of praise the angels sang...Montgomery.	229	The praise of Zion waits for thee.........Watts.
615	Sound, sound the truth abroad.............Kelly.	591	There is a blessed home.....................Baker.
484	Source and Giver of repose...............Toplady.	169	There is a fountain filled with blood..Cowper.
481	Sovereign Ruler of the skies.............Ryland.	17	There is a God! all nature speaks......Steele.
189	Sovereign ruler, Lord of all................Raffles.	524	There is a land of pure delight ....Watts.
384	Sovereign of all the worlds on high. ....Watts.	262	The Saviour kindly calls............Onderdonk.
232	Sovereign of worlds! display thy..........Voke.	59	The Saviour ! oh, what endless.........Steele.
629	Sowing the seed by the daylight fair...Anon.	134	The Son of man shall come..............Beadon.
213	Spirit Divine ! attend our prayer.........Reed.	11	The spacious firmament on high......Addison.
197	Spirit of mercy, truth and love............Kyle.	359	The Spirit in our hearts.............Onderdonk.
454	Spirit of peace! celestial Dove.............Lyte.	601	The strife is o'er, the battle done........Anon.
437	Stand up, my soul; shake off..............Watts.	319	The things of the earth, in the earth.......
260	Stand up! stand up for Jesus.........Duffield.		....(tr) Neale.
522	Still one in life, and one in death......Bonar.	575	The voice of free grace cries...........Burdsall.
176	Suffering Son of man, be near...............Anon.	529	The whole creation groans.................Anon.
327	Summer ended, harvest o'er.........Phillimore.	120	Thine earthly Sabbaths, Lord, we..Doddridge.
539	Sun of my soul! thou Saviour dear......Keble.	282	Thine forever! God of love................Maude.
191	Surely Christ thy griefs has............Toplady.	587	This is not my place of resting..........Bonar.
628	Sweet hour of prayer.....................Walford.	114	This is the day the Lord hath made...Watts.
501	Sweet is the scene when Christians..Barbauld.	473	This Lord is the Lord we adore..................
108	Sweet is the work, my God..................Watts	576	Thou art gone to the grave! but........Heber.
99	Sweet is the work, O Lord.................Auber.	50	Thou art the way, to thee alone........Doane.
175	Sweet the moments, rich in blessing....Allen.	265	Thou God of sovereign grace!............Anon.
323	Swell the anthem, raise the song......Strong.	515	Thou Judge of quick and dead......C. Wesley.
		362	Thou Lord of all above.................Beddome.
308	Tarry with me, O my Saviour.....Mrs. Smith.	83	Thou lovely source of true delight......Steele.
510	That awful day will surely come..........Watts.	499	Thou must go forth alone...................Anon.
505	That day of wrath, that dreadful....W. Scott.	224	Thou whose almighty word...........Murriott.
133	The Advent of our God............(tr) Chandler.	104	Though faint, yet pursuing.................Anon.
292	The blest memorials of thy grief................	429	Through all the changing scenes of......Tate.
439	The billows swell, the winds are.......Cowper.	315	Through every age, eternal God.........Watts.
494	The Christian would not have his lot..........	588	Thy way, not mine, O Lord............Bonar.
136	The Church has waited long...............Bonar.	599	Thy will be done! In devious........Bowring.
547	The day is past and gone...................Leland.	541	Thus far the Lord hath led me on.......Watts.
546	The day, O Lord, is spent......................Neale.	390	'Tis by the faith of joys to come..........Watts.
619	The flag hangs low, in mournful waves.......	162	'Tis finished; so the Saviour cried....Stennet.
	....Anon.	161	'Tis midnight, and on Olive's............Tappen.
559	The golden gates are lifted up...........Anon.	28	To God be glory, peace on earth...........Tate.
333	The God of Harvest praise.........Montgomery.	43	To God the only wise ....Watts.
572	The harvest dawn is near...............Burgess.	469	To Jesus, the crown of my hope......Cowper.
203	The head that once was crowned........Kelly.	548	To-morrow, Lord, is thine............Doddridge.
106	The heavens declare thy glory............Watts.	34	To thy temple I repair..............Montgomery.
500	The hour of my departure's come.......Bruce.	400	To thy pastures fair and large........Merrick.
447	The Lord himself will keep ....Kelly.	200	Triumphant Christ ascends on.........Steele.
15	The Lord is king! lift up thy voice...Conder.	228	Triumphant Zion! lift thy..........Doddridge.
102	The Lord is my Shepherd; no want		
	....Montgomery.	594	Uplift the banner! Let it float............Doane.
185	The Lord is risen indeed.....................Kelly.	603	Vain were all our toil and labor..........Lyte.
45	The Lord my Shepherd is....................Watts.		
241	The Lord of glory is my light............Watts.	19	Wait, O my soul, thy Maker's will....Lloyd.
504	The Lord will come, the earth shall...Heber.	513	Waked by the trumpet's sound..........Wesley.

INDEX OF FIRST LINES.

HYMN.	AUTHOR.	HYMN.	AUTHOR.
422	Walk in the light; so shalt thou......*Barton.*	433	When waves of trouble.................*Elliot.*
137	Watchman! tell us of the night......*Bowring.*	475	Where is my God, does he retire........*Steele.*
633	We are on our journey home........*C. Beecher.*	477	Where two or three, with sweet accord......
156	Welcome, delightful morn.............*Hayward.*		....*Stennett.*
371	Welcome, O Saviour, to my heart....*Bourne.*	419	While my Redeemer's near..............*Steele.*
491	Welcome to me the darkest night........*Anon.*	341	While life prolongs its precious light..*Dwight.*
47	Welcome, sweet day of rest..............*Watts.*	562	While o'er the deep thy servants sail........
542	We lift our hearts to thee.............*J. Wesley.*		....*Burgess.*
435	We seek a rest beyond the..............*Newton.*	140	While with ceaseless course the sun..*Newton.*
577	We praise thee, O God, for the........*Mackey.*	420	Whilst thee I seek, protecting power............
49	We sing to thee, thou Son of God........*Anon.*		....*Williams.*
631	What a friend we have in Jesus........*Bonar.*	391	Who shall the Lord's elect condemn...*Watts.*
57	What equal honors shall we bring......*Watts.*	296	Why do we mourn departing friends..*Watts.*
67	What grace, O Lord, and beauty........*Denny.*	160	Why droops my soul, with grief......*Scott.*
411	What sinners value, I resign................*Watts.*	492	Why should I murmur, or repine......*Anon.*
479	What various hindrances we meet....*Cowper.*	212	Why should the children of a King......*Watts.*
563	When adverse winds and waves arise...........	293	Why should our tears in sorrow........*Anon.*
	....*Sigourney.*	316	Why should we start, and fear.........*Watts.*
77	When along life's thorny road..........*Anon.*	503	Why should we weep for those.......*Gilbert.*
331	When in our hour of utmost need...............	8	With all my powers of heart and........*Watts.*
	....(tr) *Winckworth.*	365	With broken heart and contrite.........*Elvin.*
280	When in these courts we seek thy face........	294	With humble faith and thankful......*Stennet.*
	....*Montgomery.*	115	With joy we hail the sacred day..*Miss. Auber.*
164	When I survey the wondrous cross......*Watts.*	606	With tearful eyes I look around......*C. Elliot.*
148	When Jordan hushed his waters...*Campbell.*	272	Witness ye men and angels now.....*Beddome.*
418	When I can read my title clear..........*Watts.*	37	Worship, honor, glory, blessing............*Osler.*
496	When languor and disease invade....*Toplady.*		
149	When marshalled on the nightly........*White.*	278	Ye Christian heralds! go proclaim...*Draper.*
287	When our heads are bowed with woe............	26	Ye humble souls! approach your God..*Steele.*
	....*Milman.*	101	Ye saints proclaim abroad..............*Ryland.*
306	When overwhelmed with grief............*Watts.*	395	Your harps, ye trembling saints......*Toplady.*
95	When thou, my righteous Judge..*Huntingdon.*		

Metrical Index of Tunes and Authors.

L. M.

NAME.	HYMNS.	SOURCE.	NAME.	HYMNS.	SOURCE.
Beethoven	562	Geo. Kingsley.	Armenia	51, 510	S. B. Pond.
Duke Street	226	J. Hatton.	Avon	24	Scotch.
Federal Street	192, 230	H. K. Oliver.	Balerma	239	Simpson.
Forest	195	A. Chapin.	Bernard	421	Mozart.
Going Home	584	Dr. Wm. Miller.	Boardman	214, 453	Geo. Kingsley.
Good	605	Geo. Kingsley.	Cambridge	242, 507	R. Williams.
Gratitude	331, 491	T. Hastings.	Chestnut Street	450	H. K. Oliver.
Hallet	367, 414	Geo. Kingsley.	Christmas	130	Handel.
Happy Day	275		Coronation	48, 460	O. Holden.
Hamburg	487, 553	Dr. L. Mason.	Coventry	81	English.
Harmony Grove	20	H. K. Oliver.	Cowper	427, 533	Dr. L. Mason.
Hebron	339	Dr. L. Mason.	Cross and Crown	67	A. Chapin.
Hursley	14, 539	W. H. Monk.	Dedham	252	W. Gardiner.
Judgment Hymn	500	Dr. M. Luther.	Denfield	28, 530	Glaser.
Lambie	151, 387	Geo. Kingsley.	Devizes	434	Isaac Tucker.
Loving Kindness	56		Downs	211	Dr. L. Mason.
Luton	441	S. Burder.	Dundee	299, 494	Scotch.
Mendon	279	Dr. L. Mason, arr.	Evan	292, 417	Dr. Havergal arr.
Migdol	72, 120	Dr. L. Mason.	Fountain	169, 355	Scotch.
Missionary Chant	158, 437	C. Zeuner.	Haven	524	Dr. T. Hastings.
Northampton	565	Geo. Kingsley.	Heber	62, 527	Geo. Kingsley.
Old Hundred	3, 635	Claude Goudimel.	Henry	198	S. B. Pond.
Olive's Brow	474, 521	W. B. Bradbury.	Howard	288	Mrs. Cuthbert.
Oriel	316, 391	W. B. Bradbury.	Manoah	255	Rossini.
Rest	313, 504	W. B. Bradbury.	Marlow	113	Dr. L. Mason arr.
Retreat	410	Dr. Hastings.	Mear	295	A. Williams.
Rockingham	328	Dr. L. Mason.	Merton	85, 384	H. K. Oliver.
Sessions	7, 518		Naomi	370	Dr. L. Mason.
Stirling	10, 148	R. Harrison.	Newbold	202, 462	Geo. Kingsley.
Tallis' Ev. Hymn	69	Tallis.	Ortonville	381, 430	Dr. T. Hastings.
Uplift the Banner	594	Darley, arr.	Reiter	173	Geo Kingsley.
Uxbridge	17	Dr. L. Mason.	Rhine	373	German.
Van Hall's Hymn	124	Van Hall.	St. Martins	59	W. Tansur.
Ward	53, 162	Dr. L. Mason, arr.	Valentia	117, 272	Geo. Kingsley arr.
Ware	109, 549	Geo. Kingsley.	Walnut St. Chant	559	Geo. Kingsley.
Welton	343	Malan.	Warwick	268	S. Stanley.
Winchester	106	German.	Woodland	423	N. D. Gould.
Woodworth	364, 477, 536	W. B. Bradbury.	Woodstock	352	D. Dutton.

C. M.

			S. M.		
Antioch	127	Handel.	Badea	249	German.
Arlington	64, 497	T. A. Arne.	Barber	443	Mozart.

METRICAL INDEX OF TUNES AND AUTHORS.

NAME.	HYMNS.	SOURCE.
Boylston	132, 181	Dr. L. Mason.
Dennis	217, 304, 515	Nageli.
Dover	393	English.
Ferguson	96, 265	Geo. Kingsley.
Franklin Square	220	S. B. Pond.
Haydn	135, 396	Geo. Kingsley arr.
Kentucky	358	Western.
Laban	46, 184	Dr. L. Mason.
Lisbon	447, 546	D. Read.
Luther	465, 542	Dr. T. Hastings.
Marriage	569	
Mattoon	609	Geo. Kingsley.
Mornington	99	Lord Mornington.
Olmutz	301, 512	Dr. L. Mason arr.
Olney	467	Dr. L. Mason.
St. Thomas	245	A. Williams.
Shirland	262	S. Stanley.
Silver Street	42	I. Smith.
Thatcher	362	Handel.

H. M.
Lisher	155	German.
Lenox	153	J. Edson.

C. P. M.
Bremen	91	Dr. L. Hastings.
Wade	94	Geo. Kingsley.

11s & 10s.
Come, ye Disconsolate	555	S. Webbe.

11s.
Expostulation	104, 319	J. Hopkins.
Home	321	
Portuguese Hymn	102	J. Reading.

10s.
Eventide	579	W. H. Monk.

8s, 7s & 4s.
Golgotha	40	Geo. Kingsley.
Greenville	408	Rosseau.
Sicilian Hymn	234	Italian.
Zion	236	Dr. L. Hastings.

8s.
De Fleury	469	De. Fleury.
Inspirer and Hearer	471	

8s & 5s.
Sing of Jesus	573	German.

8s & 7s.
Autumn	142, 175	Spanish.
Golgotha	40	Geo. Kingsley.

NAME.	HYMNS.	SOURCE.
Middleton	307	
Mt. Vernon	310	Dr. L. Mason.
Nettleton	405	A. Nettleton.
Rest for the Weary	586	W. Mc. Donald.
Vespers	145	Flotow.
Vesper Hymn	179	Russian.
Wilmot	36	Weber.

7s & 6s.
All Glory, Praise &c	582	Eastern Church.
Crucifix	167	Greek.
Missionary Hymn	258	Dr. L. Mason.
Webb	165	G. J. Webb.
Yarmouth	260	Dr. L. Mason.

7s.
Comfort	189	English.
Dallas	326	Cherubini.
Hendon	284, 399	C. Malan.
Herold	204	Herold.
Horton	140, 481	Van Wartensee.
Holley	79	Geo. Hews.
Litany	187, 346	Spanish.
Martyn	75, 349	S. B. Marsh.
Messiah (double)	557	Geo. Kingsley.
Nurenberg	323	J. R. Ahle.
Pleyel's Hymn	30, 281	Pleyel.
Rock of Ages	376	Dr. T. Hastings.
Sabbath	379	Geo. Kingsley.
Scelye	208	Geo. Kingsley.
Teleman's Chant	34	C. Zeuner.
Von Weber	403, 485	Von Weber.
Watchman, (double)	137	Dr. L. Mason.

6s & 4s.
America	333	H. Carey.
Bethany	456	Dr. L. Mason.
Fatherland	458	Geo. Kingsley.
Italian Hymn	87, 224	Giardini.
Mease	613	Geo. Kingsley.
New Haven	89, 337	Dr. L. Hastings.
Olivet	222	Dr. L. Mason.

6s.
Thy Way, not Mine	588	Weber.

Miscellaneous.
Harvest Home	557	Geo. Kingsley.
The Golden Gates	559	Geo. Kingsley.
While o'er the Deep	562	Geo. Kingsley.
When Adverse Winds	565	Geo. Kingsley.
Sing of Jesus	573	German.
The Voice of Free Grace	575	Dr. Clarke.
We Praise Thee O God	577	English.

METRICAL INDEX OF TUNES AND AUTHORS.

Chants.

NAME.	HYMNS.	SOURCE.	NAME.	HYMNS.	SOURCE.
O Holy Savior	580	Sir. G. Elvey.	The Lord's Prayer	1	Gregorian.
Jesus, Lead the Way	597	German.	Gloria Patri	640	
Thy Will be Done	599	J. B. Dykes.	Gloria in Excelsis	625	
Lord, with Glowing Heart	602	Anon.	Agnus Dei	622	Layriz.
How Sweetly flowed	605	Geo. Kingsley.	A Soldier's Dirge	619	Geo. Kingsley.
Farewell! We meet &c.	617	Hastings.	It came upon the &c.	620	
Go to Thy Rest in Peace	618	Geo. Kingsley.	From the Recesses	621	Bowring.
Mt. Blanc	633	Anon.	Beautiful Zion	623	
I'm a Pilgrim	634	Anon.	Beyond the Smiling	624	D. Clark.

www.ingramcontent.com/pod-product-compliance
Lightning Source LLC
Chambersburg PA
CBHW031752230426
43669CB00007B/593